# Globalization, Development and Human Security

# Globalization, Development and Human Security

Edited by

**ANTHONY McGREW and NANA K. POKU**

polity

10229709

First published in 2007 by Polity Press

Polity Press
65 Bridge Street
Cambridge CB2 1UR, UK

Polity Press
350 Main Street
Malden, MA 02148, USA

ISBN-10:  0-7456-3086-3
ISBN-13:  978-07456-3086-1
ISBN-10:  0-7456-3087-1 (pb)
ISBN-13:  978-07456-3087-8 (pb)

A catalogue record for this book is available from the British Library.

Typeset in 10.25 on 12.5 pt Quadraat Sans Regular
by Servis Filmsetting Ltd, Manchester, UK
Printed and bound in Malaysia by Alden Press Ltd

The publisher has used its best endeavours to ensure that the URLs for external websites referred to in this book are correct and active at the time of going to press. However, the publisher has no responsibility for the websites and can make no guarantee that a site will remain live or that the content is or will remain appropriate.

For further information on Polity, visit our website: www.polity.co.uk

# Contents

# Notes on Contributors

**Peter Burnell** is Professor of Politics and International Studies at the University of Warwick. He has written widely on democratization, the political economy of foreign aid, and politics and policy in Zambia. His present research focus is a critical examination of how standard conceptions of democracy are being diffused globally through networks of democracy promotion actors based mainly in the West. Recent publications include *Democratization through the Looking Glass: Comparative Perspectives on Democratization* (2005), *Politics in the Developing World* (2005), co-edited with V. Randall, and *Civil Society in Democratization* (2004), co-edited with P. Calvert.

**Fantu Cheru** is a Professor at the School of International Service at the American University, Washington. A leading expert in African development, his previous publications include *The Planet at Risk: Mobilizing Resources for Human Security* (2005), *The African Renaissance: Roadmaps to the Challenge of Globalization* (2002); *The Silent Revolution in Africa: Debt, Development and Democracy* (1989); *Ethiopia: Options for Rural Development* (1990); and *The Not So Brave New World: Rethinking Regional Integration in Post-apartheid Southern Africa* (1992).

**Dong-Sook S. Gills** is a Senior Lecturer at the Centre for Contemporary Political Issues at the University of Sunderland. Research foci include politics and international studies, as well as the sociology of development. Among a range of publications, she is the author of *Rural Women and Triple Exploitation in Korean Development* (1999) and co-editor, with N. Piper, of *Women and Work in Globalising Asia* (2001).

**Jeffrey Haynes** is Professor of Politics at London Metropolitan University. He has more than eighty publications, including ten books. These include: *Religion in Third World Politics* (1993); *Religion and Politics in Africa* (1996); *Third World Politics* (1996); *Democracy and Civil Society in the Third World* (1997); *Religion in Global Politics* (1998); *Democracy in the Developing World* (2001); and *Politics in the Developing World* (2002). He has also edited: *Religion, Globalisation and Political Culture in the Third World* (1999); *Democracy and Political Change in the 'Third World'* (2001); and *Towards Sustainable Democracy in the Third World* (2001).

**Björn Hettne** is a Professor in the Department of Peace and Development Research at Gothenburg University, Sweden. Research interests include international political economy, regionalism (South Asia, Europe), development and conflict theory. He is the author of *Development Theory and the Three Worlds* (1995) and co-editor of *Studies in the New Regionalism, Volumes I–V* (1999–2001), with A. Inotai and O. Sunkel.

**Bonny Ibhawoh** is an Assistant Professor in the Department of History and Associate Faculty Masters in Social Justice and Equity Program, Department of Sociology at Brock University, Ontario, Canada. His research interests include contemporary African history, comparative human rights and international development studies. His forthcoming book *Imperialism and Human Rights* examines the development of the human rights movement and its humanist antecedents within the context of nineteenth-century European imperialism.

**Sandra J. MacLean** is an Associate Professor at the Simon Fraser University, Canada. Her main area of research is the impact of globalization on governance and security in developing countries and regions, with a particular focus on Southern Africa. She specializes in international political economy and comparative development, She is co-editor of *Crises of Governance in Asia and Africa* (2001) and has authored or co-authored chapters in various edited volumes.

**Anthony McGrew** is Professor of International Relations, Southampton University, and Head of the School of Social Sciences. His current research interests embrace globalization and international relations theory, military globalization and global governance. He co-authored *Global Transformations: Politics, Economics and Culture* (1999), and co-edited *The Global Transformations Reader* (2003), *Governing Globalization* (2002) and *Globalization Theory* (2007), all with David Held.

**Jane Parpart** is Professor of History, International Development Studies and Women's Studies at Dalhousie University, Halifax, Canada. Her research focuses mainly on African labour, women and development and feminist thought. Recent publications include the co-edited *Gender, Conflict, and Peacekeeping* (2005) with D. Mazurane and A. Raven-Roberts, and *Rethinking Empowerment: Gender and Development in a Global/Local World* (2002), with S. Rai and K. Staudt.

**Nana K. Poku** holds the John Ferguson Chair in the Department of Peace Studies, University of Bradford, and is Director of Research of the United Nations Commission on HIV/AIDS and Governance in Africa. His research interests include HIV/AIDS in Africa, critical security issues, migration and human security. Among his recent publications are *AIDS in Africa: How the Poor are Dying* (2005), and the co-edited *The Political Economy of AIDS in Africa* (2004) and *Global Health and Governance* (2003), both with A. Whiteside.

**Caroline Thomas** is Professor of Global Politics and Deputy Vice-Chancellor at Southampton University. Research interests include South–North relations, global development policy, international organizations and human security. Publications include *Global Governance, Development and Human Security* (2000), and the co-edited *Global Trade and Global Social Issues* (1999) with A. Taylor.

# Preface

This volume has had a rather longer gestation than we both care to admit but we hope that it has matured in the process. It has involved a true North–South collaboration, as the list of contributors attests, whilst for the editors the process has involved a sometimes frustrating intercontinental collaboration – from Southampton to Addis Ababa to Kyoto – reflecting the practical implications of uneven globalization. We would like to thank particularly our extremely patient editor at Polity, Ellen McKinlay, who provided considerable support at various stages and never despaired – or at least did not communicate it to us! The contributors to the volume also deserve praise for working to tight deadlines and responding to our editorial queries. Finally the copy editor, Jane Bainbridge, has made many helpful refinements to the text, and Neil de Cort eased the book through the production process with considerable speed. We are extremely grateful to all these people and to the many colleagues, friends and family members who have provided support, advice and (mostly) constructive criticism.

Anthony McGrew and Nana Poku

# Abbreviations and Acronyms

| | |
|---|---|
| ACP | Countries of Africa, Caribbean and the Pacific |
| AD | alternative development |
| ADB | African Development Bank |
| AIDS | Acquired Immune Deficiency Syndrome |
| AMU | Arab Maghreb Union |
| APEC | Asia–Pacific Economic Cooperation |
| ARV | anti-retroviral [drugs] |
| ASEAN | Association of South-East Asian Nations |
| ASEM | Asia–Europe Meeting |
| ASEP | Asia–Europe Parliamentary Partnership Meeting |
| AU | African Union |
| BHN | basic human needs |
| CACM | Central American Common Market |
| CARICOM | Caribbean Community and Common Market |
| CARIFTA | Caribbean Free Trade Association |
| CCEIA | Carnegie Council for Ethics and International Affairs |
| CCHS | Canadian Consortium on Human Security |
| CEE | Central and Eastern Europe |
| CHGA | Commission for HIV/AIDS and Governance in Africa |
| CIDA | Canadian International Development Agency |
| CIS | Commonwealth of Independent States |
| CLAC | Anti-Capitalist Convergence |
| CSC | Council of Swaziland Churches |
| DAC | Development Assistance Committee |
| DAN | Direct Action Network |
| DfID | Department for International Development |
| EAC | East African Community |
| EAEC | East Asia Economic Caucus |
| ECOWAS | Economic Community of West African States |
| EMIFCA | EU–Mercosur Interregional Framework for Cooperation Agreement 1995 |
| EMP | Euro-Mediterranean Partnership |
| EPZ | export processing zone |

| | |
|---|---|
| ESAF | enhanced structural adjustment facilities |
| ESCAP | Economic and Social Commission for Asia and the Pacific |
| EU | European Union |
| FDI | foreign direct investment |
| FEDEFAM | Federation of Families of the Disappeared |
| FGM | female genital mutilation |
| FH | Freedom House |
| FIDA | International Federation of Women Lawyers |
| FLACSO | Latin American Faculty of Social Sciences |
| FTAA | Free Trade Area of the Americas |
| G7 | Group of Seven leading industrial nations: Canada, France, Germany, Italy, Japan, UK, USA |
| G8 | Group of Eight: G7 plus Russia |
| G15 | Group of 17 developing countries from Asia, Africa and Latin America: Algeria, Argentina, Brazil, Chile, Egypt, India, Indonesia, Jamaica, Kenya, Nigeria, Malaysia, Mexico, Peru, Senegal, Sri Lanka, Venezuela and Zimbabwe |
| G20 | Group of Twenty: G7 plus countries regarded as 'emerging markets' |
| G22 | Group of 22 developing countries from Asia, Latin America and Africa |
| GAD | gender and development |
| GCC | Gulf Cooperative Council |
| GDP | gross domestic product |
| GIEWS | Global Information and Early Warning System (on food and agriculture) |
| GNI | gross national income |
| GNP | gross national product |
| HIPCs | heavily indebted poor countries |
| HIV | Human Immunodeficiency Virus |
| HSBC | Hongkong and Shanghai Banking Corporation |
| IAEN | International AIDS Economic Network |
| IBA | internationally based actor |
| IBRD | International Bank for Reconstruction and Development |
| ICBL | International Campaign to Ban Landmines |
| ICESCR | International Covenant on Economic, Social and Cultural Rights |
| ICRC | International Committee of the Red Cross |
| IDA | International Development Association |
| IEE – ULB | Institut d'Études Européennes – Université Libre de Bruxelles |
| IEI | International Energy Initiative |
| IFI | international financial institution |
| IGADD | Intergovernmental Authority on Drought and Development |
| IGO | intergovernmental organization |
| ILO | International Labour Organization |
| IMF | International Monetary Fund |
| INGO | international non-governmental organization |

| I-PRSP | interim poverty reduction strategy paper |
| LAFTA | Latin American Free Trade Association |
| LDC | less developed country |
| LNHO | League of Nations Health Organization |
| MDGs | Millennium Development Goals |
| Mercosur | Southern Cone Common Market (Latin America) |
| MIM | Multilateral Initiative on Malaria |
| MNC | multinational corporation |
| MOSOP | Movement for the Survival of the Ogoni People |
| MSF | Médecins sans Frontières |
| NAFTA | North American Free Trade Agreement |
| NATO | North Atlantic Treaty Organization |
| NEPAD | New Partnership for Africa's Development |
| NGO | non-governmental organization |
| NIC | National Intelligence Council |
| NIE | newly industrializing economy |
| NIEO | New International Economic Order (1974) |
| NPV | net present value |
| NRA | New Regionalism approach |
| OAS | Organization of American States |
| ODA | official development assistance |
| OECD | Organization for Economic Cooperation and Development |
| PAHO | Pan American Health Organization |
| PAR | participatory action research |
| PBS | Public Broadcasting Service [in USA] |
| PGA | People's Global Action |
| PRA | participatory rural appraisal |
| PRGF | poverty reduction and growth facility |
| PRSP | poverty reduction strategy paper |
| RRA | rapid rural appraisal |
| SAARC | South Asian Association for Regional Cooperation |
| SADC | Southern African Development Community |
| SADCC | Southern Africa Development Cooperation Conference |
| SAF | Structural Adjustment Facility |
| SAL | structural adjustment loans |
| SAP | structural adjustment programme |
| SCO | Shanghai Cooperation Organization |
| SEZ | special economic zone |
| STD | sexually transmitted disease |
| TNC | transnational corporation |
| TRIPS | Trade-Related Aspects of Intellectual Property Rights Agreement |
| UDHR | Universal Declaration of Human Rights |
| UN | United Nations |
| UNAIDS | Joint UN Programme on HIV/AIDS |
| UNCTAD | UN Conference on Trade and Development |
| UNCTAD, S-G | UN Conference on Trade and Development Secretary-General |
| UN/DESA | UN Department of Economic and Social Affairs |

| | |
|---|---|
| UNDP | UN Development Programme |
| UNDRD | United Nations Declaration on the Right to Development |
| UNESCO | UN Educational, Scientific and Cultural Organization |
| UNFPA | UN Population Fund |
| UNHCR | UN High Commissioner for Refugees |
| UNHCHR | UN High Commission for Human Rights |
| UNRISD | UN Research Institute for Social Development |
| UNU | UN University |
| WB | World Bank |
| WHO | World Health Organization |
| WIDER | World Institute for Development Economics |
| WSF | World Social Forum |
| WTO | World Trade Organization |

# Introduction

*Anthony McGrew*

Poverty and development have acquired heightened political salience on the global agenda. The campaigns of the global justice movement, the growing securitization of development in the aftermath of 9/11, widening global inequality, and the perceived threats of pandemics, migrations and failed states have contributed to a sense of renewed urgency surrounding the failure of the international community to deliver on its promises enshrined in the United Nation's Millennium Declaration of September 2000.This global covenant promulgated eight Millennium Development Goals, committing governments to realizing, *amongst other targets*, halving global poverty, by the year 2015. Progress, however, remains for the most part 'patchy, too slow or non-existent', or as the UN Secretary-General more diplomatically observed 'the world is not optimising its performance' (DFID 2005; UN Secretary-General 2004). For many critics the reasons for this have much more to do with the dynamics of contemporary economic globalization rather than simply the immobilism and failings of governments, politicians, and diplomats. Globalization, it is argued, has transformed the conditions of development and, in so doing, the prospects for a more equitable world order (Hoogvelt 1997; Thomas 2000). A principal ambition of this volume is to offer a critical exploration of this reframing of development and the prospects for development in the contemporary global political economy. In this regard, the contributors share a common intellectual aspiration to reconnect the study of development with the study of international relations or global politics, for their mutual intellectual benefit.

The justification for this will become more obvious in subsequent pages. The discussion here seeks initially to clarify the concept of globalization and to elaborate some of its more significant consequences for development. How far it is transforming the context of development is a critical focus in this respect. It then moves to a consideration of competing interpretations of this relationship, whether globalization is an engine or empire of development, before considering questions of human security and the impact of the post-9/11 war on terror on the global political economy of development.

## THE END OF THE THIRD WORLD: REBRANDING OR RESTRUCTURING?

Almost two decades ago Harris presented a controversial argument that the rise of the newly industrializing economies (NIEs) prefigured 'the end of the Third World' as both analytical category and politico-economic or ideological bloc in international affairs (Harris 1987). Increased economic differentiation, rather than underdevelopment or convergence, has continued to characterize the developing world. Amongst other factors, the rise of China and the Asian tiger economies, not to mention South Korean and Mexican membership of the OECD (the Western club of affluent states), have called into question the notion of the Third World as a useful analytical category for understanding the global political economy. Politically too, the end of the Cold War fatally undermined the logic of the neat tripartite classification of states into First, Second and Third World. In the context of the titanic struggle between capitalism and communism the idea of the Third World, largely but not completely synonymous with the non-aligned movement, retained considerable political and ideological purchase. With the fall of the Berlin Wall and the collapse of communism, as a discrete world system, it no longer made much sense to depict the world through the language and categories of the Cold War era.

A plurality of terms has evolved to signify both the shared predicament and the increased differentiation amongst the world's economically weak and vulnerable states. In both academic and popular literatures various terms such as the South, the developing or post-colonial states, the newly industrialized or emerging economies, the less developed or Fourth World have come to replace the singular signifier, the 'Third World'. Significantly the World Bank, for its own lending purposes, differentiates between five categories of states – from the low-income economies, the low and high middle-income economies to the lower and high-income OECD economies (World Bank 2005). Whilst acknowledging the end of the 'Third World' as a bureaucratic, ideological or analytical category the material predicament of global poverty, deprivation, exclusion and subordination to which originally it referred nevertheless remains a significant reality for much of humanity. Rebranding the 'Third World', however, is no mere semantic exercise but, on the contrary, a recognition of the dramatically altered context of development under the combined impacts of the end of the Cold War order and intensified economic globalization. In short, the permanent restructuring of the global political economy has precipitated both a cognitive shift in thinking about development and an associated rebranding or re-presentation of the 'Third World' problem.

Globalization has been especially critical to this restructuring of North–South relations following the demise of the bipolar world. As the Berlin Wall came down there was great concern that the South's predicament would be demoted even further on the global agenda. For much of the post-war era the competitive logic of bipolarity had turned the South into a political, ideological and sometimes military battleground between the forces of East and West. With the end of the Cold War many previously strategically significant regions or areas, most especially on the African continent, became 'strategically obsolescent'. This held out the prospect of, at best, a growing marginalization and, at worst, the exclusion of many parts of the South from the global political economy as aid flows, military assistance and economic support were withdrawn. However, such fears proved somewhat unfounded as intensifying globalization in the 1990s transformed key aspects of North–South relations although by no means uniformly so.

## GLOBALIZATION AND THE RECONFIGURATION OF THE WORLD ECONOMY

Conceptually globalization is often elided with notions of liberalization, internationalization, universalization, Westernization or modernization (Scholte 2000). However, none of these terms, as Scholte expressly argues, captures its distinctive attributes or qualities. Within the global political economy literature, globalization is generally specified in quite precise terms as 'the emergence and operation of a single, worldwide economy' (Grieco and Ikenberry 2002: 207). It is measured in respect of the growing intensity, extensity and velocity of worldwide economic interactions and interconnectedness, from trade through production and finance, to migration. In this regard it is conceived as a *process*, rather than a fixed outcome or condition, in so far as it refers to a *historical tendency* towards heightened levels of worldwide economic interconnectedness. Indeed, there is a substantive conceptual difference between the notion of a *globalizing world economy* and that of a fully or partially *globalized world economy* that implies a steady state or condition of economic integration.

Understood as a process, the idea of economic globalization also embodies the implication of an evolving *transformation* or qualitative shift in the organization of the world economy. Quite simply, over time cumulative patterns and networks of transborder economic activity dissolve the separation of the world into discrete national economic units, making the distinction between the domestic and world economy increasingly difficult to sustain for both academics and policy makers alike. In other words, globalization generates emergent or systemic properties such that the world economy increasingly operates as a single system. This structural shift is evident in, amongst other things, the formation of global markets, production networks, a new global division of labour and business competition together with global systems of economic regulation, from the World Trade Organization (WTO) to the International Accounting Standards Board.

Underlying these shifts in the scale of economic organization are contemporary informatics technologies and infrastructures of communication and transportation. These have facilitated new forms and possibilities of virtual real-time worldwide economic organization and coordination. In the process distance and time are being substantially reconfigured such that, for instance, economic and other shocks in one region, as with the East Asian crisis, can rapidly diffuse around the globe often with serious local consequences. Although geography still matters, globalization is associated with a process of 'time-space compression' – literally a shrinking world – in which the sources of even very localized developments, from commodity price rises to people-trafficking, may be traced to economic conditions on another continent.

A single worldwide economy, however, is not necessarily coextensive with a universal or planetary economy. More specifically, worldwide is generally taken to refer to *interregional* or *intercontinental* patterns of economic exchange and enmeshment. Accordingly, globalization is best conceived as embodying a *rescaling* of economic space manifested in the intensification of inter- or supraregional and multi-continental networks and flows of economic activity (Brenner 1999). It denotes, in effect, a relative *denationalization* of economic activity as significant aspects of economic life become organized increasingly on an interregional or multi-continental scale transcending bounded national economic space. This rescaling, however, is not uniformly experienced across all regions or economies since globalization is also recognizably an *uneven process*. Differential patterns of enmeshment in, or alternatively marginalization from, the worldwide economy define its 'variable geometry' (Castells 2000). This 'variable geometry' describes significant alterations to the patterns and modalities of North–South relations.

## GLOBALIZATION AND THE TRANSFORMED CONTEXT OF DEVELOPMENT

As Samir Amin concludes, although economic globalization is nothing new it has 'undeniably taken a qualitative step forward during the recent period' (Amin 1997: 31). This is articulated in transformations in trade, finance, production, migration and patterns of economic convergence.

For most of the post-war period world trade has grown much faster than world output. World exports, measured as a proportion of world output, were three times greater in 1998 than in 1950 while recent WTO estimates measure trade at around 29 per cent of world output (WTO 2001). Moreover trade now involves a larger number of countries than at any time in the recent past while developing economies today account for a growing share of world export markets in both manufactures (almost a third) and the services sector (WTO 2002). But these trade figures conceal significant transformations in the world economy such as the emergence of a new global division of labour and the intensification of global competition through trade.

Falling costs of transportation, the communications revolution, liberalization and the growth of transnational corporations have all contributed to a new global division of labour. Since 1990 developing economies have increased their share of world manufactures trade from 17 per cent to over 27 per cent (WTO 2001: 3). East Asia and other NIEs have taken on the role of the world's factories. At the same time, most developing economies have witnessed a decline in raw materials and primary products trade whilst most OECD economies and a few developing economies, such as India and Singapore, have experienced a significant rise in their trade in services. These shifts represent a new pattern of specialization (or global division of labour) within the world economy and one that is associated with an intensification of global economic competition. In both the manufacturing and, to a lesser extent, services sector the expansion of trade has increased competitive pressures on economies both North and South. It is not just that OECD economies confront cheaper imports from the world's new manufacturing zones, in

East Asia or Latin America, or lower-cost services from India and South Africa, but that competition amongst the OECD economies and with developing economies has also intensified as production and markets become globalized. Outsourcing production accounts for a significant proportion of the recent growth in world trade as firms draw upon worldwide networks of suppliers producing where greater economies of scale or efficiency gains can be realized. In this way productive and competitive forces become globalized whilst economies in different regions become more tightly intermeshed.

By comparison with trade the bulk of capital flows (some 66 per cent) is accounted for by the major OECD economies. Transborder financial flows remain highly uneven. Capital flows to developing states have fluctuated considerably over the last three decades peaking in the mid-1990s, prior to the East Asian crash, although they currently remain above the levels witnessed in the 1980s (IMF 2003). Even so these flows are concentrated amongst the principal economies of Latin America, East Asia and the European transition countries. Geography and history still exert their influence. Of course, this is not to conclude that the dynamics and volatilities of transborder financial activities have no bearing upon those on the margins, for few economies can insulate themselves against the consequences of financial contagion in what is now a single, real-time global financial system. Moreover, the evidence suggests that, for countries in the South, the ramifications and risks of deepening global financial integration, though variable, are considerable. These include significant constraints on macroeconomic policy, public spending and welfare provision, as well as impacts upon domestic investment, indebtedness and exchange rate regimes. Furthermore, as evidenced in the East Asian crisis, the financial contagion effects of crises in one region can rapidly acquire devastating economic consequences across the developing world whilst strategies to insulate economies from such events are constrained by the strictures of international financial institutions whether public (IMF, WB) or private (banks and credit-rating agencies). Such is the concern about the potential contagion effects of financial crises emanating from the South that the IMF has sought to engage the governments of the most significant developing economies in the global governance of finance through the G20 consultative arrangement (Germain 2004).

In respect of production global outsourcing is quite widespread in the most dynamic industrial and service sectors, including finance. Driving this process is the transnational corporation (TNC). According to UNCTAD (UN Conference on Trade and Development) estimates, in 2002 there were 64,000 TNCs with 870,000 affiliates and sales of $18 trillion (compared to total world exports of $8 trillion), employing 53 million people across all continents (UNCTAD 2001, 2003). By comparison with the recent past (1990) transnational production, rather than trade, has become the principal means of servicing foreign markets. TNCs account currently for more than 25 per cent of world production, 80 per cent of world industrial output, 33 per cent of world trade and 10 per cent of world GDP (Gilpin 2001: 289; UNCTAD 2001, 2003). They have become key determinants of the location and organization of production and services in the world economy, especially within the most advanced and dynamic economic sectors, integrating and reordering business activity between, and within, the world's three principal economic regions and their associated hinterlands. Over the last three decades foreign investment has become not only more geographically diffuse but also much more intense. At the turn of the new century total world (inward) FDI reached a new peak of $1,271 billion – almost four times the level of 1995 and over six times that of a decade earlier (UNCTAD 2001: 3). With the slowdown in the world economy it has declined dramatically, to just over $651 billion in 2002, but has recently begun to recover (UNCTAD 2003: 2). Even so, the scale of FDI remains over ten times that of 1982 and significant flows (more than $10 billion) reach more than twenty-four developing economies compared to seven in 1985 (UNCTAD 2001: 4). FDI has become increasingly important (measured in terms of the ratio of FDI to GDP or FDI to domestic investment) to economic growth in both advanced, but also, and most especially, developing, economies. This is evident from the rise of NIEs in Asia and Latin America. De-industrialization across OECD economies is causally linked with the industrialization of many developing economies as production is shifted to lower-cost locations. Over time the cumulative impact of capital mobility, along with the expansion of trade, has contributed to structural changes in the world economy.

Amongst the most significant of these structural changes is the evolution and consolidation of a new worldwide division of labour. As noted there has been a visible shift in the location of manufacturing production from OECD economies outwards to NIEs in East Asia, Latin America and other parts of the developing world. To a much more limited degree, a similar trend is evident in some aspects of service provision, most notably in data processing and information provision (WTO 2001). At the same time the raw material sector, measured as a proportion of world FDI and trade, has declined such that many developing economies increasingly have entered, or seek to enter, the manufacturing (and even services) business. As a result the geography of world economic activity has been transformed in recent years with important consequences for the distribution of economic power and wealth, and ultimately for the politics of global economic relations (Crafts 2003; Gilpin 2001).

A further, and related, structural change has been the intensification of transnational and interregional competition for market share, technological advantage and rapid product innovation. Such competition is no longer necessarily best conceived as occurring between self-contained national economic units, in so far as the new geography of world economic activity links distant markets through the operations of giant multinational corporations (MNCs) and interregional production networks. In this respect economic and corporate competition is globalized since it transcends regions biting deeper into national economies and magnifying the consequences of local competitive conditions and economic differences with significant consequences for the developing world. Thus competition between supermarket chains in the UK for agricultural produce turns farmers both at home and in developing economies into direct competitors.

By comparison with capital, labour remains relatively immobile. That said, labour flows are much more geographically extensive and, in terms of direction, are an almost mirror image of capital flows in so far as they have become primarily South to North (Castles and Miller 2002; Chiswick and Hatton 2003). Outward flows of labour are a predominantly developing country phenomenon and, despite greater restrictions, somewhat surprisingly they are on a scale equivalent to the mass migrations of the early twentieth century (Chiswick and Hatton 2003: 74). Though diverse in origin and final destination, global, as opposed to regional, migration has grown enormously over the period 1950–2000 (Chiswick and Hatton 2003). So too has skilled labour migration from South to North. These developments reflect tendencies towards the integration of labour markets across the North–South divide. Perhaps of greater significance are the political consequences of increased legal and illegal migration. In the aftermath of 11 September 2001, this has contributed to, amongst other things, the growing securitization of development and migration policies. Human security, rather than simply military security, concerns have acquired a salient influence upon the development agenda. For in a globalized context the consequences of failing states, immiseration, barbarity and poverty in the world's periphery find their expression in significant migrations of the dispossessed. In the post-Cold War epoch some of the poorest developing states have acquired the mantle of perceived security threats because of the potentially significant regional and global social consequences of their domestic instability. Development, as it was in the Cold War, is becoming (re-) securitized, as geographical distance no longer insulates the North from the consequences of deprivation, poverty and political turmoil in the South.

Whilst in the last fifty years poverty has declined 'more than in the previous 500' the decline has been highly uneven (UNDP 1997: 2). Three related global patterns are evident: the growing polarization between the richest and poorest in the world economy, the segmentation of the global workforce into the winners and losers from economic globalization, and the growing marginalization of the losers from the benefits of development. As the UNDP (UN Development Programme) Report on Human Development states, all the key indices of human development 'have advanced strongly in the past few decades' and these 'advances are found in all regions of the world' (pp. 2–3). However, at the same time the ratio of the incomes of the world's poorest peoples to the richest has more than doubled from 30:1 in 1960 to a staggering 78:1 (p. 9). Furthermore the richest 20 per cent of the world's people have seen their share of world income increase from 70 per cent in 1960 to 85 per cent in 1996 whilst the poorest 20 per cent had to get by on a dwindling proportion of world income down from 2.3 per cent in 1960 to 1.4 per cent in 1996 (Castells 1998: 81).

Although the polarization between rich and poor in the global economy is intensifying there is also evidence to suggest that those countries largely bypassed by globalization are amongst the poorest (Birdsall 1998). In this respect globalization is reordering developing countries into clear winners and losers such that it operates to the advantage of the 'more dynamic and powerful countries in the North and the South' (UNDP 1997: 87). This pattern of exclusion is also replicated within countries, both North and South, as communities and locales closely integrate into global production networks and markets reap significant rewards whilst others survive on the margins. Thus within OECD economies inequality, unemployment and social exclusion have increased as many low-skilled and semi-skilled jobs have been relocated to more profitable ventures in developing countries (Rodrik 1997; Castells 1998). Globalization brings with it a horizontal segmentation of the workforce, within rich and poor countries alike, into winners and losers. As Castells observes, 'Globalization proceeds selectively, including and excluding segments of economies and societies in and out of the networks of information, wealth, and power that characterize the new dominant system' (Castells 1998: 162).

One consequence of this segmentation is that many of the least developed economies and locales have become increasingly marginalized within the global economy (Hoogvelt 1997; Duffield 2001; Castells 1998). According to this argument, globalization is associated with a new architecture of domination and subordination, inclusion and exclusion, within the global political economy. As Hoogvelt concludes:

> Globalization has rearranged the architecture of world order. Economic, social and power relations have been recast to resemble not a pyramid but a three-tier structure of concentric circles. All three circles cut across national and regional boundaries. In the core circle we find the elites of all continents . . . They are encircled by a fluid, larger social layer who labour in insecure forms of employment, thrown into cut-throat competition in the global market . . . The third, and largest, concentric circle comprises those who are already effectively excluded from the global system. (Hoogvelt 1997: 239–40)

This, in turn, has shaped the politics of development.

For many developing states 'the real choice . . . is not how best to fight globalization but how best to manage it' (Haass and Liton 1998). In the wake of the East Asian crash many developing economies in the region, from Malaysia to South Korea, came under enormous external pressure to alter, if not abandon, the developmental state model of economic development in favour of a more liberal market strategy (Godement 1999; Mallett 1999). Until the crash, many East Asian governments demonstrated that it was possible, in a globalizing economy, to combine rapid economic growth with strong state direction of the economy whilst simultaneously maintaining social cohesion. The developmental state model represented a distinctive model of capitalism, which differed in significant ways from its European and American counterparts. Whilst its obituary is premature it is nevertheless clear that the Asian financial crisis has precipitated its transformation. Amin, and many others, argue that under conditions of globalization the spectrum of development strategies that may be pursued successfully by states is significantly restricted (Amin 2003). This, in turn, has quite significant consequences for state sovereignty and autonomy – the right to and capacity for self-governance.

Amongst subordinate states the constraints of world order, whether in the age of empires or the Cold War era, have always figured large in the determination of national policy. Moreover, whilst the poorest states in the world may have all the constitutional and legal attributes of statehood, a significant number lack the vital capacities and resources to act as such, being, in Jackson's words, 'quasi-states' (Jackson 1990). For the majority of developing states the intensification of globalization in recent decades poses a distinct challenge to the capacity for self-governance although, of course, the ability to moderate that challenge varies considerably. It is not that global financial markets or institutions dictate the specific policies of governments but rather that they configure the agenda or the parameters within which strategic choices concerning national development are made. As Grugel observes of Latin America, 'the options appear to governing elites to have shrunk to either successful liberalization or unsuccessful liberalization; any search for alternatives has disappeared from domestic agendas' (Grugel 1991).

Somewhat paradoxically this narrowing of development possibilities is occurring just at the historical moment when democracy, as a system of governance, has become more widely institutionalized within the global South. Following the end of the Cold War the 'third wave' of democratization, as Huntington refers to it, has encompassed virtually all regions of the globe, from South America to South Asia. Governments in these fragile 'third wave' democracies, however, regularly have to confront controversial trade-offs between the principles of democratic self-governance and the operation of global market forces. This is particularly evident in their relationships with multilateral agencies, such as the World Bank and IMF, which in return for assistance require market-conforming development strategies, from liberalization to fiscal prudence, in strict accordance with the neoliberal Washington Consensus. At the same time multilateral agencies, donors and lenders continue to advance a good governance agenda, which involves, if not demands, the deepening and widening of democratic practices. Under these conditions the stability and consolidation of democracy becomes highly problematic not least because poverty and underdevelopment provide weak foundations for its flourishing.

## DEVELOPMENT OR DOMINATION?

Considerable controversy abounds as to whether these transformations associated with globalization represent a new 'opportunity structure' for developing states or alternatively a new phase of subordination. In their popular radical treatise *Empire*, Hardt and Negri argue that globalization is creating a historically novel form of global domination (Hardt and Negri 2000) – 'empire' not in its statist or orthodox sense, but as a dynamic, decentred and diffusing global market system which both unites and divides the world under the rule of capital as opposed to any particular Capitol. By contrast Dollar and Kraay, amongst others, consider globalization as inherently more benign, enhancing the development prospects of states and diffusing wealth and power globally as is evident in the rapid rise of China and India over the last two decades (Dollar and Kraay, 2002). In between these somewhat radically polarized interpretations are a range of nuanced positions, from the work of

Hoogvelt, Castells and Mittelman, which though highly critical of globalization emphasize its contradictory character, to the work of Bagwhati, Wolf and perhaps even Sen, which present a qualified endorsement of liberal globalization (Hoogvelt 1997; Castells 1998; Mittelman 2000; Bagwhati 2004; Wolf 2004; Sen 1999). At issue in these virtual conversations are not only differences of interpretation concerning world economic trends but also significant differences of a theoretical and normative kind. Recurring issues in these conversations concern the causal connections between globalization and global exclusion; poverty and inequality; development and underdevelopment; democratization; and the growing securitization of development in the wake of 9/11.

In her analysis of globalization Hoogvelt argues, as noted, that it creates new patterns of inclusion and exclusion in the global political economy (Hoogvelt 1997). It is highly selective, such that patterns of enmeshment in the global economy vary not just between North and South, but also within states and locales both North and South. By comparison with the epoch of European world empires, the world's poorest nations and rural communities are largely marginalized or excluded from the new global order. If anything the bulk of the world's population, as Hirst and Thompson concur, has experienced a significant process of economic and political de-globalization over the last century as empires have given way to national independence (Hirst and Thompson 2003). Duffield too argues that the current global order is defined much more by a process of selective inclusion than it is by global integration (Duffield 2001). If globalization is more accurately understood as a process of selective or differential inclusion or incorporation into the world economy this has highly significant systemic consequences for the development possibilities of many societies. According to UNCTAD, lack of foreign investment and capital impedes development (UNCTAD 2001).

This selective inclusion figures prominently, as an explanatory factor, in many analyses of the impact of globalization on world poverty and inequality. For Castells there is a strong relationship between globalization and the worsening trends in world poverty and inequality (Castells 1998). It is responsible, he argues, for the emergence of a Fourth World (the world's very poorest nations and communities in which deprivation and immiseration are prevalent) and a growing polarization between rich and poor across the globe. Amin, Hoogvelt, Milanovic and Reddy and Pogge also identify a connection between globalization and increasing global poverty and inequality (Amin 2003; Hoogvelt 1997; Milanovic 2002; Reddy and Pogge 2003). However, these conclusions are hotly disputed by the studies of Salai-i-Martin, Dollar and Kraay, Wolf and Firebaugh, amongst others (Salai-i-Martin 2002; Dollar and Kraay 2002; Wolf 2004; Firebaugh 2004). Not only do these authors conclude that global poverty is in decline and global inequality is reducing but also that globalization, in creating the conditions for sustained economic growth, is the engine of development. Of course the debate is somewhat less polarized than this summary implies, since most authors are careful to qualify their analyses and conclusions. Even so, the current orthodoxy of academics tends to advance the former argument, that of the practitioners the latter. This remains a crucial debate, not just because of its policy implications, but also since it is central to the wider issue as to whether the consequences of globalization for development can be judged generally benign or malign.

Development, according to Sen, is not to be judged simply in terms of levels of industrialization or economic growth (Sen 1999). These are principally, he argues, the means by which development, understood as the realization of 'expanding human freedoms', is realized (p. 2). Whether globalization contributes to development in its more restricted or expanded conception, or both, is the subject of considerable controversy. Much of the current neoliberal development orthodoxy, emanating from international financial institutions and official development agencies in the form of the Washington Consensus, emphasizes liberalization and integration into the world economy as the key to development. As Dollar and Kraay conclude, there is a strong relationship between development and openness – those economies, as in sub-Saharan Africa, least integrated into the world economy are amongst the least developed whilst those, as in East Asia, which are highly integrated have high growth rates (Dollar and Kraay, 2002). This neoliberal orthodoxy, however, is challenged by other studies which suggest a much more complex relationship between liberalization and patterns of economic development (Wade 2004). For instance, China and South Korea have witnessed rapid economic growth but in relatively closed economies whilst many Latin American states liberalized rapidly in the 1990s but witnessed low growth rates. As Ugarteche (2000), amongst many others, suggests, the neoliberal orthodoxy presents a false dilemma since countries can gain from engaging with the global economy without fully liberalizing. Thus the key issue for developing countries is how liberalization and integration with the global economy is pursued and managed. Globalization, in this interpretation, has differential consequences for developing economies depending upon their geo-economic position, domestic economic structure, state policies and the terms of engagement with the world economy. In the case of some states, amongst them the world's poorest, globalization has been associated with patterns of distorted development, if not underdevelopment, as a consequence of their selective inclusion in, or structural exclusion from, the global economy (Hoogvelt 1997; Amin 2003). Under conditions of globalization, differential, or uneven, development remains a dominant feature of the world economy (Hoogvelt 1997).

For Sen, one of the most crucial elements of development is 'the pre-eminence of political freedoms and democracy' (Sen 1999: 147). As the third wave of globalization intensified in the final decades of the twentieth century, so too did the third wave of democracy. Huntington's classic study suggests that the latter was only loosely associated with the former whilst the end of bipolarity was much more significant (Huntington 1993). Recent studies appear to confirm this conclusion. Grugel argues that the consequences of globalization for democratization in the developing world, most especially the consolidation of democracy, have been, and remain, problematic. She concludes that its consequences are contradictory in so far as it contributes both to the diffusion of democratic norms and institutions but also to the destabilization of processes of democratic consolidation (Grugel 2004). This tension is perhaps most dramatically articulated in the case of those many new democracies which have been subjected to the disciplines of structural adjustment policies by the international financial institutions. But even for many OECD states the operation of global market forces imposes, to various degrees, constraints upon the exercise of popular sovereignty or democratic self-governance. For the majority of developing states these constraints, as noted previously, tend to be highly significant in so far as they constitute the parameters of feasible development strategies (Thomas 2000). Some even argue that, under these conditions, many developing states are best described as low intensity democracies rather than authentic democratic polities (Gills and Rocamora 1993). Amongst developing states, globalization and democratization are far from complementary processes but rather best conceived as in dynamic tension.

In an interconnected world whether democratization succeeds or fails may have dramatic ramifications for regional and global security. As in the Cold War, when the domestic politics of Third World states acquired global strategic significance, similarly today, in the context of a globalized world, political instability, internal conflict and state failure amongst developing countries are perceived as threats to regional and global security. For the consequences of state failure or domestic turmoil in one region can rapidly destabilize neighbouring societies and regions with sometimes quite significant economic, military or political implications for distant states. Localized conflict, in an integrating world, may come to acquire significant systemic consequences. By its very nature globalization is associated with the expansion and intensification of mutual vulnerabilities. The same infrastructures that facilitate the globalization of economic and social activities also facilitate the transnational organization of criminal and terrorist activity. As the events of 11 September 2001 demonstrated, globalization, combined with the complexity of modern societies, has generated new sources of mutual vulnerability and insecurity for states, from terrorism and organized crime to global pandemics. In this context poverty, development, conflict and instability in the South become of heightened global strategic interest. One major consequence of growing mutual vulnerabilities, according to Duffield, has been the accelerating securitization of development (Duffield 2001).

Increasingly multilateral agencies and donor governments coordinate their development activities and policies, targeting them upon strategic zones of conflict and instability in the South (Duffield 2001). This has been especially the case, following 9/11, in respect of official foreign aid disbursements. As Woods observes, these appear to signal the replacement of a development-led approach by a security-led approach (Woods 2005). Official aid and development, to a degree, have always been shaped by the logic of security, especially at the height of the Cold War. What, however, is distinctive about this re-securitization of development is the expanding security agenda. Everything from the ecology to the economy is reinterpreted through the security lens whilst globalization functions to magnify such potential and distant threats.

The danger is that securitization may provoke a covert, and sometimes overt, process of militarization. Amin suggests this is already occurring in the form of a US-led 'militarization of globalization' (Amin 2003). Securitization also harbours the potential risk that legitimate rationales or pretexts for, and modes of, external intervention in the domestic affairs of developing states are expanded. In this regard the progressive notion of human security, or protective security as Sen refers to it, which is conceived as an alternative to orthodox or realist discourses of security, may unintentionally widen the parameters of legitimate interventionism. Framing development in terms of human security, as is currently the dominant progressive view, paradoxically may expose its subjects to new insecurities. In the context of the war on terror, globalization and the securitization of development are likely to remain mutually reinforcing.

To the extent that globalization is transforming the context of development, so it has elicited a rethinking of national development strategies. This has been linked with the emergence of three distinctive strategic responses: regulation, regionalism and resistance. Whereas the campaign for the NIEO (New International Economic Order) in the 1970s sought to rewrite the rules of the world economic order, the current struggle is largely over the terms of globalization: how to regulate it in the interests of the world's poor. Collectively and individually developing states have sought to exploit the rules of the global governance complex in order to advance development goals. Governments in the emerging economies of Asia and Latin America are increasingly resorting to the WTO trade dispute settlement mechanisms in their conflicts with the EU and the US since, in a rule-based system, might has less chance of trumping right. Of course, the WTO is also used by the more powerful to annul some of the traditional protection that the poorest states have received and to advance the trade liberalization agenda. This has been combined with collective attempts, as with recent G20 moves to ensure the WTO Doha Trade round gives priority to development, to demand reforms to both the institutions and the rules of global economic governance. Following the East Asian crash in 1997, reforms to the rules and architecture of global finance have dominated the international financial agenda as financial stability acquired priority. In the case of the IMF there have been moves to widen consultation and participation in rule-making beyond the G7 to embrace the more representative G22 – a formal grouping which includes the major developing states from each world-region. The non-aligned movement have also recently formed the G15 of leading developing states which seeks to establish a role as a kind of 'poor man's G7' (Sindharan 1998). These developments reflect one of the most fundamental challenges of globalization to existing modes of global economic governance, namely how to ensure its effective regulation in the interests of the weak rather than the strong. Given the limited successes (to date) in reforming the global governance complex it is no surprise that states and peoples in the developing world have turned to alternative strategies.

Whereas the strategy of *tiers-mondisme* in the 1970s sought to build global solidarity amongst developing nations and ultimately a degree of de-linking from the global capitalist economy, recent years have witnessed a profound shift towards the new regionalism as a political strategy for engaging with a globalizing world. Underlying this new regionalism amongst developing states and emerging economies is a recognition that, in a more interconnected and less stable world order, effective development policies are 'possible only in concert with others, such as regional trading groups . . . By forming such groups, poor countries combine increased competition with economies of scale and a better division of labour – while retaining some protection from competition from more advanced countries' (UNDP 1997: 91). New regionalism also potentially enhances the bargaining power of subordinate states within the institutions of global economic governance. By comparison with the strategy of *tiers-mondisme* it also supports a form of international solidarity, which can take account of the enormous diversity amongst developing states, in terms of levels of industrialization, geopolitical situation, history and culture, and forms of governance. Amin refers to this new regionalism as 'polycentric regionalism' since it is a strategy for eroding the old North–South hierarchy and building a more pluralistic world order (Amin 1997). Furthermore, rather than being constructed in opposition to globalization it is, on the contrary, buttressed by growing enmeshment in the global political economy. For the new regionalism constitutes a form of 'open regionalism' with the object of deepening global engagement whilst at the same time creating an institutional and political capacity to 'modify the conditions of globalization' (Gamble and Payne 1991; Amin 1997: 75). However, the limits to regionalism are all too evident in the potential it has to intensify interregional competition and conflict as well as to erode global solidarity. As a political strategy new regionalism is thus by no means purely benign in development terms.

Finally, as non-governmental agencies become more active on development issues they 'challenge traditional approaches to development, which place the state at the centre of the process' (Dickson 1997: 155). Recent years have witnessed a vigorous 'globalization from below' as social movements, citizens' groups and communities build transnational alliances and coalitions to resist and contest the terms of neoliberal economic globalization by promoting an alternative programme which aims 'to make markets work for people, not people for markets' (UNDP 1997: 91). What connects these diverse movements is an alternative vision of development, which starts from the assumption that 'all economics is local' and which seeks above all the empowerment of peoples, human security and environmental sustainability through selective engagement with, rather than systematic de-linking from, the world economy (Thomas 2000). But there are also significant divisions and differences of interests and priorities between these social movements, not least on grounds of gender, culture and priorities (Cheru 1997). Whether alternative development is a viable strategy for reducing world poverty and realizing the UN's millennium development goals remains a deeply contested issue both within and outside the development community.

## GLOBALIZATION, DEVELOPMENT AND HUMAN SECURITY

In the chapters that follow, much more substantive scrutiny is given to the issues raised in this introduction. Most particularly they interrogate further the argument that globalization is transforming the context of development, whether for better or for worse. Moreover they critically assess the notion of human security and how this connects to the growing securitization of development in response to the 'war on terror'. Whether human security evolves into a new technology of social control as opposed to an emancipatory discourse remains to be judged.

Collectively the chapters present a radical critique of current development orthodoxies from a range of different perspectives and specialisms. Whilst, with qualifications, they acknowledge the ways in which globalization has transformed the context of development, they are rightly sceptical of any claims that it has fundamentally altered the power relations between North and South, or rich and poor states in the global political economy. In this respect the volume stresses the complex relationships between globalization, new modes of domination and uneven development in the global system. Its distinctive perspective on these issues arises from a shared commitment to the dissolution of the artificial intellectual divide between the study of global politics (or global political economy) and the study of development. For too long the great divide between them has impoverished our understanding of both. Moreover, until fairly recently, the globalization debate has been dominated by a preoccupation with its consequences for the states and societies of the OECD world. This volume is a contribution to the redressing of these twin deficits by reuniting global politics and development studies through the themes of *global development* and *human insecurity* which are 'as relevant to the advanced industrialized world as . . . to those conventionally labelled "developing" ' (Phillips 2005: 266).

The volume is organized into two distinct parts: the first explores the relationship between globalization and the changing context of development; and the second examines how globalization impacts upon human security in the developing world.

Part I commences with an analytical essay by Björn Hettne surveying the transformation of world order and its implications for development. He examines the relationship between globalization and the strategy of new regionalism. Discussing the impact of 9/11 and the reassertion of US unilateralism he concludes that the new regionalism is perhaps a more robust response to globalization than its critics acknowledge. Peter Burnell takes up the issue of the development consequences of 9/11, exploring its implications for the pattern of official aid flows. Whereas, in the early 1990s, globalization was associated with the diminution of official aid and its replacement with private finance he argues that, in more recent years, the uneven nature of globalization has altered the politics of aid. The result has been a revival and refocusing of aid along with, in the aftermath of 9/11, its increased securitization. He points, however, to the emerging contradictions between the multiple objectives – strategic, political, developmental – of aid and its limited capacity to address the implications of uneven globalization.

Fantu Cheru's chapter examines the implications of financial globalization for developing economies, and in particular how it has contributed to growing indebtedness and restricted access to credit. He dissects the implications of multilateral measures such as HIPC – the Heavily Indebted Poor Countries Initiative – for development amongst the world's poorest states. And he concludes that the key problem confronting indebted countries in the South is that 'Efforts to reform economies at the national level have often been derailed by market failures at the global level' (chapter 3, p. 80). In the final chapter of part I Jeffrey Haynes examines how globalization has both reinforced and constrained processes of democratization in developing countries. From the perspective of comparative political analysis he surveys the Third Wave and assesses the causal role of global factors in the diffusion of democratic norms and institutions. In doing so he demonstrates the limits of much orthodox comparative political analysis in failing to integrate global and external factors into accounts of democratization in developing countries. He concludes with the problem of democratic consolidation and emphasizes the contradictory impact of globalization which although 'important at the transition stage of democratization' may be 'often less central to efforts to institutionalize and sustain democracy' (chapter 4, p. 89).

Whereas part I provides an overview of the changing context of development, part II focuses exclusively upon the implications of globalization for development, from within a human security perspective. Accordingly, it commences with an analytical overview of the human security framework by Caroline Thomas. The chapter provides a critique of the concept of human security but nevertheless argues that it remains essential to understanding how globalization transforms the conditions and prospects for real development – as defined by Sen in terms of the expansion of human capabilities or freedoms (Sen 1999). Drawing upon this discussion she explores the implications of globalization, through an analysis of global trade, for human security across the South. She concludes that the current global social crisis, articulated in the unprecedented scale of impoverishment and human insecurity, requires taming globalization in ways which make it 'commensurate with human security' (chapter 5, p. 128). Taking up the theme of human insecurity, Sandra MacLean's chapter presents a cogent examination of the limitations of the existing global health regime in dealing with the challenges to the health of the world's poorest communities posed by globalization. She commences by reminding the reader that, in the international classification of diseases, the single largest killer and source of ill health across the globe is given by the code Z59.5 – extreme poverty. Mapping the new health inequalities of globalization she argues that a different approach is needed to global health governance, which brings together health, security and development policies to address the problem of extensive human insecurity. In this regard, analysing the political economy of global health is an essential step towards reframing global development policies to deal with the failings of the global health regime. She identifies in the current global politics of health, whether the activities of transnational social or global health campaigns, such as the anti-tobacco coalition, the growing institutionalization of the human security agenda.

Failings in the global health regime are amplified in Nana Poku's discussion of the AIDS pandemic. His chapter assesses the scale of the global AIDS epidemic and its implications for development and human security in Africa. Such is the economic and social dislocation caused by the disease that in some sub-Saharan countries the epidemic represents a serious threat to national security, in respect of the functioning and reproduction of the state apparatus. Moroever, the failings of the global AIDS regime and the constraints of structural adjustment policies severely limit the effectiveness of national government responses to the pandemic. Under these conditions, as Poku argues, the prospects for development and human security are considerably weakened. Bonny Ibhawoh links the discussion of human security to the issue of human rights in the developing world. He traces the links between globalization and the emergence of a cosmopolitan moral order, in the form of human rights norms. Rather than understanding this relationship in terms of a dialectic, in so far as globalization is conceived as advancing and restraining the human rights project, he suggests it is a trilemma or triple-edged sword. Thus globalization diffuses the rights discourse at the same time as economic globalization constricts its effective realization, which in turn invites a counter-reaction or reactive impulse by human rights activists in the developing world to reclaim or reassert those rights. In exploring the globalized politics of human rights within the developing world he presents a fresh but critical perspective on the transformative potential of this new politics of rights. Indeed he concludes that this represents a partial reinvention of globalization with human rights at its core.

In the penultimate chapter Dong-Sook Gills expands this discussion of 'globalization from below' to an exploration of the global politics of resistance to neoliberal globalization. In doing so she provides a holistic analysis of the political economy of globalization and how it relates to the rise of grass-roots movements of resistance in developing societies. These movements seek to replace the primacy of the global market with the primacy of human security. She examines this global politics of resistance through a focus on the World Social Forum (WSF), as the principal voice of the global social justice movement. Characterizing this as an emergent form of global anti-capitalist struggle she identifies in these new social forces of resistance significant problems in respect of cultural diversity, representativeness and strategic priorities, which limit the potential for its institutionalization. In sum, strategies of resistance towards globalization confront the dilemma of 'finding ways of coordinating diverse grass-roots movements under a more structured organization without compromising the strength of decentralized movements' (chapter 9, p. 205). In the final chapter Jane Parpart considers how the globalization of governance norms, such as the good governance agenda, is highly gendered with significant consequences for the empowerment of women in developing societies. There is, as Sen observes, a significant gender aspect to the analysis of development and human security (Sen 1999). This chapter discusses the limits and contradictions of the good governance agenda as it impacts upon women in developing societies. It concludes that strategies 'to empower women that do not take into account the way women (and men) are situated in an increasingly global economy are bound to fail' (chapter 10, p. 216). In short, analyses of the relation between globalization and human security which neglect the gender dimension remain, at best, significantly flawed.

## MAKING GLOBALIZATION WORK FOR THE POOR: A CONTRADICTION IN TERMS?

One of the most pressing questions confronting the international community is whether it 'can manage the globalization process in a way that. . . . offers a more equal sharing in its benefits' (UNCTAD 1998: 5). The evidence of recent years, most especially in the derisory progress towards achieving the Millennium Development Goals, suggests that it cannot. Despite assaults on the neoliberal Washington Consensus global development policy appears to remain firmly anchored to a very particular ideology of capitalist development. Moreover appeals for a global 'New Deal' between rich and poor states have been overtaken by the global war on terror. The more recent militarization of globalization and associated securitization of development do not bode well for enhancing the global human condition. The contributions to this volume go some way to understanding how this failure to tame globalization has occurred and its implications for development and human security. Although globalization has transformed the context of development it has yet necessarily to transform for the better the prospects for real development (in Sen's terms) and human security for the majority of the world's most vulnerable communities.

### References

Amin, S. 1997: *Capitalism in the Age of Globalization*. London: Zed Books.

Amin, S. 2003: *Obsolescent Capitalism*. London: Zed Books.

Bagwhati, J. 2004: *In Defense of Globalization*. Oxford: Oxford University Press.

Birdsall, N. 1998: Life is unfair: inequality in the world. *Foreign Policy*, 111, 76–93.

Brenner, N. 1999: Beyond state-centrism? Space, territoriality and geographic scale in globalization studies. *Theory and Society*, 28 (1), 39–78.

Bryant, R. C. 2003: *Turbulent Waters – Cross-Border Finance and International Governance*. Washington, D.C.: Brookings Institution.

Callinicos, A. 2003: *An Anti-Capitalist Manifesto*. Cambridge: Polity.

Castells, M. 1998: *End of the Millennium*. Oxford: Blackwell.

Castells, M. 2000: *The Rise of the Network Society*. Oxford: Blackwell.

Castles, S. and Miller, M. 2002: *The Age of Global Migration*. London: Palgrave.

Cheru, F. 1997: The silent revolution and the weapons of the weak: transformation and innovaton from below. In S. Gill and J. Mittelman (eds), *Innovation and Transformation in International Studies*, Cambridge: Cambridge University Press.

Chiswick, B. R. and Hatton, T. J. 2003: International migration and integration of labor markets. In M. D. Bordo, A. M. Taylor and J. G. Williamson (eds), *Globalization in Historical Perspective*, Chicago: Chicago University Press, 65–120.

Crafts, N. and Venables, A. J. 2003: Globalization in history: a geographical perspective. In M. D. Bordo, A. M. Taylor and J. G. Williamson (eds), *Globalization in Historical Perspective*. Chicago: Chicago University Press, 323–72.

DfID 2005: *MDG Factsheets*, at www.dfid.gov.uk/pubs/file/mdg-factsheets/poverty.

Dickson, A. 1997: *Development and International Relations*. Cambridge, Polity.

Dollar, D. 2004: *Globalization, Poverty and Inequality since 1980*, World Bank Policy Research Working Paper 3333, June. Washington: World Bank; at www.ibrd.org.

Dollar, D. and Kraay, A. 2002: Inequality is no myth. *Foreign Affairs*, 81 (4 July).

Duffield, M. 2001: *Global Governance and the New Wars*. London: Zed Press.

Firebaugh, G. 2003: *The New Geography of Global Income Inequality*. Cambridge, Mass.: Harvard University Press.

Firebaugh, G. 2004: Accounting for the decline in global income inequality. *American Journal of Sociology*, 110 (2), 283–312.

Galbraith, J. R. 2002: A perfect crime: inequality in an age of globalization. *Daedalus* (Winter), 11–25.

Gamble, A. and Payne, A. 1991: Conclusion: the new regionalism. In A. Gamble and A. Payne (eds), *Regionalism and World Order*, London: Macmillan.

Garrett, G. 1998: Global markets and national politics. *International Organization*, 52.

Germain, R. 2004: *The International Organization of Credit*. Cambridge: Cambridge University Press.

Gills, B. and Rocamora, J. 1993: *Low Intensity Democracy*. London: Pluto Press.

Gilpin, R. 2001: *Global Political Economy*. Princeton: Princeton University Press.

Godement, F. 1999: *The Downsizing of Asia*. London: Routledge.

Gordon, D. 1988: The global economy: new edifice or crumbling foundations? *New Left Review* 168, 24–65.

Grugel, J. 1991: Latin America and the remaking of the Americas. In A. Gamble and A. Payne (eds), *Regionalism and World Order*, London: Macmillan.

Grugel, J. 2004: *Democratization*. Basingstoke: Palgrave.

Grieco, J. M. and Ikenberry, G. J. 2002: *State Power and World Markets*. New York: Norton.

Haass, R. N. and Liton, R. E. 1998: Globalization and its discontents. *Foreign Affairs* (May/June).

Hardt, M. and Negri, A. 2000: *Empire*. Cambridge, Mass.: Harvard University Press.

Harris, N. 1987: *The End of the Third World: Newly Industrialising Countries and the End of an Ideology*. London: New Amsterdam Books.

Hirst, P. and Thompson, G. 1999: *Globalization in Question*. Cambridge: Polity.

Hirst, P. and Thompson, G. 2003: Globalization – a necessary myth? In D. Held and A. McGrew (eds), *The Global Transformations Reader*, 2nd edn, Cambridge: Polity, 98–106.

Hoogvelt, A. 1997: *Globalisation and the Postcolonial World – The New Political Economy of Development*. London: Macmillan.

Huntington, S. 1993: *The Third Wave*. Norman: University of Oklahoma Press.

IMF 2003: *World Economic Outlook*. Washington, D.C.: IMF.

Jackson, R. H. 1990: *Quasi-States: Sovereignty, International Relations and the Third World*. Cambridge: Cambridge University Press.

Keohane, R. and Nye, J. 2003: Globalization: what's new? What's not? (And so what?). In D. Held and A. McGrew (eds), *The Global Transformations Reader*, Cambridge: Polity, 75–84.

Lindert, P. H. and Williamson, J. G. 2003: Does globalization make the world more unequal? In M. D. Bordo, A. M. Taylor and J. G. Williamson (eds), *Globalization in Historical Perspective*, Chicago: Chicago University Press, 227–75.

Mallett, V. 1999: *The Trouble with Tigers*. London: Harper Collins.

Milanovic, B. 2000: True world income distribution, 1988 and 1993. *Economic Journal*, 112, 51–92.

Mittelman, J. H. 2000: *The Globalization Syndrome*. Princeton: Princeton University Press.

Phillips, N. 2005: Whither IPE? In N. Phillips (ed.), *Globalizing International Political Economy*, Basingstoke: Palgrave Macmillan, 246–70.

Reddy, S. G. and Pogge, T. W. 2003: *How Not to Count the Poor*. New York: Columbia University, 37.

Rodrik, D. 1997: *Has Globalization Gone Too Far?* Washington, D.C.: Institute for International Economics.

Rowthorn, R. and Wells, J. 1987: *De-Industrialization and Foreign Trade*. Cambridge: Cambridge University Press.

Salai-i-Martin, X. 2002: *The Disturbing 'Rise' of Global Income Inequality*. Cambridge, Mass.: National Bureau of Economic Research, 72.

Schmidt, V. 2002: *The Futures of European Capitalism*. Oxford: Oxford University Press.

Scholte, J. 2000: *Globalization – A Critical Introduction*. Basingstoke: Palgrave.

Sen, A. 1999: *Development as Freedom*. Oxford: Oxford University Press.

Silver, B. J. 2003: *Forces of Labor: Workers' Movements and Globalization since 1870*. Cambridge: Cambridge University Press.

Sindharan, K. 1998: G-15 and South–South cooperation: promise and performance. *Third World Quarterly*, 19 (3), 357–73.

Thomas, C. 2000: *Global Governance, Development and Human Security*. London: Pluto Press.

Ugarteche, O. 2000: *The False Dilemma – Globalization: Opportunity or Threat?* London: Zed Books.

UNCTAD, S.-G. o. 1998: *The Least Developed Countries 1998 Report*. Geneva: UNCTAD.

UNCTAD 1998: *World Investment Report*. Geneva: UNCTAD.

UNCTAD 2001: *World Investment Report*. Geneva: UNCTAD.

UNCTAD 2002: *World Investment Report*. Geneva: UNCTAD.

UNCTAD 2003: *World Investment Report*. Geneva: UNCTAD.

UNDP 1997: *Human Development Report 1997*. Oxford: Oxford University Press.

UNDP 1998: *Globalization and Liberalization*. New York: UNDP.

UN Secretary-General 2004: *Report on the MDG*. New York: UN Office of the S.-G., UN.

Wade, R. 2004: Is globalization reducing poverty and inequality? *World Development*, 22.

Wolf, M. 2004: *Why Globalization Works*. New York: Yale University Press.

Wood, E. M. 2003: *Empire of Capital*. London: Verso.

Woods, N. 1999: Order, globalization and inequality in world politics. In A. Hurrell and N. Woods (eds), *Inequality, Globalization and World Politics*, Oxford: Oxford University Press.

Woods, N. 2005: The shifting politics of foreign aid. *International Affairs*, 81 (2), 393–409.

World Bank 2005: *Classification of Countries*, at www.ibrd.org.

World Trade Organization 2001: *World Trade Report*. Geneva: WTO.

WTO 2002: *World Trade Report*. Geneva: WTO.

Part I

# Globalization and the Transformed Context of Development

# 1 Globalism, Regionalism and Interregionalism

*Björn Hettne*

*This chapter explores the relationship between globalization, the emergence of the new regionalism, and development strategies. It commences with an analytical discussion of the idea of new regionalism and then examines how globalization, amongst other factors, has led to an expansion in regional formations across the globe but especially in the South. It goes on to present a comparative assessment of this new regionalism and its implications for global governance, concluding with a discussion of the future of regionalism in the post-9/11 world.*

## INTRODUCTION: REGIONS AND REGIONALISM

In considering the world order implications of ongoing globalization and regionalization and also the effects of 11 September on the future formation of regions and interregional relations, this chapter builds and elaborates on results from the UNU/WIDER international research project on the 'new regionalism'.[1] The original thrust of this project was to explore the role of the regional factor in global transformation from the mid-1980s under the assumption that this regional wave was 'new'. It differed from the 'old' in a number of ways: it took shape in a multipolar world order; it was a more voluntary process from within the emerging regions; it was often described as 'open', and thus compatible with an interdependent world economy; it was resulting from a comprehensive, multidimensional societal process; and it formed part of a global structural transformation, or globalization, in which also a variety of non-state actors were operating at several levels of the global system.

### Approaches

Some conclusions drawn from contrasting old and new regionalism were: (1) the focus on the multitude of actors which points beyond state-centric approaches; (2) the focus on the 'real' region in the making, rather than the formal region defined by member states, which also implied a substantivist, multidimensional view of the region; and (3), the focus on the global context – the process of globalization – as an exogenous formative factor not really considered by old regionalism theory. Globalization and regionalization are interlinked processes.

The New Regionalism approach (NRA) employed in the project tried to consider these aspects, particularly those focused on conditions related to what is called globalization. Since the regional impact of globalization differs in various parts of the world, the actual process of regionalization also differs between emerging world-regions, thus giving shape to many regionalisms and, ultimately, even a modified global structure. Globalization shapes regionalization and vice versa.

Globalization and regionalization processes, however, interact under different conditions of 'regionness', creating a variety of pathways of regionalization. These different pathways, particularly in what used to be called the Third World, are the subject of this chapter. A future perspective in which regions mediate to form increasingly dense interregional structures as an extension of regionalization, in the long term possibly leading to what I call multiregionalism, is also suggested and tentatively explored here. In this way the chapter moves the emphasis from regionalism to transregionalism, and, by implication, world order. The strong emphasis on the new regionalism in the project meant that other world order options and the way they could relate to regionalization were neglected, which narrowed the scope as far as future options are involved. This limitation is quite natural since the original research programme was about regionalism as a new empirical phenomenon, but in order to grasp the current process of global transformation a broader approach to world order is needed (Hettne and Odén 2002). Regionalism, seen as a 'return of the political', thus has to be related to governance and global forms of governance, particularly what will be discussed here as trans-, inter-, and multiregionalism.

The approach taken here is an understanding of contemporary regionalism as well as emerging transregionalism from both an endogenous perspective, according to which regionalization is shaped from within by a large number of different actors, and an exogenous perspective, according to which regionalization and globalization are intertwined articulations of global transformation. The ultimate outcome of this double process may be a regionalized world order.

The endogenous perspective strongly underlines the historical continuities between old and new regionalism. It is therefore important to explore the contextual – conditions relevant in each specific case. Here a focus on the transformation of territorial identities becomes relevant.

The theoretical inspiration, as far as the exogenous perspective is concerned, is the historical/dialectical perspective implied in Karl Polanyi's 'Great Transformation' and the so-called 'Double Movement'. These concepts were originally developed to explain the rise and fall of market society in the nineteenth and early twentieth century; they are here applied to changes of the current international political economy, i.e. globalization, interpreted as a Second Great Transformation (Hettne 1997).

## Conceptualization

In spite of the enormous literature to date, there is little consensus on the terminology of regionalism. This is how the terms will be used in this chapter.

■ *Regions* must be understood as processes; they are not geographical or administrative objects but subjects in the making (or un-making); their boundaries are shifting and so is their capacity as actors, which here is referred to as the level of *regionness*.

■ *Regionalism* is the ideology and political project of *region-building*, but the concept also denotes the whole complex or phenomenon as such, i.e. the study of regions. The New Regionalism thus refers to the study of new regions or the recent process in the formation or transformation of regions.

■ *Macroregions* and *microregions* (the former supranational and the latter often subnational, but may nevertheless also be transnational) are structural expressions of interrelated processes. *Growth triangles* and *economic corridors* are varieties of transnational microregions. *Subregions* are distinct parts of large macroregions, such as the new Europe. They represent more dense supranational cooperation.

■ *Regional cooperation* refers to joint efforts by states to harmonize their national economies.

■ *Regional integration* connotes a more purposeful cooperation among neighbouring states and can also be seen as the outcome of regional cooperation.

The *formal* or institutionalized region is of course more easy to define, but the process of *regionalization* is going on partly independently from the institutionalization process, and covers many dimensions and many actors. It is a process of region-formation, whether this is planned or unplanned.

Region-building, as an expression of the ideology of regionalism, has mainly been a European phenomenon. In the rest of the world regionalization happens in more informal ways, largely as a response to globalization, but also as a way of managing crises, such as the many state collapses in West Africa and elsewhere (Grugel and Hout 1999).

Microregionalism and transregionalism are two relatively new phenomena, belonging to the era of New Regionalism. Transregionalism will be discussed in more detail in the final section. Microregions are complex and varying. There are many reported cases from Europe and South-East Asia, but a beginning has been made to identify microregionalism also in Africa (Söderbaum 2002). A common element is a larger room-for-manoeuvre for microregional actors, be they local governments, civil society or firms, but the incentives driving these actors differ. It seems that some of them react more to globalization than to regionalization. Globalization has as one of its most significant consequences a decreasing state-control over local actors. However, as macroregions are being shaped, they also provide a political framework, legitimizing a more independent behaviour from subnational regions, which may and often do create transnational microregions.

Regionalization has structural consequences beyond the particular region, as stressed in the New Regionalism approach. *Transregionalism*, thus, refers to structures mediating between regions, if one can use the word *interregionalism* in a formal way; and if it thus constitutes a form of world order: *multiregionalism*. Like the new regionalism, transregional arrangements are voluntary and cooperative.[2]

If by region we mean instrumental regions with some actor-capacity, we can make a distinction between intracontinental and intercontinental transregionalism. Intracontinental regional organizations such as the AU (African Union) and OAS (Organization of American States) are usually weak paper organizations without actor-capacity, and therefore also lack intercontinental relations of any importance. Regional organizations of a more substantive kind below the continental level which develop relations between continents, have more actor-capacity, and their mutual relations therefore gain a certain significance as we shall see in the concluding section.

## THE FORMATION OF REGIONS

Regional integration and regional cooperation are concepts associated with the first wave of regionalism. The other concepts have been developed more recently in the context of the new regionalism. The new regionalism goes beyond free trade arrangements to include also other economic, as well as political, security, social and cultural issues. The political ambition of establishing regional coherence and regional identity is of primary importance. As a political project I call this ambition 'the pursuit of regionness' (Hettne 1995a).

### Regionness

The level of 'regionness' defines the position of a particular region or regional system in terms of regional coherence, identity and actor-capacity, which can be seen as a long-term endogenous historical process, changing over time from coercion, the building of empires and nations, to more voluntary cooperation, transcending the Westphalia logic.

Regions are, as was stressed above, always evolving and changing. Like a nation, a region is an 'imagined community', and like a nation it has a territorial base. This *regional space* is the first step on the staircase of 'regionness'. It is a geographic area, delimited by more or less natural physical barriers. The region is thus rooted in territory and is, in social terms, organized by human inhabitants, at first in relatively isolated communities, but more and more creating some kind of translocal relationship. Region as a *regional complex* implies ever widening translocal relations between the human groups. Such relations of embryonic interdependence subsequently constitute a 'security complex', in which the constituent units, normally some sort of 'states', are dependent on each other, as well as on the overall stability of the regional system. Region as *international society* can be either organized or more spontaneous. In the case of a more organized cooperation, region is defined by the list of countries that happen to be members of the organization in question. Such a region could be called the 'formal' region, in contrast to the process of regionalization from below, creating the 'real' region. The states are still the dominant actors, but the pattern of relations is regulated and 'society-like'. A region as *community* takes shape when an enduring organizational framework (formal or less formal) facilitates and promotes social communication and convergence of values and actions throughout the region. Finally, region as an *institutionalized polity* has a more fixed structure of decision-making and stronger actor capability or 'actorship'.

Since regionalism is a *political project*, and therefore created by human actors, it may, just like a nation-state project, fail. In this perspective a region in decline means decreasing regionness and ultimately a dissolution of the region itself. This is what has happened in the Balkans. Another 'implosive' region is South Asia. A third is Central Africa. The trend is ominous.

## Regionalism as response

Globalization is a challenge provoking a regionalist response. One of the basic assumptions about the new regionalism held by the UNU/WIDER project was that it was an integral part of globalization. This raised the issue of how to conceive globalization in theoretical terms. Since globalization by definition is a worldwide, multidimensional process about which there can be no meaningful explanatory theory, we have to choose a more specific and delimited entry point. In the theory of economic history associated with the above-mentioned Karl Polanyi an expansion and deepening of the market is supposedly followed by a political intervention 'in defence of society'; the expansion of market exchange constituting the first, and the societal response the *second*, movement, together making 'the double movement'. It is important to note that both movements, albeit through different dynamics, are engineered by political forces and actors. The first movement implies a deliberate institutionalization of market exchange and the destruction of institutions built for social protection, a destruction euphemistically called 'deregulation' or even 'liberalization'. The resulting turbulence and social unrest leads to a re-regulation; new institutions of social welfare adapted to the new political economy are created as part of the transformation. In the historical transformation analysed by Polanyi, these institutions formed part of the modern nation-state. The dysfunctions associated with the second movement and its various forms of political regulation then lead to a renewed defence of market solutions as an escape from illegitimate 'rent seeking' behaviour on the part of the political class.

In accordance with the double movement thesis, asserting that market exchange and political regulation (mediated by social movements) constitute the basic dialectics of a changing political economy, globalism, or the globalist project, is here seen as an effort to institutionalize the market system on a global scale; and trends towards the creation of regional formations throughout the world as one political attempt (among others) to manage the social turbulence implied in such unprecedented deregulation, unprecedented in terms of its global scope. This does not mean that globalization is uniformly 'economic' and regionalization 'political'. In both processes political decisions, shaped by contesting social and political forces, are crucial, and the consequences in terms of distribution of resources are deeply political. As was stressed above, the distinction between economic and political must not be exaggerated. Here 'political' normally will refer to efforts at creating political communities on various levels of the world system; but depoliticization is nevertheless also political in its redistributive consequences.

If market-led globalization is the first movement in a second great transformation, what should we expect from a second movement? The fundamental problem with market-driven economic globalization (corresponding to the ideology of globalism) is selectiveness. Not everybody can be included. These exclusivist implications lead to a 'politics of identity', as loyalties are being transferred from civil society to 'primary groups' (defined as the smallest 'we-group' in a particular social context), competing for scarce resources. This can be described as some sort of regression into pre-Westphalianism – a world with a reduced role for the nation-state as we know it. Concepts which have been used in this context are 'durable disorder' or, in metaphorical terms, 'a new medievalism' (Gamble 2001). The mainstream understanding of this is that the 'new wars' constitute abnormal crises in an otherwise normal transition process. Mark Duffield (2002) has interpreted this as a new political economy rather than as a temporary crisis. The overall significance of this route is a downward (from the state) movement of authority and governance to subnational regions, localities and social groups, while supranational forms of governance remain embryonic. This is a scenario to be avoided.

We should therefore expect various political forces to shape the future course of globalization, i.e. to 'politicize' it (in the sense of democratic, civil society control). This will be done in competition between forces that are neither mutually compatible nor necessarily benevolent from different normative positions that we may have (Falk 2002). 'Resistance is localised, regionalised, and globalised at the same time that economic globalisation slices across geopolitical borders' (Mittelman 2000: 177).

I thus conceive 'contemporary globalization' (Held et al. 1999) primarily as a further deepening of the market system, which, including its disturbing social repercussions, now takes place on a truly global scale. We should expect not a uniform response to this transformation, but, as history shows, many forms of resistance, constructive as well as destructive (Gills 2000). Regionalism is one of them. The following section presents an overview of emerging regionalisms in the world. The concluding section discusses world order implications of this trend.

## A WORLD OF REGIONS

The process of regionalization has transformative structural consequences on various levels, such as microregionalism, macroregionalism, subregionalism and transregionalism. Microregions are subnational but very often cross borders of neighbouring countries, thus becoming transnational, for instance in the case of Öresund (Denmark and Southern Sweden). Subregions, which are supranational, emerge within larger macroregions, such as the European Union, and may facilitate cooperation among a grouping of states having particular interests and problems in common. Examples of such subregions in Europe are the Visegrád group in Central Europe, the Baltic area, the Mediterranean, etc. Often microregions coincide with so called 'historical regions' formed long ago, but they also constitute completely new forms of cross-country cooperation between subnational regions, which suddenly find themselves in a more advantageous location due to the overall change in the political/administrative landscape.

There are thus many endogenous regionalisms as well as many different manifestations of the dialectics of the double movement. This makes it important to understand the varying nature of emerging regional formations in the North as well as in the South. What is suggested here is a tentative map of the new regionalizing world.

## Types of regions

A rough distinction can be made between three structurally different types of regions: core regions, peripheral regions and, between them, the intermediate regions. How do they differ from each other? There are two basic criteria. The regions are, first, distinguished by their relative degree of economic dynamics and, second, by their relative political stability. The borderlines are non-permanent. Rather one could think of the hierarchical structure as zones that the regions enter or leave depending on their economic position and political stability, as well as their level of regionness. This means that the regions may be differently situated and defined on different occasions, or at different times in world history (Hettne 1998).

The economic policy position is similarly unstable. The growth path relying on neoliberal adjustment can quickly be reversed. In spite of being politically incorrect, the interventionist orientation inherent in an intermediate position may be brought out, questioning the hegemonic economic philosophy currently in place. Furthermore as the regions grow, incorporating peripheral areas, they become increasingly heterogeneous. This means that they contain their own intermediate and peripheral areas (North–South regions). This pattern is visible for very large countries (Brazil, China) as well. A new geopolitical landscape is thus taking shape in the world, warranting a new political geography.

Let us now look at these structural levels in more empirical terms, i.e. identify what geographical areas we are talking about, and to what extent there are regional organizations to represent them.

## Globalization as 'Triadization'

The core regions, namely Europe, North America and East Asia, are economically advanced; they also have stable political regimes, exercising global power. The three core regions make a large part of the world economy. 'Triadization' (i.e. the increasing dominance of the EU, NAFTA (North American Free Trade Agreement) and East Asia) is for many what globalization is really about. They organize for the sake of being better able to control and to gain access to the rest of the world, i.e. the world outside their own region. One important means of control is ideological hegemony.

The three core areas constituting the Triad have different traditions in this respect. It has become common to speak of three forms of capitalism: the unregulated capitalism of North America, the administered capitalism of East Asia, and the social capitalism of Europe. Probably, the two latter are better prepared to handle the growing demands implied in a second movement, at least as far as state intervention and redistributive policies are concerned.

The currently predominant economic philosophy in the core is neoliberalism, which therefore also, with varying and perhaps declining degrees of conviction, is preached throughout the world. The stronger economies demand access to the less developed in the name of free trade; regionalization (open regionalism) may be a push in that direction. We can thus speak of 'neoliberal regionalism', although it may sound a contradiction in terms. This is the 'stepping stone', rather than 'stumbling bloc', interpretation of regionalism with respect to its relation to globalization. There are, however, different emphases among the core regions due to their contrasting traditions, differences that may become more important, depending on which of the current types of capitalism turns out to be more viable in the longer run. At present neoliberal globalization faces many counterforces.

Europe has become the paradigm of regionalization; it serves both as a *model*, stimulating other regions to become more integrated, and as a *threat*, provoking other regions to be prepared for a protectionist turn in the world economy. Europeanization, or regionalization in Europe, can be described as a process of homogenization with convergencies taking place in terms of political regimes, security arrangements and economic policies as well as other policy areas, leading to an ever increasing level of regionness, not only in the EU (formal regionalism) but throughout continental Europe and within its subregions and microregions (informal regionalization). Europe is also a paradox in terms of integration and disintegration. The process of economic homogenization, so far associated with globalization, has led to a state of liberal hegemony. Democracy and market will therefore provide the basis for future integration. However, this process is not free from conflicts and setbacks. On the contrary, the process of integration is accompanied by processes of social exclusion as well as processes of national disintegration. The immigration and asylum regime has been strongly in focus lately, due to increasing populist and anti-immigration sentiments in an increasing number of countries. A smooth balance between processes of integration and disintegration can therefore not be taken for granted. Internally the European region is becoming increasingly heterogenous due to the enlargement, ultimately making the 'formal' and the 'real' region coincide. Thus 'Europe' has to be understood through its constituent subregions, as well as its microregions. The fifth enlargement, from fifteen to twenty-five, which took place in 2004, increased the EU size and population without adding much to its GDP. The EU is thus more and more becoming a North–South region, a process that started with Spain, Portugal and Greece and may end up with Turkey (*The Economist*, 7–13 December 2002). The controversial issue of whether 'Europe' is to be understood as a historical civilization rooted in Christendom or as a set of human values was, hopefully, settled at the Copenhagen summit in December 2002.

The other two core regions, that is North America and East Asia, so far lack a regional political order. This is particularly true for East Asia, where serious tensions between nation-states are right below the surface, at the same time as the economic miracle after the recent crisis is being put in question. In terms of security the whole region is marked by a rather low level of regionness, although this is compensated for by a dense transnational economic network. East Asian regionalism is thus often described as *de facto* regionalism, whereas regionalization in Europe takes place *de jure*. This having been said, it is obvious that on levels other than the interstate level, there has been an impressive process of regionalization on the ground through the combination of Japanese capital and Chinese diaspora entrepreneurship. Another important factor – whether primarily associated with globalization or regionalization is unclear – are the so-called growth triangles that link parts of national territories into transnational but subregional production zones, market-driven but state-assisted (Mittelman 2001). This is similar to the development of 'microregions' in Europe and the 'corridors' of Africa.

On the North American continent the core is constituted by the USA, Canada and Mexico, organized in NAFTA. This organization thus has an internal hierarchy and regional division of labour, with the USA in the centre, Canada and Northern parts of Mexico in a more subordinate position, and the rest of Mexico as an internal periphery, to which we can add Central America and the Caribbean as well. In spite of not being formally part of NAFTA they are integrated in the North American market and have no alternatives to this.

As far as NAFTA is concerned, the USA as the dominant North American state represents neoliberal capitalism. Canada and Mexico are historically more interventionist, but have adapted to the hegemonic discourse, which is more controversial in their domestic politics. Even in the core itself there are problems on the social and political front, indicating the beginnings of a 'second movement'. Reference was earlier made to social disturbances in Europe.

## Regionalism between state and market

The intermediate regions, for instance Central Europe, the Latin American Cone and South-East Asia, are linked to one or the other of the core regions, not only geographically (the 'near abroad') but also in the sense that they have strong economic relations with a particular core region and try to or are pressured to pursue similar economic policies. As they conform to the criteria of 'core-ness', that is, sustained economic development and political stability, they will gradually be incorporated into the core. This implies maintaining economic growth in a context of openness and deregulation, as well as eliminating and if necessary repressing domestic conflicts. A failure may mean sinking into the periphery.

This means that 'politics of distribution' characteristic of social capitalism has been put aside for the time being; the praise for free trade is here, nevertheless, somewhat more reserved, which is what one would expect in a context of developmentalism. The recurrent financial crises in South-East Asia and Latin America have enforced the inherent scepticism of blind subordination to the principles of free trade. The recent social collapse in Argentina has further underlined this.

The dominant perspective prevalent both in South-East Asia and Latin America is nevertheless 'open regionalism', which means open economies in principle but with some preference for one's own region in practice. Regulation is by no means excluded. Central Europe has been a waiting room for NATO (North Atlantic Treaty Organization) and EU candidates. The subregion is organized in the Visegrád group, but there has been little genuine subregional cooperation. Once they become full EU members they will probably have good reasons to articulate common interests. The three Baltic countries, Estonia, Latvia and Lithuania, as well as Slovenia, having escaped from the Balkan imbroglio, joined the EU in 2004. The former countries have reoriented themselves more or less completely away from the post-Soviet area and towards the West. Although they are often lumped together, they differ a lot in terms of history and culture, and there is so far little, apart from their shared Soviet experience, to make them into a subregion. However they are showing signs of becoming part of a Nordic-Baltic region, and have also based their subregional cooperation on the Nordic model.

The *post-Soviet area* is now in the process of being reintegrated by Russia in the form of the Commonwealth of Independent States (CIS). The CIS may perhaps lay the ground for a future core region but this is, at least in the short run, an uncertain prospect. This large area is very weak in terms of regionness. The historical Soviet Union can best be seen as an empire, an enlargement of the old Russian empire; as has been the case with declining empires, the constituent parts belonging to different natural regions move in different directions: European, Caucasian and Central Asian. The two latter are treated below as peripheral regions. Apart from Russia, the European part consists of Ukraine, Belarus and Moldova, all rather turbulent countries, the last mentioned also being among the poorest of the world. This underlines the disconnection between being post-colonial and being poor in the emerging world system.

North Africa is sometimes, being part of the Arab world, treated as part of the Middle East. It is at the same time the 'near abroad' of Europe. Algeria, Libya, Mauritania, Morocco and Tunisia are since 1989 organized in the Arab Maghreb Union (AMU), which later Egypt also joined. The region has, as part of the Mediterranean region, been a candidate for intermediate status, but, due to the enduring domestic unrest in Algeria (with spill-over risks in the neighbouring countries) and repressive political structures in the others, a rather weak one. Putting an end to this destructive process is necessary in order to avoid sinking into the periphery. The instability of this subregion is the main reason behind the Barcelona Process to be discussed below.

Latin America constitutes the 'near abroad' (or 'backyard') of the North American part of the Triad. Parts of it are thus in the process of becoming North Americanized, but its southern bloc, Mercosur (Southern Cone Common Market), is still putting up some resistance to neoliberal logic and to the US cultural influence. The engine behind Mercosur is Brazil, which by its size alone gives the region an intermediate position. The Southern Cone is, however, badly weakened by recurrent crises, reaching alarming proportions in Argentina. The future relationship between NAFTA and Mercosur is crucial but hard to foresee.

South-East Asia, primarily the six original ASEAN (Association of South-East Asian Nations) countries together with Vietnam, repeats the development pattern of East Asia, to which this region is increasingly linked economically as well as in security terms. The countries in ASEAN, being comparatively small, are mostly outward-oriented and, as far as the original group (ASEAN-6), is concerned, in various phases of an NIC-type development path. Malaysia and Singapore are leading, Indonesia is lagging behind. The more recent members, Burma and the former Indo-Chinese countries, particularly Cambodia and Laos, are lagging far behind in terms of economic development and political stability and can thus be seen as a peripheral subregion of ASEAN. Problems on the international market usually reinforce domestic authoritarianism due to the strong two-way causal relationship between economic growth and political stability. 'Developmental authoritarianism' constitutes the homogenizing political factor for which the ASEAN countries are often criticized by the West in human rights terms.

There are recurrent expressions of a more exclusivist Asian regionalism within the larger region. The Malaysian Prime Minister Mahathir once proposed the formation of an East Asian Economic Caucus (EAEC; Leong 2000). This was meant to be a sort of Asian response to the threat of European and North American 'fortresses'. The EAEC proposal slowly gained support among other ASEAN countries and to some extent China, whereas Japan took a more sceptical attitude. It is currently not on the agenda, but neither is it dead and buried. China is pursuing Asianization in various forms.

The Cambodian conflict has been of major concern for the ASEAN countries, which shows how a national crisis becomes regionalized and the regional organization is given incentives to act in the interest of the region. In this case the UN successfully cooperated with regional actors. Of importance for the successful outcome was the lack of ethnic divisions and the strong accumulated urge for peace in the war-torn country. Another major crisis erupted in Indonesia, when East Timor, after massacres carried out by Indonesian militia, became another case for UN intervention. From a regionalist point of view the low profile of ASEAN was disappointing but, in view of the consensual and non-interventionist tradition of that organization, not surprising. However, some of the ASEAN countries have been active in crisis management, and there were certainly lessons learned in the process. Coastal China follows in the footsteps of South-East Asia and is, together with Hong Kong and Taiwan, becoming part of a Greater China subregion. The most dynamic areas are the special economic zones. South Pacific (organized in South Pacific Forum) is also being drawn by Japanese capital into the larger East Asia economic space.

## The need to regionalize

The peripheral regions are politically turbulent and economically stagnant. War, domestic unrest, and underdevelopment constitute a vicious circle which make them sink to the bottom of the system, creating a zone of war and starvation. Consequently they have to organize, i.e. to regionalize, in order to arrest a threatening process of marginalization and complete collapse. At the same time their regional arrangements, if they exist at all, are as fragile and ineffective as their state structures and civil institutions. This weakness notwithstanding, they must first of all tackle acute domestic violence and poverty. Their overall situation thus makes 'security regionalism' and 'developmental regionalism' more important than the – at this point rather irrelevant – creation of free trade regimes, or even adhering to the more cautious 'open regionalism'. They have objective reasons to be more introverted and more interventionist than they are allowed to under the present hegemonic order. This tendency is what lies behind the (from a globalist position) alarmist protectionist ('stumbling bloc') interpretation of the new regionalism. Many of the peripheral regions are also geographically more distant and isolated.

Starting again from the perspective of the EU, the Balkans is a region that can be only negatively defined as an explosive regional security complex and consequently constituting a dangerous 'near abroad', something that recent history dramatically underlines. Greece, only partly involved in the region, due to its EU membership, and Turkey, a bridge to the Middle East, are the stronger actors. Of former Yugoslavia, Serbia/Montenegro, Bosnia, Kosovo and Macedonia are Balkan, together with two former 'East European' countries, Bulgaria and Romania, now on their way to the EU. Because of these different historical alignments all countries have lost whatever little tradition of cooperation they once might have been involved in. Regionalization was more due to coercion and conquest than to voluntary cooperation. The current degree of regionness in the Balkans is thus low indeed. It can, however, at this point only increase.

Two post-Soviet areas are situated in the periphery. Caucasia makes up part of southern Russia (i.e. Northern Caucasia), with Chechnya, Dagestan and other autonomous republics, and an area south of the Caucasian mountain range (Transcaucasia), where there are three post-Soviet countries, Armenia, Georgia and Azerbaijan, with complex external and internal relations. Also in this case the region is united through its many problems rather than by any positive cooperative schemes. In terms of regionness and security it is a regional complex.

In Central Asia major changes and new alignments can be expected, but in the present turbulence, magnified after 9/11, it is hard to tell exactly what changes will take place. The geopolitical importance of the region has undoubtedly increased. The Shanghai Cooperation Organization (SCO), originally established as a bulwark against Talibanism, is an indication of this. Members are Russia and China plus four Central Asian countries. Now its purpose is rather to balance the USA, which has become a major actor in the subregion (*The Hindu*, 13 February 2002).

Moving to Latin America, the Andean region as well as Central America and the Caribbean are here seen as peripheral subregions of Latin America. They hold this position due to several handicaps such as small-sized countries and rather one-sided resource endowment in the two latter, and a tradition of unruly populist politics in the former. All three regions were early organized into formal regions – the Andean Group 1968, Central American Common Market (CACM), and CARIFTA (Caribbean Free Trade Association) 1968, replaced by CARICOM (Caribbean Community and Common Market) 1973 – but the experience was not very successful. The Andean Group – a rather ambitious proposition for its time – with Bolivia, Chile, Colombia, Ecuador, Peru and Venezuela, was consciously designed to be more developmentalist than the Latin American Free Trade Association (LAFTA). It lapsed into passivity because of political reasons (the Chilean coup). The structural problems of the Andean countries are reflected in their peculiar political development (criminalization and populism). As mentioned above, Central America and the Caribbean (the Caribbean Basin) economically form part of North America and have little room for manoeuvre as far as economic policy is concerned.

The Middle East is a region originally defined from outside and thus more of a social construction than other regions. It has an unsettled and explosive regional structure which in this respect can be compared to the Balkans. The ethnic pattern is extremely heterogenous. The states are incoherent, and several regimes compete for regional hegemony or dominance. There is an enormous gap between the political elites and the masses. The level of regionness is low, and, to the extent that a stronger regional identity will emerge, it will be confined to various subregions, the North African Maghreb countries (or Western group, organized in the AMU), the Mashreq countries (or Eastern group organized in the Arab League) and the Gulf area (organized in the Gulf Cooperative Council, GCC).

In the East Asian part of the Triad, the countries in the former Indo-China subregion of South-East Asia have, together with Burma, recently become ASEAN members, in spite of their economic and political problems. Like the southern enlargement of the EU, this one may in the longer run stabilize the whole region through better control over a potentially destabilizing North–South division. Inland China, which has not been part of the modernization process, is lagging far behind the rest of China in terms of economic development. There are also ethnic tensions emerging in some provinces. This may endanger the coherence of the Chinese state/empire and destabilize the intermediate Chinese region; i.e. ultimately the coastal areas, as well.

South Asia has so far shown a low level of 'regionness', because of domestic violence and the tension between the two major powers. India and Pakistan are also diverging in terms of regime type due to fundamentalist trends in both countries. Bangladesh, Sri Lanka, Nepal, Bhutan and the Maldives all share a suspicious attitude towards the regional great power. Security is thus the main problem. South Asia has been described as 'the most dangerous place in the world'. The region was traditionally inward-looking, since the regional great power strongly emphasized self-reliance, non-alignment and bilateralism. For similar security reasons, the smaller countries encouraged external links to decrease their dependence on the regional power. The crucial interstate conflict between India and Pakistan is a conflict that defines the regional security complex and provides a key to its transformation into a regional security community. Cooperation within the regional organization SAARC (South Asian Association for Regional Cooperation) is, however, extremely weak, because the conflict in the region will continue to paralyse SAARC for some time to come, but at the same time promising, since controversial problems can be handled within one organization. The early evolution of SAARC coincided with serious internal conflicts. It is a proof of the inherent soundness of the idea of regional cooperation that a number of meetings took place in spite of ongoing disturbances. However, more recently SAARC meetings have been cancelled due to the increased tension. The events of 11 September 2001 brought this region into the very centre of world politics.

The real periphery of the world is in many senses Africa. The 53 African countries, represented on the continental level by the African Union (AU; formerly the Organization of African Unity), are grouped into more than 200 regional bodies. Apart from the formal regions, there are more important informal networks transcending state borders; these networks can be seen as embryonic regional civil societies. To the extent that one can speak of a new regionalism in the African context, the trend should rather be from single issue organizations to consolidated, multidimensional regions, ranging from economic development to security. On the whole the level of regionness is very low in Africa, and there are even some geographical areas which largely lack experience of regional cooperation. North Africa was dealt with above as an intermediate region. There are as in Asia several distinct regions and subregions within the continent (Hettne 2001).

In West Africa, where the major regional initiative ECOWAS (Economic Community of West African States) had been more or less paralysed long ago, there have been unexpected signs of a somewhat more active regionalism, in terms of a regional security regime, provoced by Liberia, Sierra Leone and Ivory Coast.

Central Africa, once dominated by former Zaire, now the Democratic Republic of Congo, is today a region only in the sense of being a geographical area and security complex, with a high level of violence. Efforts at external interventions have been confused and ineffective. Recent warfare and its consequences in terms of changing regional power structures suggest that a new pattern of alliance is emerging.

East Africa constitutes a traditional region formed by colonial bonds, but also culturally integrated through the Swahili language. In the north-eastern Horn of Africa subregion the record of conflict is much longer than the record of cooperation. Even in the Horn, a pattern of regional cooperation is slowly beginning to emerge. Countries in the region (Somalia, Djibouti, Ethiopia, Eritrea and Sudan) did (in January 1986) establish the Intergovernmental Authority on Drought and Development (IGADD).

The Eastern group of Kenya, Tanzania and Uganda formed one area of historical integration by colonialism, but later divided by national rivalries and even war (the Tanzanian invasion of Uganda under Idi Amin). Furthermore, Tanzania joined the Southern Africa Development Community (SADC) and for political reasons oriented itself towards the South. The 'old' and imposed regionalism that failed miserably has in the last decade been revived by a 'new', more spontaneous regionalism. In 2001 the first summit of the reborn East African Community (EAC) took place in Arusha. The community is said to be private business- and civil society-led. The treaty (article 5) emphasizes peace and security as one of its fundamental objectives. The inspiration from the EU is obvious.

In Southern Africa several subregional initiatives in the spirit of the new regionalism, at least in terms of declared objectives, have been taken. One example is SADCC (Southern Africa Development Cooperation Conference), now SADC, covering fourteen countries. The main function of SADCC was originally to reduce the dependence on South Africa with designs of coercive regional dominance through the destabilization of 'hostile' neighbouring regimes.

The grouping of regions, subregions or even parts of larger states into the three categories suggested above is necessarily problematic, which by itself is an indication of the complex dynamics of globalization, regionalization and transformations on the state level. 'Subregions' are in my terminology not subcontinental areas but more distinct regional groupings within a larger region, for instance the Horn of Africa in East Africa.

In order to make meaningful comparisons between regions, it is important to take cognizance of not only the historical differences expressed in culture and politics, but also the structural position. That peripheral regions are called 'peripheral', because they are stagnant, turbulent and war-prone, is of course no explanation of their status, merely a structural analysis of their relative positions in the world system, in terms of underdevelopment and conflict-proneness. These crucial dimensions are closely linked. Underdevelopment generates conflicts, and conflicts prevent necessary steps to regulate the economy. To the extent that the structural criteria change by purposive political action, the region 'moves' from one structural position to another.

It seems likely that attempts to reach intermediate status by quickly linking up to the world market in some cases will lead to deeper internal divisions with destabilizing consequences. This leaves those parts of the countries in the intermediate zone which control state power with a great responsibility for countering the process of peripheralization and internal disintegration. The only way for these poor and violent regions to become less peripheral in structural terms is to become more regionalized, i.e. to increase their levels of 'regionness'. Otherwise, their only power resource would rest in their capacity to create problems for the core regions ('chaos power'), thereby inviting or provoking some sort of external engagement. To pretend that market-led globalization will solve their problems is either stupid or cynical. These concerns are real and warrant some institutional response, such as regionalism.

## INTERREGIONALISM AND GLOBAL GOVERNANCE

To conclude this survey of the role of the regional factor in the formation of world order, I shall investigate the new empirical phenomenon of transregionalism and its varying manifestations. I shall also discuss a purely normative model of world order that I call 'regional multilateralism' or, for short, 'multiregionalism', which if fully developed would be a possible model of global governance. A 'society of states' in the classical post-anarchy model associated with Hedley Bull (1977) is not the last word in political organization. The possibility of global human community should not be excluded, but a structure of interlinked regional political communities, constituting a base for interregionalism, is logically prior to it. This can only come about through the dialectics of the globalization process as a part of a 'second movement'.

The disrupting social consequences of deterritorialization implied in this process of market-led globalization may generate political forces to halt and modify the process of globalization in order to guarantee territorial control, cultural diversity and human security. Instead of cultural homogenization, there must be an intercivilizational dialogue on the level of the macroregions; such a dialogue would necessitate a reasonably symmetric power base for regionally based civilizations; instead of asymmetry and polarization, the structural gap between regions must be bridged, and the vertical structure of the world order horizontalized through the strengthening of weak and incoherent regions (increasing regionness) in the periphery. Of importance is also that intermediate regions are capable of advancing their interest in changing the structure of comparative advantages rather than simply adapting to the received pattern of comparative advantages.

## Levels of 'interregionness'

Are there any empirical trends pointing in this direction? I think there are, but it will be a very long process for them to be realized in concrete structures. In the introduction I distinguished between transregionalism, interregionalism and multiregionalism as, as it were, different levels of 'interregionness'. The distinctions may be useful for the purpose of categorization, but in reality the lines are not that easy to draw. Transregionalism refers in general to relations between regions, and these relations may differ in terms of comprehensiveness. By the concept of transregionalism I also, however, refer to weaker forms of relations between regions, or countries within different regions (transregional interstate bilateralism).

As formal macroregions, assuming a political actor role, are emerging, there will necessarily also arise a need for more organized contacts between the regions as subjective actors. Interregionalism is thus a more organized and formal relationship, already possible to identify in the empirical world in a few cases, as we shall see below. This is the more significant arrangement as it may have long-term consequences for the structure of world order.

Multiregionalism, still a rather speculative idea, is a form of regionalized world order, which may or may not become real. This is the end point of the process. Coexisting regional communities, i.e. transregionalism or perhaps interregionalism, may be the best world order we can hope for in the medium to long term. In the long term there is a possible line from transregionalism over interregionalism to multiregionalism or, if we put it differently, higher degrees of interregionness.

Interregionalism, expressing the more comprehensive relations of the new regionalism, can provide a compromise between Westphalian and post-Westphalian logic, or between territorialism and supraterritorialism. As compared to market-led globalization in a world of nation-states, interregionalism is more rooted in regional territorial formations, and in contrast to multilateralism, it is a more exclusive relationship. The partners are defined in the interregional agreement.

Looking at the existing formal interregional arrangements, which include two or more regional organizations (interregionalism), or simply groupings of states from different geographical regions (transregionalism), there is so far no clear picture on the horizon. Consequently, it is premature to speak of interregionalism as a form of transnational, not to speak of global, governance. But the trend pointing in that direction may be important, particularly as a counter-trend towards US unilateralism.

## Patterns of transregionalism

To establish some order in this emerging cobweb of transregional relations, one can distinguish between relations within the Triad on the one hand, and relations between the core regions of the Triad and their various regional partners outside on the other. Unsurprisingly, power balance concerns, as well as the somewhat different economic ideologies referred to above, result in a degree of tension in the former relations.

Transregional links within the Triad are constituted by various transatlantic (US–EU) agreements, APEC (Asia–Pacific Economic Cooperation), where the USA is the driver, and the ASEM (Asia–Europe Meeting) process, involving the EU and selected Asian countries. The institutionalized transatlantic links are weak, not to speak of interregional arrangements between the EU and NAFTA, which as a matter of fact are non-existent. The reason for this is that the USA prefers bilateralism, which of course prevents the building of institutions of interregionalism.

The fifteen member-strong forum for APEC, set up in 1989, is a comprehensive organization. In my view it is not adequate to describe the huge area covered by APEC as a region, which is often the case; rather it is a transregional organization, expressing the US hegemonic interest in the area, just like the transatlantic community (organized within NATO). The ASEM process in contrast seems to be more susbstantive, which may be explained by the need felt by European and Asian partners to relate to, and perhaps to try to balance, the US dominance.

Often the EU constitutes the core or hub in these intercontinental arrangements, because of its regionalist ideology of the Union, whereas the USA participates in transregional arrangements, such as APEC, for more globalist reasons, i.e to promote free trade globally, using the transregional organization merely as a platform. It is interesting to compare 'oceanic' APEC with 'territorial' ASEM, the former being an interstate arrangement across regions, and the latter a semi-formal relationship between the EU and ASEAN minus Cambodia, Laos and Burma plus China, Japan and South Korea. The selectiveness on the side of the EU in the case of ASEAN participants has to do with human rights considerations.

What is interesting about the ASEM process is the fact that a political space is created, which increasingly is made use of by actors other than governments. ASEP (Asia–Europe Parliamentary Partnership Meeting) is a parallel body and at its meeting in Manila in August 2002 the participants took a very strong stand against US unilateralism (*Frontline*, 27 September 2002). ASEM Peoples' Forum is an interesting example of civil society making use of not only a regional but also an interregional arena for promoting its views vis-à-vis political and market actors. ASEM is thus a more comprehensive, multidimensional type of collaboration in spite of limited formalization. The uniqueness of ASEM is that it is one of the few international organizations of political importance of which the USA is not a member. This is what makes it interregional rather than multilateral. Multilateral regionalism (or multiregionalism) would imply systematic relations between all regional organizations, making up a form of global governance, a sort of 'European world order'.

The EU–Mercosur relationship is in formal terms an even more fully-fledged example of interregionalism, since there exists an agreement (1995) between two regional organizations (EMIFCA) with formal status since 1999. This so-called Rio de Janeiro Process, which started in 1999 with a summit between the two partners, has a similar objective to ASEM, i.e. to bring the two continents of Europe and Latin America closer in a number of policy areas. The interregional cooperation includes a political dialogue and substantive financial support to Mercosur's institutional development (Sanchez Bajo 1999). Here there is a competition with FTAA (the Free Trade Area of the Americas), which would include the USA and the whole of Latin America (minus Cuba as long as Castro remains in power). Europe can thus be seen as challenging the US hegemony in the southern part of Latin America with the support of Mercosur. Furthermore the EU–Mercosur trade is larger than the Mercosur–NAFTA trade, and the EU is also the most imporant source of investment for Mercosur. These competitive relations are part of the dynamics of regional and interregional developments and underline the need to study the dialectics of competing regionalisms (Molvik 2002).

ASEM is symmetric, EMIFCA somewhat less symmetric, in their way of operation, whereas the EU relation to ACP (Countries of Africa, the Caribbean and the Pacific) is rooted in colonial and neocolonial relations. Somewhere in between one can situate the Barcelona Process, i.e. cooperation between the EU and its Mediterranean neighbours, where peace and stability is the primary aim. Apart from countries in North Africa, also Israel and the Palestinian Authority also participate in this process, which underlines what problems are involved in the Euro-Mediterranean Partnership (EMP), but also the need for it. There are no simple solutions to security crises.

In the most obvious way, the Mediterranean region, in reality an explosive regional security complex, is a social construction, an EU invention motivated by compelling security concerns.

## Multiregionalism or unilateralism? Implications of 9/11

Many of the transregional arrangements described above are without doubt feeble and contradictory, but they nevertheless signify an interest in, and a growing need for, interregionalism in a more viable form.

A regionalized world order derived from still embryonic, transregional formations would challenge the homogenizing tendency of contemporary globalization by working for a multicentric world order, with self-centred but not autarchic regions, each rooted in historical civilizations. The regions should be internally multicultural, similar to the historical empires, which for a much longer time than the homogenizing nation-states system have provided humanity with a relevant polity, combining stability with reasonable tolerance minorities.

Being an outflow of the new regionalism, the different forms of interregional arrangements are voluntary and fundamentally cooperative, in contrast to a world order based on hegemony or, worse, dominance. The regions should, furthermore, coexist in a normative universe of converging cosmopolitan values, created through processes of intercivilizational dialogue and intersubjective understanding. This utopia differs a lot from the 'unilateralist movement' and 'the war against terrorism', which at present mark world politics.

How are these regional arangements and the feeble transregional system affected by 9/11 and the 'war against international terrorism'? Today we are thus certainly far away from realizing such a model. The 'war against terrorism' strengthens neo-Westphalian forms of governance. Since this 'war' has become a unilateralist movement, strengthening US dominance, the European-led regionalist movement is facing bad weather conditions. Even the levels of regionness within various regions are badly affected by authoritarian and coercive tendencies and regional hegemonism or rather dominance, creating suspicions within the region. The unprecedented aggressiveness of the Iraeli state, the war threat against Iraq, the declaration of Iran as 'evil', the rivalry between India and

Pakistan, the insurrection in Nepal, the crisis in Indonesia after the Bali suicide bombing, the US anti-terrorist intervention in the Philippines, the renewed demonization of North Korea are some examples of the current world disorder.

These drawbacks and obstacles may not, however, prevent the regionalist movement from resuming its course and ultimately overtaking the unilateralist movement. Rather an exhaustion of unilateral power (or 'imperial overstretch'), which is rather likely, may in due time reinforce this process. Africa and Latin America are two regions that lost importance in the US geopolitical perspective, which means that the opportunity for regional arrangements actually increases here. Mercosur already shows some signs of revitalization. Of crucial importance is the future transatlantic relationship and the capacity of an enlarged but more heterogeneous Europe to balance the USA (Wallace 2002). Of importance also is the relative role of military versus civil or 'soft' power in the struggle against terrorism. In the short term 9/11 has definitely changed the balance in favour of unilateralism and militarism. In the longer term the current role division between war-making and nation-building is unsustainable.

One problem for Europe is of course the absence of one authoritative voice. The foreign policy doctrine of interregionalism is not expressed by a president, as in the case of the Bush doctrine of pre-emptive warfare. The European doctrine has been expressed many times by temporary office holders. For instance Hans-Dietrich Genscher said with reference to interregional relations, in a preface to a book published in 1990 (Edwards and Regelsberger 1990: vii–viii), that 'the path of political dialogue and economic cooperation embarked upon by the EC in a spirit of true partnership is proving to be the path of the future'. The European model of international relations was more recently (26 September 2001) argued for by the Belgian Prime Minister Mr Verhofstadt, then President of the European Union, in suggesting a G8 based on a more adequate regional representation: 'we need to create a forum where the leading continental partnerships can all speak on an equal footing: the European Union, the African Union, Mercosur, ASEAN, the North American Free Trade Agreement, etc.' (quoted from Hveem 2002). There is an EU doctrine on international relations and world order, but no foreign policy. This is perhaps the most important difference between the EU and the USA.

### Notes

1 WIDER is the World Institute for Development Economics in Helsinki and belongs to the family of United Nations University-sponsored research institutes.

2 This conceptualization is inspired by the IEE-ULB conference 'Between Regionalism and Globalism: European Union Transregional and Interregional Trade Strategies', Brussels, 18–19 October 2002. In particular, I want to mention the useful framework developed by Vinod K. Aggarwal and Edward A. Fogarty in their paper with the same title as the conference. Albeit intended for the analysis of regional trading arrangements, the framework has a wider application.

## References and Further Reading

Bull, H. 1977: *The Anarchical Society.* Macmillan: London.

Duffield, M. 2002: Reprising durable disorder: network war and the securitization of aid. In B. Hettne and B. Odén (eds), *Global Governance in the 21st Century: Alternative Perspectives on World Order*, Stockholm: EGDI, 74–105.

Edwards, G. and Regelsberger, E. 1990: *Europe's Global Links. The European Community and Inter-Regional Cooperation.* London: Pinter Publishers.

Falk, R. 2002: The post-Westphalia enigma. In B. Hettne and B. Odén (eds), *Global Governance in the 21st Century: Alternative Perspectives on World Order*, Stockholm: EGDI, 147–83.

Gamble, A. 2001: Regional blocs, world order and the new mediavalism. In M. Teló (ed.), *European Union and the New Regionalism*, Aldershot: Ashgate.

Gills, B. K. (ed.) 2000: *Globalization and the Politics of Resistance.* London: Macmillan.

Grugel, J. and Hout, W. 1999: *Regionalism Across the North-South Divide: State Strategies and Globalization.* London and New York: Routledge.

Held, D. 1995: *Democracy and the Global Order: From the Modern State to Cosmopolitan Governance.* Cambridge: Polity.

Held, D. et al. 1999: *Global Transformations.* Cambridge: Polity.

Hettne, B. 1995a: Introduction: the international political economy of transformation. In B. Hettne (ed.), *International Political Economy: Understanding Global Disorder*, London: Zed Books.

Hettne, B. 1995b: *Development Theory and the Three Worlds.* London: Macmillan.

Hettne, B. 1997: The double movement: global market versus regionalism. In R. W. Cox (ed.), *The New Realism. Perspectives on Multilateralism and World Order*, Tokyo: United Nations University Press.

Hettne, B. 1998: Globalism, regionalism and the new Third World. In N. Poku and L. Pettiford (eds), *Redefining the Third World*, London: Macmillan, 69–87.

Hettne, B. 2001: Regional cooperation for security and development in Africa. In P. Vale, L. A. Swatuk and B. Odén (eds), *Theory, Change and Southern Africa's Future*, Basingstoke: Palgrave, 83–110.

Hettne, B., Inotai, A. and Sunkel, O. (eds) 1999/2001: *Studies in the New Regionalism. Volumes I–V.* London: Macmillan Press.

Hettne, B. and Odén, B. (eds) 2002: *Global Governance in the 21st Century: Alternative Perspectives on World Order.* Stockholm: EGDI.

Hveem, H. 2002: Geopolitics vs globalization? The political economy of inter-regional relations. Paper for *Symposium on American, European, Russian Foreign Strategies and China*, Chinese Academy of Social Sciences, Beijing. 9–11 April.

Leong, S. 2000: The East Asian Economic Caucus (EAEC): Formalized regionalism being denied. In B. Hettne et al. (eds), *National Perspectives on the New Regionalism in the South*, Basingstoke: Macmillan, 57–107.

Mittelman, J. H. 2000: *The Globalization Syndrome. Transformation and Resistance.* Princeton: Princeton University Press.

Mittelman, J. H. 2001: Subregional responses to globalization. In B. Hettne et al. (eds), *Comparing Regionalisms. Implications for Global Development*, Basingstoke: Palgrave, 214–33.

Molvik, S. 2002: *Mercosurs utvikling. Makt og idéer i soramerikansk nyregionalisme*. Oslo: Oslo universitet.

Polanyi, K. 1945: Universal capitalism or regional planning. *London Quarterly of World Affairs*, January 1945.

Polanyi, K. 1957: *The Great Transformation*. Boston: Beacon Press.

Sanchez Bajo, C. 1999: The European Union and Mercosur: a case of interregionalism. *Third World Quarterly*, 22, 927–41.

Söderbaum, F. 2002: *The Political Economy of Regionalism in Southern Africa*. Göteborg: Padrigu.

Teló, M. (ed.) 2001: *European Union and the New Regionalism*. Aldershot: Ashgate.

Wallace, W. 2002: Living with the hegemon: European dilemmas. In E. Hersberg and K. Moore (eds), *Critical Views of September 11*, New York: The New Press, 95–108.

# 2 Foreign Aid: Reports of its Death Greatly Exaggerated

*Peter Burnell*

*Following years of relative decline official foreign aid (multilateral and bilateral) has begun to rise. Peter Burnell seeks to explain why and whether it represents a significant transformation in global development prospects. Following an examination of past and current trends in aid disbursements the discussion turns to an explanation of the significant shifts underway, linking these to the impact of 9/11 and the subsequent securitization of development. This leads to an examination of the effectiveness and impact of aid with particular reference to political conditionality and the contradictions between the various objectives of aid, from democratization, to securitization, to liberalization.*

## INTRODUCTION

This chapter explores the reasons why the reports circulating in the early 1990s that foreign aid was in terminal crisis were premature. After introducing the terminology of international assistance, and noting the grounds for pessimism some years ago, it proceeds to explore the present mood and future prospects. Aid's reviving fortunes in one sense are explained in terms of a growing awareness of the uneven implications of globalization and the after-effects of the terrorist events of 11 September 2001 in the United States. The chapter concludes with some words of caution, especially regarding political development aid, which was fashionable in the 1990s.

## THE FOREIGN AID BUSINESS

The Development Assistance Committee (DAC) of the Organization for Economic Cooperation and Development (OECD), which accounts for over 95 per cent of all official development assistance (ODA), defines ODA as resources transferred on concessional terms for the promotion of the economic development and welfare of developing countries. Alongside ODA the post-Cold War era has witnessed the growth of 'official aid'. That shares ODA's concessionary qualities but is destined chiefly for thirteen former communist bloc societies – 'transition economies' – together with a slowly increasing number of graduates from among ODA recipients, most notably Israel. In addition to official flows from governments and multilateral organizations such as the International Development Association (IDA) and various UN bodies, there is the voluntary assistance of non-governmental organizations (NGOs), many of them relying heavily on official support. There is much less military aid now than at the height of the Cold War. But because aid is fungible with respect to the ends that it actually serves, analytical distinctions between military aid, development aid and humanitarian assistance can be artificial in practice.

ODA peaked in the early 1990s and subsequent trends appeared to confirm predictions of inexorable decline. All major donors reduced ODA relative to gross national income (GNI): by 2000 the DAC states provided a smaller share (0.22 per cent) than at any time since the late 1940s, thereby moving away from the 0.7 per cent target adopted by the UN General Assembly in 1970. The reasons are well known. Pre-eminent was the collapse of the Soviet Union, which dramatically reduced US support for aid (bilateral and multilateral) driven by national security and geopolitical strategic concerns for the entire period when the US was top donor, that is from the late 1940s to 1990. Second, a widespread perception set in that there was growing 'aid fatigue', fuelled by doubts about aid's effectiveness even with respect to the ethically-rooted development objectives, from both the political left and the more influential political right. Third, in many countries the increasingly onerous foreign debt overhang appeared to confirm these doubts, suggesting that new aid, particularly loans, would compound the problem (see chapter 5). Fourth, an ideology of international political economy that privileges private capital flows and trade over aid is very much ascendant; also, it locates responsibility for ensuring development in the developing countries themselves. Fifth, some favourable developments made certain kinds of aid look less essential, such as the end of violent conflict in Mozambique (the expectations were that post-apartheid South Africa would promote growth throughout the region), and Central America. A more stable Middle East involving peace between Israel and the Palestinians looked a real possibility after the 1991 Gulf War.

On the 'donor side', in Japan, the largest ODA provider for most of the 1990s, financial and economic deterioration caused support to sag towards the end of the decade. Germany's willingness to continue its historically large aid budgets was undermined by the financial, economic and political costs of reunification. The EU, vying to be the world's fourth largest donor (together with member states' bilateral aid, the EU accounts for just over half of all ODA), became increasingly preoccupied with its own internal agenda: enlargement to the east (which will be expensive for EU finances), deeper political integration, and preparations for the single currency. Aid budgets were a soft target as member states sought to restrain public spending so as to satisfy the convergence criteria for monetary union. In Britain, an incoming Labour government endorsed the Conservative Party's animus against overt increases in direct taxation; inevitably it would face growing pressure to spend more on such domestic social priorities as health, education, pensions and public transport. The newly rich countries of East Asia showed no inclination to share the burdens of international assistance, let alone fill the gap left by Saudi Arabia and the Soviet Union, who were major donors in the past. Then came the Asian financial crisis (1997), which generated requests for massive financial support from the international community including the International Monetary Fund (IMF). Up until then dramatically increased foreign corporate investment and commercial bank lending to a few developing countries in East Asia (primarily China) and Latin America was making ODA look relatively increasingly insignificant. So, all told there were considerable grounds for thinking aid faced secular decline. Poor countries in Africa particularly were doubly concerned, fearing there would be aid diversion favouring former Soviet bloc countries, by West European donors especially.

## TEN YEARS ON

Over the 1990s annual flows of ODA in real terms declined by around 10 per cent, and by 40 per cent to sub-Saharan Africa, which has the highest concentration of least developed countries. Signs of a recovery began to appear in 1998; a small real-terms decline (to $51.4 billion) in 2001 owing partly to dollar appreciation. More significantly, recent pledges suggest that trends have finally turned the corner.

Prior to an international conference on Financing for Development, held in Monterey in March 2002 – an event that some observers were writing off well before it began – the US unexpectedly revealed proposals to increase its bilateral aid for developing countries, linked to economic policy and governance conditionalities. The increase (as clarified on 19 March) involves an extra $10 billion over 2004–6, of which $5 billion would appear in 2006, subject to Congressional approval. This 'Millennium Challenge Account' followed an EU pledge to increase ODA by up to $7 billion annually by 2006. All EU member states agreed to raise their contribution to at minimum the EU's current average (0.33 per cent of GNI), so raising the average to 0.39 per cent. Norway and Canada aimed to provide 1 per cent of GNI. The combined US and EU pledges would raise the DAC ODA:GNI ratio from 0.22 per cent to 0.24 per cent if annual real income growth averages 2.5 – still a long way from the 0.33 per cent of 1990–2. The US pledge, while a reversal of recent declines and implying a real-terms increase in aid of around 40 per cent by 2006 over 2003, still leaves aid's share of the federal budget and of gross national product (GNP) at historically low levels (Shapiro and Birdsall 2002).

It is difficult not to see the EU and US announcements as a form of competition to avoid the moral 'low ground', with implications for their respective claims to influence international policy towards development cooperation particularly in multilateral forums. Also at that time the US was looking for diplomatic support for its global campaign against terrorism and belligerence towards Iraq (one of three states in President Bush's so-called 'axis of evil'). The US administration was also conscious of European criticism of its increasingly unilateralist tendencies and absolutely weak contribution to 'international burden sharing' in aid (the

US's proportional share having fallen continuously since the early 1960s). At 0.11 per cent of GNI now and only 0.02 per cent given to the least developed countries, the US compares unfavourably with every other DAC country, despite regaining (from Japan) the position of largest donor in 2001 (Japan's ODA decline of 18 per cent in real terms in 2001 owed much to yen depreciation).

Of course even modest promises are not always kept. Moreover they look insignificant compared to the challenge posed by world poverty, or to US defence expenditures or the anti-developmental effects of agricultural protectionism in the North. The Millennium Challenge pledge might raise just over 1 per cent of the world's poorest people over the threshold of absolute poverty (a dollar a day). This is well short of the UN's Millennium Development Goal, of halving the proportion of people living in extreme poverty by 2015 with specific targets for increasing educational enrolment and reducing infant and child mortality and maternal mortality – all reckoned to require at minimum a doubling of world aid. Furthermore there remain disagreements over funding the IDA, whose interest-free loans are crucial to those very poor countries that cannot attract international private capital especially as they cannot even service their existing debts.[1] The US government wants the World Bank to convert at least half of its lending into grants. European critics claim this will erode its funding base (repayments by borrowers to the IDA were $13 billion between 1992 and 2001). Dependence on – and political vulnerability to – donor governments would be increased. A compromise reached in July 2002 commits 18–21 per cent of IDA resources as grants for interventions like AIDS programmes within a total budget pledge by governments to the IDA of $23 billion over the next three years – 18 per cent more than was agreed for the previous three years.

Nevertheless, there is an improved climate for aid. Observers chose to interpret the Millennium Challenge as a signal that the US is now more open to persuasion that aid *might* be developmentally efficacious in certain circumstances; in the words of Jeffrey Sachs, the 'US is waking up from a twenty-year sleep in the development field. We can forgive them not immediately knowing everything that has been happening during their slumbers' (*Financial Times*, 25 March 2002). This has been greeted with relief, even though important long-term issues regarding the international financial architecture for development support remain to be addressed, which means more cases of financial collapse like that of Argentina remain a distinct possibility. Japan, hitherto top donor, shows no inclination to exercise global leadership over aid's overall purpose and direction. The EU too has proven unable to fix on a coherent vision for its development cooperation and apply it rigorously; its aid implementation is notoriously bureaucratic. But while the publications mill on aid never stopped working overtime ('nothing attracts quite like the manner of its passing'), there is more enthusiasm now to move the debate forward (Burnell and Morrissey, 2003). One example is the endeavour to unlock 'added value' in our understanding of complex issues of development and aid by combining interest in aid effectiveness with the analytical framework offered by public goods theory. The World Bank and United Nations Development

Programme are both supporting the research. The demand for international/global public goods of all descriptions, which currently account for only 9 per cent of aid (a further 30 per cent is allocated to national public goods) looks bound to increase, so increasing the demands for yet more aid (Velde 2002).[2] Indeed, issues of international concern where aid could make a constructive contribution range ever more widely, from meeting refugee and humanitarian crises – in the 1990s a significant growth area for aid *inside Europe*, as in the Balkans – to attacking drugs production and trafficking. And target-setting remains in fashion; thus for example at the UN World Summit on Sustainable Development in Johannesburg in September 2002 there was agreement to halve the number of people without access to sanitation and safe water to 1 billion by 2015, which will require substantial amounts of aid.

Economists have regained the courage to reassert some good news about aid, where previous years had highlighted the doubts and reservations (Collier 1999). This trumpets the positive association between aid inflows and economic growth; and reminds us that even aid not directed into investment can still benefit welfare and development. Poverty has moved closer to centre stage in the discourse and the policy rhetoric. For example the subtitle of the World Bank's *World Development Report 2000–01 – Attacking Poverty* – reactivated the poverty-focus of its 1990 report; even critics allow that 'in some ways the report really is a step forward' (Boer 2001). This follows decades in which much aid was largely driven by geopolitical imperatives and pursuit of economic and commercial advantage, with the 1980s specifically being called a 'lost decade for poverty' because of the adverse impact of the structural adjustment conditionalities that were attached to much ODA.

A significant milestone in the emergence of a new forward-looking consensus on aid was identified with the OECD's publication in 1996 of *Shaping the 21st Century: The Contribution of Development Co-operation*, which set clear targets for global poverty reduction and social development (Thérien and Lloyd 2000). Then came the World Bank's research report *Assessing Aid. What Works, What Doesn't, and Why* (1998), which restated the argument that aid can be an effective instrument against poverty so long as it goes to countries characterized by the right political will, appropriate policies and institutions and adequate governance. Also, aid was found to be twice as effective in poverty reduction in post-conflict situations (Collier 2002). The Bank claims that additional assistance of $1 billion would now raise 284,000 people above absolute poverty compared with only 105,000 people ten years ago, by focusing on 'good policy' countries. Such countries receive a growing share of IDA lending.[3] A standard requirement now is that the governments write poverty reduction strategy papers in consultation with representatives from society, for endorsement by the Bank and IMF. In April 2002 the Bank doubled the target number of countries selected for fast-track support to achieve the UN's goals for education. Although the revised total (ten) remains modest, expressions of approval from the likes of Oxfam and Action Aid are a refreshing contrast with the vituperation that NGOs routinely heaped on the Bank in the past.

Finally, the end of the Cold War did more than liberate aid from certain political constraints. It provided an enabling environment for new political objectives and aid rationales in the form of democracy, 'good governance' and human rights, pursued directly via projects and programmes or through adding political conditionalities to other conditionalities already attached to ODA. The belief that political reform might serve economic liberalization in formerly statist and authoritarian regimes was particularly important for aid to retain some measure of support in the US. The Clinton presidency pushed the idea that support for democratic transformation of Central and Eastern Europe would serve American interests. New dimensions in the academic study of aid have emerged in consequence, and generated some intriguing new agendas of inquiry, this time involving not just economists but political scientists and international relations experts. For example how can the effectiveness of political aid be measured and do the methodologies allow meaningful comparison with the returns to more conventional development aid? Are political conditionalities likely to be any more successful than the mixed record of economic conditionalities?

So, despite the ill omens ten or more years ago, reports of aid's death were greatly exaggerated in terms of both the resource flows and the attention given to aid and accompanying mood music. Comparatively speaking the indicators are most positive in Britain. As one of its earliest initiatives Tony Blair's 'New Labour' government enhanced the displacement of the Department for International Development (DfID) by giving its political head a seat in cabinet, and signalled meaningful increases in its budget. Both the Prime Minister and Gordon Brown, Chancellor of the Exchequer, voice personal support for international development cooperation. Brown has given both rhetorical and practical support for substantial debt relief to poor countries, and endorsed calls for a doubling of world aid (Dixon and Williams 2001). Of course for aid's strongest supporters these developments can never be enough, but lively public debate is an improvement on stale debate or no debate at all. Even contributions like the suggestion that the World Bank has undergone a 'tragic deterioration' and is now in crisis (under John Wolfensohn's presidency) can be interpreted as praise indeed (*Financial Times*, 28 August 2001). They reflect the myopic beliefs of right-wing American bankers and economic purists who regret recent Bank initiatives to consult representatives of poor communities and incorporate competent NGOs in its policy process, and the inclusion of gender and environmental considerations. The darker side of globalization and the rise of terrorism to the top of the US government's international political agenda are also now helping to drive a renewed interest in development aid.

## REVIVING AID

Explaining aid's revival could become entangled in long-running theoretical debates over the relative importance of structure and agency, ideas and interests, the push and pull of endogenous and exogenous forces. A full audit of influential factors would tease out relationships between demand and supply side forces as mediated by both formal and informal institutions, by private and public sector actors at national, international and subnational levels. Only two factors will be visited here: globalization, and the consequences of the events of 11 September 2001.

## Globalization

The meaning of the term globalization and the historical origins of the phenomenon are highly contested (see Introduction and chapter 1). Contemporary usage varies from simple propositions about increases in world trade and foreign direct investment to ideas about the increased interconnectedness of peoples more generally and the emergence of supraterritoriality. Different social science disciplines offer different perspectives; and globalization's meaning and significance are contested *within* disciplines or sub-disciplines like international relations. That said, there are implications for aid.

One side of the debate rejects the World Bank's view that the number of people in absolute poverty and inequality among the world's households are both declining. Instead, it maintains that globalization's effects are unequal and there are losers (whatever the unit of analysis – households, larger social groups, whole countries or regions), both relative and absolute, chiefly in the developing and post-communist worlds. The realistic option is not to try to reverse the tide of globalization but to make an intelligent use of policy instruments to optimize its effects, capture the benefits and *reduce or compensate* for the harmful consequences. This implies a role for concessionary transfers. They can support the casualties of globalization (peoples whose livelihoods are disrupted) and societies so peripheral that they will not experience the potential benefits but cannot make progress in isolation either (around 2 billion mainly very poor people are reckoned to live in countries that are neither globalizing nor developing). Victims of the uneven distribution of benefits face growing powerlessness at all levels, as a result of increasing social and economic inequalities. Wade goes even further, from claiming that world income distribution is becoming more unequal to arguing that 'incomes in the lower deciles of world income have probably fallen absolutely since the 1980s' and the number of people in absolute poverty may well have increased (Wade 2001).[4]

There are several different issues here; needless to say, if assistance is to help then different forms must be directed to different situations. There remains much analytical work to be done to refine our understanding of how different interventions can achieve the desired effects. Over the years researchers have accumulated plenty of case lore about what does *not* work well, or may not work at all. But assured knowledge about the secrets of success and, equally important, confidence that the solutions are transferable and can be replicated or scaled up remain elusive. That 'the road to hell is paved with good intentions' is a staple reflection among specialists in international development cooperation, applying even to the NGOs.

So, awareness of the negative side of what has come to be called or associated with globalization strengthens the case for international assistance, whether the reasoning be grounded in morality and justice or the security of the rich world (more on that below). That is except for the critics that think much more radical action is required, arresting globalization or tempering the neoliberal economic premises upon which it is based. Hence for example Mosley believes the strategy outlined by DfID will not serve the poor in all situations (Mosley 2001).[5] He judges aid's leverage insufficient, especially given that the donor countries maintain significant trade distortions where it suits their immediate interests, notwithstanding their insistence on market-based solutions for developing countries (government spending on subsidies in the North approximates six times the level of ODA). Of course extreme critics still say aid is worse than useless anyway, not merely irrelevant in an inequitable world trade regime. Some believe it simply prolongs the agony, diverting attention from what really needs to be done – the abolition of international capitalism.

## The events of 11 September 2001

It has become *passé* to say the terrorist attacks on the World Trade Center and Pentagon are the sort of 'events that changed the world', altering the way we understand contemporary world politics and the prospects for global stability and peace. The consequences for aid have been positive but ambiguous.

The heightened sensitivity to international terrorism has provoked a return to the kind of foreign policy behaviour associated with old-fashioned realpolitik. The consequences have included, inter alia, offers of debt relief to Pakistan including US economic support of $600 million and relaxation of aid sanctions (imposed in 1990 in response to fears about nuclear proliferation). Pakistan's support was critical to the US military operations in Afghanistan. Japan was called on to show solidarity and reward General Musharraf's, just as it was over sharing the financial costs of the 1991 Gulf War. In former Soviet Central Asian republics the US quickly made offers of aid in return for use of military bases. Turkey – a long-standing recipient of American aid – also found itself well placed to benefit, given its strategic location and as a mainly Muslim country.

There is an assumption of issue linkage between Islamic fundamentalist belligerence against the US and the conflict between Israel and the Palestinians. The US will be obliged to maintain assistance to 'moderate regimes' as in Jordan and Egypt (a major recipient of US aid since the Camp David Agreement of 1978). Aid's usefulness as a bribe or reward exchanged for political concessions without much heed to its developmental effects, could well return to fashion (it never really went away).[6] Israel's defiance of President Bush by prolonging its military incursions into Palestinian areas in April 2002 indicates we should not make simplistic assumptions about aid as weapon in intergovernmental relations. Indeed, Israel's reliance on the US (for 'security assistance' of around $3 billion annually including $1.8 billion in military aid) seems to be a classic example of reverse dependence; and Israel wields considerable influence over US policy in the region (Clarke 1997). But the Middle East situation also offers opportunities for large-scale humanitarian and post-conflict reconstruction assistance. International donors were called on to provide $2 billion in emergency assistance for the Palestinian economy for 2002 alone (unlike the first intifada, 1987–92, when the costs fell to Israel as being responsible for civil administration of the Palestinian territories). Substantial aid would have to be part of any political deal to create an internationally recognized Palestinian (provisional) state, something that looks inevitable eventually. If friendly regimes come about in Iraq (post-Saddam) and Zimbabwe (post-Mugabe) that will trigger significant aid inflows there too.

Afghanistan itself is a dynamic new aid frontier. It was promised up to $4.8 billion ($1.8 billion for 2002 alone) from the international community at a pledging conference in Tokyo in January 2002. Much larger sums will be needed over the next ten years. Acceptance of that fact sits uneasily alongside the knowledge that for (formerly) failed states it is difficult to use large aid volumes effectively without becoming aid dependent (the Afghan government barely has a tax base). But even the World Bank accepts the argument for budgetary support in this case. The state of East Timor presents another new candidate for ODA. Elsewhere, the US administration aims to increase its provision for security assistance to the authorities in Colombia, in what looks like 'mission creep' from its original involvement in providing material support to counter-narcotics operations, becoming more engaged in the war against 'left-wing terrorism' there.

To many the events of 11 September graphically confirmed the case for the rich world to be more proactive in tackling world poverty. Blair told his hosts in Ghana, 'There are times in politics when it is possible to do what was thought to be impossible a short time before . . . This is such a time. Let the developing and the developed world create together that decent prosperous future' (Tony Blair quoted in *Financial Times*, 9/10 February 2002). The proposition that extreme poverty, resentment at gross international inequalities and a sense of despair all provide fertile ground for 'anti-system behaviour' like international terrorism is more believable than saying that such behaviour stems from these 'causes' alone.[7] In Arab countries of the Middle East other factors such as US support for Israel and repression by their own governments also play a part. And the appetite for and the means to impose violent 'system change' may actually increase after passing a certain threshold of economic development.

Even so, the problems posed to the rich world by 'rogue states' and fragile or failing states (of which there are several) is much better appreciated now than when the US marines and then a United Nations force withdrew from the chaos in Somalia (1995). Thus President Bush's earlier reluctance to see the US being drawn into providing support for nation-building or state reconstruction in countries like Afghanistan could be difficult to sustain, and appears already to be waived in Iraq's case. The 'logic of neoimperialism is too compelling', given the dangers to global security of non-involvement (Mallaby 2002). The connections between poverty and other conditions that are construed as threatening, such as large-scale movements of illegal migrants and the rapid transmission of disease across borders, are also now widely appreciated. Such concerns particularly affect EU countries in their relations with the Maghreb, and could increase as the EU enlarges to the east, making its proximity to struggling economies in Belarus, Ukraine and Russia appear that much closer.

The political dimensions are never far away. Thus for example in sub-Saharan Africa the idea of a New Partnership for Africa's Development (NEPAD) has been warmly welcomed by Blair especially. The idea, which emerged out of Africa (Nigeria and South Africa in particular), suggests a willingness to acknowledge Africa's share of the responsibility to improve human rights, political accountability and economic management, and end civil conflict. In return for progress there would be more aid (a requirement of $64 billion annually has been mentioned) and trade concessions. The idea of peer review mechanisms in Africa is central to the proposal. Africans' reluctance to openly criticize Zimbabwe's flawed presidential election in March 2002 (the Common Market for Eastern and Southern Africa observer mission proclaimed it was conducted credibly, freely and fairly) has not boosted donor confidence. Indeed, following the adverse report of the Commonwealth election observers Blair reputedly threatened to withdraw Britain's support from NEPAD if South Africa's President Mbeki resisted moves to suspend Zimbabwe from the Commonwealth (*The Independent*, 21 March 2002).[8] Those moves in turn helped ensure NEPAD's place on the agenda of the G8 summit in June, which produced conditional pledges to Africa worth £4 billion annually. While the sums look grossly inadequate, UN Secretary–General Kofi Annan considered the outcome 'a turning point in the history of Africa and indeed the world' (*The Independent*, 28 June 2002).[9] At least NEPAD has mobilized discussion of Africa's plight, though it seems unlikely to stimulate a 'Marshall Plan for Africa'. Of course sceptics doubt the commitment of Africa's leaders to deliver their side of the bargain; and anti-capitalist/anti-globalization protestors argue they should not even try, seeing NEPAD as but another elite-formulated, top-down initiative.

In sum, questions about whether economic progress, even if it does reduce poverty, can solve all the problems intimated in this section, and how aid might best contribute, are highly disputed both in development studies and among aid practitioners. In aid and development the past tendency for 'magic bullets' to disappoint the hopes that were vested in them at first has generated a general attitude of caution, nowhere more apparent than in the recent history of political development aid.

## HAS POLITICAL DEVELOPMENT AID HIT THE BUFFERS?

If aid generally faces a more promising future than seemed likely a decade ago then political development aid could be a partial exception. A significant increase in international cooperation for democratization, or democracy assistance, followed the collapse of the Soviet Union (Burnell 2000). In social science the 'new institutionalism' claims that politics matters – no mere epiphenomenon of 'deeper' economic and social structures. Thus political institutional reform – engineered or underwritten by international technical and other assistance – can make a difference to the way countries are governed, irrespective of their economic situation. This belief provided some intellectual underpinning to political development aid. Recently, the political commitment appeared to be given new endorsement by President Bush's address on national security strategy to Congress (20 September 2002). Bush declared '[we will] use our foreign aid to promote freedom and support those who struggle non-violently for it, ensuring that nations moving toward democracy are rewarded for the steps they take' (*Financial Times*, 21/22 September 2002).

However, there is always a lag between the inauguration or dramatic expansion of a new kind of activity and the devising of a suitable methodology to evaluate results and appraise the performance. The story in regard to democracy assistance is not wholly encouraging. The evidence so far has underlined the difficulties facing attempts to promote any or all of the following: a rigorous respect for the rule of law, by power-holders in particular; a durable system of competitive party politics that steers between single-party dominance and excessive political pluralism or hyperfactionalism; a sustainable increase in the strength and vitality of civil society; intercommunal trust and cooperation in societies where deep-seated divisions exist. Even the limited objective of consolidating judicial autonomy looks elusive, in the absence of much more wide-ranging changes to the social, cultural and political context. As international involvement in trying to reform previously undemocratic or illiberal institutions intensified, so we were bound to appreciate more the obstacles and complexities. And even in respect of democracy projects or programmes, practitioners have yet to establish a consensus on 'best practice', in the face of a growing body of criticism by independent analysts (Carothers 1999). Problems have arisen similar to those that have long beset more conventional ODA, including relations with NGO 'partners', not least in civil society projects. One conundrum is how to generate a sense of 'ownership' and promote indigenous sustainability. Another is how to overcome the limitations of 'butterfly projects' that have little impact at the macro level, preventing replication or 'scaling up'. In what sense is 'partnership' really meaningful in this context anyway?

One of the more obvious sites where power and wealth meet in the political economy of aid is in attaching certain political conditionalities to ODA. The calibration of an optimal mix of assistance to political projects/programmes with 'positive conditionalities' (inducements of economic development/financial aid in return for improvements in democracy, human rights or 'good governance') and 'negative conditionalities' (threatened sanctions in the event of non-compliance) remains, at best, experimental. The *economic* conditionalities that became the norm in the 1980s were conceived on the grounds that it was essential to get economic policies and institutions 'right' if development was to happen. By and large they embodied the Washington Consensus on orthodox monetary and fiscal policy and structural/sectoral economic adjustment. By the 1990s this theorizing was overtaken by the realization that an essential (albeit not sufficient) prerequisite could be to 'get the politics right' first. The simple view was that sound economics would then take over and poverty reduction follow in due course, although both of these inferences are highly debatable. So, enter political conditionalities, albeit with some confusion over whether democracy, human rights and 'good governance' are all equally valuable and cover the scope for tension between them and their constituent parts. In this political development soup many donors have come to prioritize reducing the levels of corruption, portraying that as essential not just for democratic consolidation and economic renewal but for addressing poverty too.

Alas, just as analysts have come to doubt the effectiveness of economic conditionality in meeting its stated economic objectives and remain dubious about its social achievements,[10] so there are several reasons to doubt the chances of political conditionalities faring any better (Killick 1998; Crawford 2001). The NEPAD can be interpreted in two ways, neither of them complimentary. It could be a tacit acknowledgement by the West that some alternative, more consensual approach to levering political change is required. Alternatively it betokens a possibly desperate attempt to strengthen the instrument of conditionality, by invoking the threat of sanctions even against reform-minded states in a region for failing to bring their more obdurate neighbours into line. Surely the former will not willingly risk jeopardizing the West's promise of rewards for NEPAD and their own country's stake because of some misguided commitment to African solidarity with reactionary regimes?

But, first, on the donor side it is more difficult to formulate the political objectives in a clear and agreed language that will allow progress/regress to be measured objectively and furnish a sound basis for judging policy compliance, which is essential to agreeing on the next steps. Fine-tuning the conditionalities in second and subsequent 'rounds' is an even more imprecise art than in the case of economic targets or objectives and conditionalities. Our understanding of the relationships between the sort of stipulations typical of political conditionalities and the wider political impact (anticipated and actual) and of the temporal dimensions is far more tentative than what we think we know about how to manage national financial and economic affairs.

Moreover there is competition from the donors' other foreign policy concerns as well as their position as net winners from economic globalization. These concerns include their economic objectives such as the adoption of the Washington Consensus and national commercial advantages, as well as more strategic political concerns, like US support for regimes that guarantee oil and military bases to the US. Democratic conditionalities may be subordinate to other political conditionalities, such as the British government's (failed) bid to make European Union ODA conditional on recipient cooperation in controlling illegal migration.[11] The US faces a choice between maintaining good relations with certain illiberal regimes in the Middle East or pressing them to be more representative of and responsive to their societies' views (which means pro-Palestinian sentiments). Put differently, no donors trouble China – easily the largest aid recipient in the 1990s – with political conditionalities, unlike small, debt-distressed least developed countries that have few bargaining resources.

That there may often be a clash of political objectives could be unavoidable and, of course, need not be thought illegitimate. For instance in countries emerging from civil war or military rule it might be more helpful to reward steps towards a peaceful transfer to civilian rule and signs of political stabilization than to dwell on irregularities in the electoral process that would query the new government's legitimacy. Nigeria's presidential election in February 1999 was just such a case. EU aid to Macedonia is another example, which also illustrates the EU's capacity to mismanage aid.[12] Rather different is the situation created by reactions to the events of 11 September 2001. President Bush's robust line against the 'axis of evil' has been criticized for undermining putative political reformers in Iran, Iraq and North Korea. Elsewhere, Egypt for example, illiberal regimes have used the US's commitment to defeating terrorism as an excuse to intensify repression and silence dissent at home, where increasingly radical anti-government opposition seems to be made more likely by Israel's treatment of the Palestinians and US support for Israel.

On the recipient side of aid conditionalities it is self-evident that authoritarian regimes will be more willing to make economic than political concessions if the latter imply a democratic advance that would threaten their interest in retaining power. Many ruling elites have shown themselves adept at neutralizing the potential domestic political fallout from structural economic adjustment, for instance by externalizing the responsibility for any painful economic measures. And just as many rulers have dissimulated in deferring to donor political demands in principle, such as by holding elections, while frustrating the very purpose, namely the establishment of more legitimate and accountable government. Irrespective of whether conditionality is primarily understood to be a coercive instrument, a bribe, an exchange, or an exercise in persuasion, the chances of achieving 'ownership' of the conditions look remote in respect of political conditions and authoritarian rulers. In contrast, economic policy conditions are taken on board where they actually further the interests of the power-holders. For example the privatization of state-owned enterprises has in many countries profited members of the ruling elite, who gain the assets cheaply and operate them as private monopolies.

Another signal weakness in respect of political conditionalities is the absence of a true counterpart to the central enforcer and coordinator that the World Bank provides when chairing donor consortia and consultative groups. The Articles of Agreement of the Bretton Woods institutions rule against political goals. And when the member states of the 'international community' privilege the high politics of bilateral diplomacy over collective action there can be contradictions and inconsistencies in the political demands they articulate through their aid relations. That unique hybrid, the European Union, is no exception. Members will hide behind the EU's collective stance when it 'talks tough', as when spelling out conditions to its seventy-eight Africa–Caribbean–Pacific partners as institutionalized (previously) in the Lomé Conventions and now in the Cotonou Agreement. But individually they are not above defaulting on EU solidarity and showing much greater lenience when pursuing bilateral relations with favoured states, so undermining the formal EU position.

Finally, political conditionalities could be wholly redundant anyway not just for non-aid-receiving countries but where the main threats to democracy and so forth come from actors largely beyond the control of elected governments. In some cases that means the security services and the military, which may have praetorian inclinations as in Turkey or where, as in Serbia, there is resistance to being called to account for crimes against humanity.[13] In other cases it refers to terrorists/guerillas/freedom fighters; there may even be a debilitating combination of both state and non-state actors whose behaviour lies beyond the reach of a fragile regime and external political conditionalities. Hence in regard to the EU's offer of 1 billion euros' support for reconstruction in Afghanistan, the EU Commissioner for External Affairs expressly rejected the setting of specific conditions, notwithstanding the EU's desire to see fiscal transparency, opium poppy eradication and moves towards a more ethnically mixed government.[14] For the West, there are many countries like Pakistan where helping to strengthen the state's ability to govern, maintain order and collect taxes must look at least as attractive as promoting democratization. Democratization can be highly destabilizing and, far from immediately bearing out the 'democratic peace' hypothesis, could threaten to convert some countries into even greater threats to regional stability or wider international security. For a time in 2002 certain European governments considered delaying World Bank funding to Pakistan to apply pressure not for political liberalization or democratization, but for greater efforts to control cross-border terrorism in India. The US rejected that proposal, fearing it might destabilize the Pakistani regime.

In general, then, attaching political conditionalities to aid is probably more effective at promoting some political objectives (liberalization, or democratic transition, for example) than others like democratic consolidation. That is not just because donors 'tend to have a natural bias in favour of the incumbents whom their funding buttresses' (de Walle 2002). It is because 'consolidation', whether understood as democratic 'deepening' or longevity, requires that democratic values be internalized in society. Attempts at imposition are misguided, unless the indigenous political culture and, possibly, social and economic conditions change in ways that make democratic consolidation possible. Generally speaking, political conditionality might be more effective at retarding democratic reversal in situations where the rulers are minded to undermine or dismantle democracy and ignore the rule of law rather than promote sustainable democracy. But specific examples like Zimbabwe's President Mugabe (with assistance from Libya) indicate that nowhere will it deter leaders intent on getting their way, even where ODA is desperately needed.[15] Meanwhile, the limitations of politically conditioned aid say nothing about the potentially greater efficacy of other kinds of leverage. Thus in Central and Eastern Europe many observers believe the 'carrot' of EU accession has exerted a significant positive influence on the pace and direction of economic and political reform in many of the countries (Lewis 2003).

## CONCLUSION

This chapter does not set out to defend aid against its critics. Nor does it claim that henceforth there will be a continually rising trend in the real volume of aid or its quality. Indeed, for many least developed countries substantially increased aid inflows would create problems because of their limited absorptive capacity. Instead it notes that for much of the 1990s aid seemed to many to be in terminal decline. As recently as 2000 Hopkins judged aid's future 'precarious' (Hopkins 2000: 423). This was because of the disappearance of much of the familiar rationale offered by traditional realist approaches to international politics, and growing doubts about the strength of more liberal and idealist arguments that presume aid is able to foster economically sustainable development. Thus the DAC's reclassification of ODA to Israel as official aid, in 1997, could be construed as a defensive rather than bullish manoeuvre, aimed at securing the US's commitment to maintain massive support to Israel in spite of a dwindling ODA budget. At the same time it indicates the continuing presence of powerful political rationales.

Indeed, with hindsight it is now possible to say that the situation of multiple driving forces and a plurality of objectives that has long characterized aid has become more pronounced than ever. That, combined with the defence of vested interests by numerous governmental, intergovernmental and non-governmental institutions involved in aid, explains aid's survival and the more recent developments that could reverse the decline. These include vigorous high-level political discussions and official pledges to increase ODA, the possibility that new frontiers will be opened up or revisited in parts of Central Asia, the Middle East and sub-Saharan Africa, and the unremitting efforts by policy-oriented economists and others to strengthen the developmental case for aid. Even the ethical case briefly received an unusual amount of attention, in the form of the United Nations World Conference on Racism (in Durban, August 2001). European leaders were reminded there of the damage done to Africa by the slave trade and colonialism, and of Africa's entitlement to reparations to tackle the legacy.

However, the persistence of both a realpolitik of aid drawing on the age's enlarged understanding of national and international security threats and requisites, and more purely developmental concerns centred on reducing poverty, continue to make uneasy bedfellows. Regardless of how much/little credit is given to alms-racing in securing the West's victory in the Cold War and to relegating socialism as a competing ideology, there can be no doubting that aid's ability to advance developmental goals was heavily compromised in the past. That experience, combined with a growing perception among the interested public that aid's economic conditionalities were undermining social development in Third World countries, risked damaging popular support for aid in the 1980s. Put differently, the regional, country and sectoral allocations of ODA and its terms and conditions would all have been very different if goals of addressing poverty or correcting and compensating for the adverse social consequences of globalization had enjoyed clear priority. That essential point is equally valid with respect to current and future flows.

What is more, the commitment to using aid to encourage neoliberal economic reform and to ameliorate/reduce poverty may not only be contradictory (in the short term, at least), as some critics maintain; it may not even be compatible with the promotion of democratization. Notwithstanding the thesis that democracies do not make war on other democracies, political liberalization and democratic opening can be so politically destabilizing as to worsen the economic and social conditions (as in Milosevic's former Yugoslavia), possibly threatening the West's security and other foreign policy goals. Thus even the seemingly benign agenda of manipulating aid for the purpose of substituting oppressive regimes now looks more questionable than it did in the early 1990s. Both the commitment to such a policy and the performance in practice have been found wanting; there is a long way to go to perfect the art of democracy assistance or 'positive conditionalities'. Indeed a discernible trend in recent thinking takes us back to the modernization approach pioneered by Seymour Martin Lipset in the 1960s, which suggested that the best way to advance the long-term prospects of stable democracy is to improve the socio-economic conditions. While politically convenient in cases where a donor's immediate objectives appear to be served by maintaining the political status quo (Egypt, for example), or where there appears no realistic alternative (China), recent trends do still add weight to the case for making the war on poverty aid's overriding objective.

Thus although at one level aid's prospects look brighter now than for some considerable time, it is premature to say that the judgements passed by historians in the future will be any kinder than the often damning verdicts on aid that social scientists have made in the past. For one thing history tells us that aid pledges do not always materialize in practice. For another, because of the variety of political reasons for aid-giving we cannot be sure that aid will be substantially reallocated to countries with policy environments that favour its effective use for poverty reduction. Also, history tells us that in countries with weak institutions an increase of badly designed aid can actually harm the prospects for sustainable development and democratically accountable, sound and effective governance.

### Notes

1  IDA net disbursements of $3.7 billion in 1999 (down from $5.2 billion in 1997) go to around eighty eligible countries totalling 2.3 billion people.
2  Poverty reduction is but one of the global public goods; others are peace and environmental goods.
3  In *Assessing Aid* (Washington, D.C.: World Bank) the World Bank claimed that 1 per cent of GDP in assistance translates to a sustained increase in growth of 0.5 percentage points of GDP, and in countries with sound management it reduces poverty by 1 per cent. A $10 billion increase in aid to those countries would lift 25 million people a year out of poverty, or 7 million if distributed more widely (www.worldbank.org/research/aid/aidtoc.htm, pp. 14; 3).

4 The relationships between economic openness, growth, poverty and inequality are all in dispute.

5 The DfID White Paper *Eliminating World Poverty: Making Globalisation Work for the Poor* prioritizes growth as a necessary condition for sustained reduction in absolute poverty, not reductions in inequality. Cammack (2001) argues that the White Paper aims more at developing global capitalism than at eliminating poverty.

6 Planned US aid of $11.6 billion for 2003 includes $2.2 billion for the Economic Support Fund for countries like Israel and Egypt based on considerations of special economic, political or security needs and other US interests.

7 Michel Camdessus, Managing Director of the IMF, says at least one-third of the separate discussion during the 'retreat' among heads of state at the Monterey conference was devoted to the possible link between poverty and terrorism (*The Courier*, 2002, 6). According to Jessica Mathews, President of the Washington, D.C.-based Carnegie Endowment for International Peace: 'it is clear that the new U.S. interest in aid and development stems from the anti-terrorism connection' (Carnegie Endowment Policy Brief 2001: 9).

8 Clare Short, then Secretary of State for International Development, explained that failure to condemn Zimbabwe's elections would endanger the 'prospects of NEPAD, not as a collective punishment but by reputation, but that did not happen' (2002: 9).

9 European leaders and Canada pushed unsuccessfully for larger sums, against US and Japanese intransigence. However, £13 billion was promised over ten years to a programme to destroy Russia's unwanted nuclear stockpile.

10 Social conditionalities as manifested in Poverty Reduction Strategy Papers are too recent for there to be useful evaluations.

11 Floated in advance of an EU summit of leaders in June 2002, there was strong opposition from inside the cabinet and from some EU governments like France.

12 Following a highly critical evaluation by independent consultants commissioned by EuropeAid (set up by External Affairs Commissioner, Chris Patten), donors, including the EU, approved $515 million of new aid – more than double the amount predicted beforehand – at a pledging conference on 12 March 2002. This aid was supposed to bolster a peace deal reached between Macedonia's government and ethnic Albanian 'rebels' in August 2001 that had looked close to collapse.

13 For example in April 2002 the US froze $40 million in aid to former Yugoslavia over the non-extradition of war crimes suspects indicted by the International Criminal Tribunal in The Hague.

14 Patten: 'I don't think there is any country where you would be mechanistic about conditionality' (*Financial Times*, 21 May 2002).

15 UK Foreign Office Minister Baroness Amos, replying to MPs asking for even just one example of British influence in Zimbabwe before or since the March 2002 presidential elections: 'I cannot give . . . that kind of assurance . . . We are all deeply frustrated' (*Financial Times*, 15 May 2002).

### References and Further Reading

Boer, L. 2001: Attacking poverty: rediscovering the political economy. *Third World Quarterly*, 22 (2), 288.

Burnell, P. (ed.) 2000: *Democracy Assistance*. London: Frank Cass.

Burnell, P. (2001) Promoting parties and party systems in new democracies: is there anything the 'international community' can do? In K. Dowding, J. Hughes and H. Margetts (eds.), *Challenges to Democracy*, Basingstoke: Palgrave, 188–204.

Burnell, P. and O. Morrissey (eds.) 2003: *Foreign Aid in the New Global Economy*, Cheltenham: Edward Elgar.

Cammack, P. 2001: Making the poor work for globalisation? *New Political Economy*, 6 (3), 397–408.

Carnegie Endowment Policy Brief 2001: *Special Edition 18* (September), 9.

Carothers, T. 1999: *Aiding Democracy Abroad. The Learning Curve*. Washington, D.C.: Carnegie Endowment for International Peace.

Clarke, D. L. 1997: US security assistance to Egypt and Israel: politically untouchable? *Middle East Journal*, 51 (2), 200–14.

Collier, P. 1999: Aid 'dependency': a critique. *Journal of African Economies*, 8 (4), 528–45. *Financial Times*, 25 March 2002.

Collier, P. 2002: Aid: new challenges to traditional modes of development assistance. *The Courier* (EU-ACP), 191 (March–April ), 26.

*The Courier – ACP-EU Development Cooperation*, 192, May–June 2002, 6.

Crawford, G. 2001: *Foreign Aid and Political Reform*. Basingstoke: Palgrave.

DfID 2000: *Eliminating World Poverty: Making Globalisation Work for the Poor*, White Paper.

Dixon, R. and Williams, P. 2001: Tough on debt, tough on the causes of debt? New Labour's third way foreign policy. *British Journal of Politics and International Relations*, 3 (2), 150–72.

*Financial Times* 28 August 2001, 9/10 February 2002; 15 May 2002; 21 May 2002, 7 June 2002; 21/22 September 2002.

Hopkins, R. (2000) Political economy of foreign aid. In F. Tarp (ed.), *Foreign Aid and Development: Lessons Learned and Directions for the Future*, London: Routledge, 423.

*The Independent*, 21 March 2002; 28 June 2002.

Killick, T. 1998: *Aid and the Political Economy of Policy Change*. London: Routledge.

Lewis, P. 2003: Central and Eastern Europe. In P. Burnell (ed.), *Democratization Through the Looking-Glass*, Manchester: Manchester University Press.

Mallaby, S. 2002: The reluctant imperialist. *Foreign Affairs*, 81 (2) (March/April), 6.

Mosley, P. 2001: Making globalisation work for the poor? *New Political Economy*, 6 (3), 394–6.

Shapiro, I. and Birdsall, N. 2002: How does the proposed level of foreign economic aid under the bush budget compare with historical levels? Center for Global Development's Center on Budget and Policy Priorities, at www.cbpp.org/3-14-02 foreignaid.htm.

Short, C. 2002: Secretary of State for International Development, Keynote

lecture to Southern African Regional Poverty Network, 4 April at
www.SARPN.ORG.ZA/Activities/april2002/clareshort/lecture.php, p. 9.

Thérien, J. and Lloyd; C. 2000: Development assistance on the brink. *Third World Quarterly*, 21 (1), 25.

Velde, D. W. te 2002: 'Aid financing for international public goods? *ODI Opinions* (February), at www.odi.org.uk/publications/opinions.

Wade, R. 2001: The rising inequality of world income distribution. *Finance and Development*, 38 (4), 39.

Walle, N. van de 2002: Africa's range of regimes. *Journal of Democracy*, 13 (2), 74.

World Bank (1998) *Assessing Aid*. Washington, D.C.: World Bank, at www.worldbank.org/research/aid/aidtoc.htm, pp. 14; 3.

Youngs, R. 2001: *The European Union and the Promotion of Democracy. Europe's Mediterranean and Asian Policies*, Oxford: Oxford University Press.

# 3 The Heavily Indebted Poor Countries (HIPC) Initiative: Old Wine in a New Bottle?

*Fantu Cheru*

*Debt is amongst the most politically controversial topics on the global agenda with huge consequences for development trajectories and possibilities. In this chapter the focus is upon how the debt crisis has arisen, its implications for development generally (but with specific attention to the most indebted economies in Africa) and an exploration of why current attempts to resolve it have failed. It commences with an examination of global and regional trends in indebtedness and initial responses to these in the form of structural adjustment policies. The human and development consequences of these policies and debt are explored and the subsequent responses, most especially the HIPC Initiatives. The conclusion argues that debt and the global (mis)management of credit remain significant barriers to effective development.*

## INTRODUCTION

For almost twenty years, the international financial institutions (IFIs) and Western creditor governments were engaged in a self-deceptive and destructive game of managing the Third World debt problem from afar and by forcing unpopular economic policies down the throats of powerless countries in the belief that the bitter medicine of macroeconomic adjustment would ultimately put these countries on a path to prosperity and debt-free existence. Two decades later, however, many poor countries are in a worse condition than when they started implementing IMF/World Bank mandated structural adjustment programmes. Structural adjustment programmes have failed to create a framework either for sustained economic recovery, or for enabling the poor to benefit from market reforms. The debt 'hangover' has had a crippling effect on the achievement of human development targets. This is particularly more pronounced in sub-Saharan Africa, which has undergone two decades of adjustment without making a dent on the extreme level of human deprivation (Mkandawire and Soludo 1999).

Africa's burden of illegitimate foreign debt represents the single largest obstacle to the continent's development. So long as African countries are forced to spend almost $15 billion per year repaying debts to G8 governments and international financial institutions, they will be unable to address their urgent domestic needs. The constant outward flow of desperately needed resources undermines poverty reduction initiatives and cripples efforts to cope with the devastating impact of the HIV/AIDS crisis. Without freeing the continent from the shackles of debt, it would be impossible to stem the spread of the pandemic in the continent (Cheru 2002).

This chapter examines the politics of policy reform in low-income Africa, and specifically the double standard applied by the creditor countries in dealing with the debts of middle-income Latin American and low-income African countries. While the Latin American debt was promptly dealt with by Western creditors because of the risk it posed to the stability of the Western banking system, equal attention was never given to the debt burden of the poorest African countries whose debts were largely owed to multilateral financial institutions. Finally, the chapter examines the adequacy of the Heavily Indebted Poor Countries (HIPC) Initiative, which was introduced in 1996 to address the problem of debt owed by low-income countries to the multilateral development banks. While twenty-six countries have benefited so far from HIPC debt relief, recent analysis by the IMF and the World Bank concluded that the net present value (NPV) of debt-to-exports ratio could be above the 150 per cent threshold at their completion points (IMF/World Bank 2002: 9). There is clear evidence that the initiative is not working and that a fundamentally different approach is needed to deal with poor countries' debt once and for all.

## AFRICAN DEBT AND THE POLITICS OF INDIFFERENCE

At the beginning of 1999, the total foreign debt owed by developing countries was $2.1 trillion. The regional distribution of this debt was as follow: $792 billion for Latin America; $340 billion for Africa (of which $175 billion was owed by sub-Saharan Africa); $972 billion for Asia (United Nations 2000: 276–7, tables A.36–38). Yet, by most conventional indicators, such as the ratio of debt to GNP, sub-Saharan Africa's debt burden was 133 per cent of its GNP compared to 41.4 per cent for Latin America and 28.2 per cent for Asia. In terms of ratio of external debt to exports, the figures are striking: 202 per cent for Latin America; 340 per cent for sub-Saharan Africa; and 121 per cent for Asia (United Nations 1998: 171). In short, Africa is considerably more 'debt-stressed' than Latin America.

There is another important difference between Latin American and African debt. While most of Latin America's debt is owed to commercial banks, most of the debt owed by African nations is to official donors and multilateral organizations such as the World Bank, the IMF and the regional development banks. For low-income countries (defined by the World Bank as those with per capita GNP below $785), multilateral debt increased by some 544 per cent between 1980 and 1997, from $24.1 billion to $155 billion, as credit from other sources dried up and repayments mounted. Multilateral debt constitutes 33 per cent of the long-term debt burden of the most impoverished countries (United Nations 1998: 165). For middle-income countries, the corresponding percentage is 15 per cent. Neither agency is permitted, under existing rules, to reschedule or write off debt; and repayment to both have to be met in full.

The growing importance of the IMF and the World Bank as creditors has made debt management less flexible. As more and more Third World countries ran into greater difficulties servicing their huge loans made to them by Northern banks and multilateral institutions in the 1970s, pressure to adopt structural adjustment grew strong as a wide range of bilateral and multilateral donors insisted upon economic reform as a condition for the disbursement of funds and for rescheduling the debt. By the end of 1985, twelve of the fifteen debtors designated as top-priority debtors – including Argentina, Mexico and the Philippines – had submitted to structural adjustment programmes (Cavanagh et al. 1985). Over the next seven years, structural adjustment loans (SALs) proliferated as the economies of more and more Third World countries came under the surveillance and control of the World Bank and the IMF. Cooperation between the two institutions was brought to a higher level with the establishment in 1988 of the Structural Adjustment Facility (SAF) to closely coordinate both institutions' surveillance and enforcement activities.

The countries of sub-Saharan Africa, with their poor credit rating, have largely been turned into an IMF/World Bank 'macroeconomic guinea pig' since they depend largely on resources from the multilateral institutions. Out of the total of 47 countries in the region, 30 were implementing adjustment programmes in 1999 jointly administered by the World Bank and the IMF. Whereas the number of IMF standby arrangements declined from a high of 132 in the 1981–5 period to 49 in 1996–8, the number of enhanced structural adjustment facilities (ESAF) grew from 18 in 1986–90 to a record high of 99 in 1991–5 and 96 in the 1996–8 period (IMF 1998: table 8). Very high proportions of ESAFs were with the countries of sub-Saharan Africa. Since most of these countries have very weak political structures, an IMF–World Bank condominium has been imposed over them under the guise of providing aid. As a result, these countries have pretty much ceded their sovereignty to the IMF and the World Bank (Mkandawire and Soludo 1999; Cheru 1990).

The basic philosophy of structural adjustment programmes has been to persuade indebted countries to 'export their way out of the crisis' through closer integration into world markets, while devoting less attention to the expansion of public expenditure to boost production for domestic needs. The IMF calls this 'demand management'. It is meant to ensure that more of debtor nations' resources will be used to produce exports to be sold for dollars that can then be used to pay debts. Among the conditions typically required by the IMF and the World Bank are the following (Kahn 1990; Mosley et al. 1991):

■ deep reduction or elimination of subsidies and price controls, which distorted internal prices for a number of goods and services;

- drastic reduction of trade and exchange controls designed to protect the local economy from foreign competition;

- high interest rates to fight inflation, promote savings and allocate investment capital to the highest bidders;

- privatization of state-owned firms;

- reduction of the role of the state, not only in the economy but also in the provision of social services such as health, education and social security;

- indiscriminate export promotion through devaluation of the currency.

These policies are uniformly applied to all debtor countries requesting assistance from the IMF regardless of the special circumstances of each country experiencing balance-of-payments difficulties. Two decades later, from Argentina to Ghana, state intervention in the economy has been drastically curtailed, protectionist barriers to Northern imports have been eliminated wholesale, restrictions on foreign investment have been lifted and, through export-first policies, internal economies have been more tightly integrated into the capitalist world market.

While it is generally true that some debtor countries have witnessed varying degrees of growth following reform, there are few countries where macroeconomic stability and policy-induced growth have been consistent over the medium term (Killick 1991). Demand management policies have had a regressive impact by reducing the amount of resources available to purchase necessary imports, leading to severe import strangulation, depriving industry and agriculture of needed input. Moreover, as indebted countries flooded the world market with their coffee, cocoa and other goods, this created a glut in the market and a precipitous decline in their earnings. Instead of graduating from debt, indiscriminate market reform of liberalization and deregulation has taken these countries in the wrong direction. Investment in the productive sectors of the economy has dwindled as resources are shifted to the export sector to expand the volume of exports in order to earn badly needed foreign exchange to service their external debt.

More importantly, economic adjustment has been achieved on the back of the poor. Debt-servicing requirements have detracted funds from necessary spending in the areas relevant for the promotion and protection of human rights, as defined in the principal human rights treaties.[1] Consequently, living standards for the majority of Africans have declined (Weissman 1990). Increasing malnutrition, declining school enrolments and rising unemployment and poverty threaten the social fabric of highly indebted poor countries (Cornia et al. 1987). Increasing globalization, which has pushed many poor countries to the margins of the world economy, compounds this situation (Chossudovsky 1997). Reform has been necessary to satisfy the demands of external creditors for servicing debt and not adequately internalized as domestic requirements for pursuing human-centred growth and development.

## INDEBTEDNESS AND THE HUMAN CRISIS

The World Bank and the IMF have single-handedly managed the Third World debt crisis since the 1980s, without any regard for the social and economic costs of macroeconomic adjustment. The dramatic situations of heavily indebted countries affected by war, natural disasters and the HIV/AIDS pandemic have not been given the special attention they deserve. In the social sector, debt servicing and the adjustment policies pushed to free up foreign exchange needed to service the debt have worsened social welfare (Kanji 1995). The cuts mandated by adjustment have been indiscriminate, thereby jeopardizing the following fundamental human rights.

■ *The right to food*    There is convincing evidence demonstrating that nutritional levels decrease among poor segments of the population as a result of the removal of food subsidies. Growing unemployment has a similar result. The switching effect of agricultural policies, primarily from food crop production for local consumption to generation of foreign exchange through the production of coffee, tobacco or cotton, has resulted in a drastic decline in food production, reduced nutritional levels and increased malnutrition (Mukherjee 1994; Ziegler 2001).

■ *The right to education*    Article 26 of the Universal Declaration of Human Rights declares that all people have the right to education. The Convention of the Rights of the Child has also established the right to early development and education. Thanks to extraordinary efforts during the 1960s and 1970s, the percentage of children completing at least four years of primary education reached 50 per cent or more in almost all developing countries. But since the 1980s, increasing debt and the consequent implementation of structural adjustment programmes has led many governments to freeze or cut educational spending (Tomasevski 1995). Primary schooling has often suffered disproportionately, and there was significant slippage in sub-Saharan Africa. The percentage of six- to eleven-year-olds enrolled in school dropped from a high of 55 per cent in 1979 to 45 per cent in 1995 (UNESCO 1996).

■ *The right to health*    Health is one of the fundamental human rights embodied in Article 25 of the 1948 Universal Declaration of Human Rights. The goal of 'Health for all by the year 2000' agreed upon in the Alma Alta Declaration has been severely undermined by cutbacks in government health budgets as social and development objectives have been superseded by financial imperatives (World Health Organization 2001; Cornia et al. 1987). The imposition of 'user fees' for primary health care drove large numbers away from public health services, contributing to increased rates of sexually transmitted diseases. Moreover, cutbacks in the public sector helped send health professionals to the private sector or abroad and reduced investments in health-care delivery systems (Turshnet 1994).

In the face of widespread public criticism, however, the World Bank and the IMF held fast insisting that not only are structural adjustment programmes working, but also they are a necessary element of long-term transformation. In early 1994, the Bank released a progress report on Africa, *Adjustment in Africa: Reform, Results and the Road Ahead*, to defend its failed policy of structural adjustment (World Bank 1996). By manipulating selective data of cross-country analysis, and without revealing the significant objection to the report's conclusion from internal Bank economists, the Bank claimed that African countries which implemented structural adjustment programmes in the 1980s experienced greater positive growth than those that did not. Two years earlier, a draft World Bank study stated, 'World Bank adjustment lending has not significantly affected growth and has contributed to a statistically significant drop in investment ratios' (World Bank 1992). Of the six countries the Bank put forward as adjustment 'successes' – Ghana, Tanzania, the Gambia, Burkina Faso, Nigeria and Zimbabwe – four had deteriorating rates of investment and two had negative GDP growth rates during their respective adjustment periods.

A similar verdict was delivered on the ineffectiveness of the IMF's ESAF by a report prepared by a team of external evaluators hired by the Fund Executive Board in 1996 (Botchwey et al. 1998). The evaluation team concluded that while ESAF-supported economic reforms generally have positive effects on growth and income distribution, they do entail temporary costs for certain segments of the population. This calls for appropriate compensatory measures to be built into programme design to protect such groups, including the provision of well-targeted assistance and the allocation of adequate resources for social sectors.

## CREDITOR STRATEGY: A DECADE OF COMPLACENCY!

The indifference of Western creditor governments to the plight of poor people in low-income indebted countries was clearly evident in the piecemeal approach adopted by the G7 governments since 1987. Successive debt-relief initiatives introduced by the G7 governments with great fanfare have done little more than apply ill-conceived, short-term palliatives to what is arguably the most intractable obstacle to Africa's recovery.[2] The G7 debt reduction initiatives were set and reset arbitrarily rather than based on serious assessment of the needs of each country.

The reason for this arbitrary approach is not difficult to figure out. For twenty-five years, the guiding principle of official debt relief has been to do the minimum to avert default, but never enough to solve the debt crisis. The HIPC Initiative, though presented as a major break from past practices, is guided by the same logic of damage control. A mixture of debt relief and repeated rescheduling operations has so far prevented extensive default on Africa's debt. Indeed, between 1987 and 1996, there were 166 debt-restructuring agreements with official creditors in the Paris Club, of which 96 cases involved African countries (United Nations 1998: 172, table A.35). Although these debt-restructuring initiatives helped to reduce some debt, their overall impact on reducing the debt burden of poor countries was negligible as these proposals gave considerable latitude to participating creditor countries to take the strategy that is less costly to them. A good illustration of this point is the 'Toronto Terms' introduced during the G7 Toronto meeting in 1989. The creditor nations agreed on a 'menu' option for rescheduling nonconcessional debt. These included the following options:

1  cancel 3.3 per cent of debt service covered by the agreement and reschedule the rest with 14-year maturity and 8-year grace period;
2  reduce interest rates by 3.5 percentage points or 50 per cent, which ever is less, and reschedule with 14-year maturity and 8-year grace;
3  extend grace to 14 years, and maturity to 25 years. In addition, aid debt will be rescheduled over 25 years with 14 years' grace, at existing concessional interest rates.

Options (1) and (2) involved immediate cost to creditor governments and immediate relief to the debtor. Option (3) merely increases debt stock and future debt service as deferred interest payments are capitalized and added to the total debt stock. The less than generous options provided by the G7 governments to the poorest countries in Africa is in stark contrast to the massive debts owed by the Latin American debtors to commercial banks. Considering the magnitude of the debt and the threat to the Western banking system, the response was swift as both the 1985 Baker Plan and the 1989 Brady Plan demonstrated.[3] Both the Baker and Brady plans tried in general to use a more appealing and aggressive strategy, employing measures to induce commercial banks to rewrite existing contracts to exchange debt either for secured liquid assets on better terms or for cash. For example, the Brady Plan made it possible to replace a portion of outstanding debt with 'Brady bonds' having a lower face value and a longer repayment schedule  (Browne 1999).

Finally, the various G7 proposals (i.e. Toronto, Trinidad and Naples terms) gave paltry attention to the debt owed by low-income African countries to multilateral development banks. For most of the world's impoverished countries, multilateral debt looms larger than other debts because of the status of the IMF and the World Bank as 'preferred creditors' assigned them by the G7 industrialized countries. For many African countries, debt servicing to the IMF and the World Bank account for 36 per cent of total debt-service payments. Because of the preferred creditor status of these two institutions, payments of multilateral debt take priority over private and bilateral debt.  Borrowing governments have special incentives to stay current with their multilateral debts because they do not want to jeopardize their access to more concessional forms of finance needed to support recovery.

## THE HIPC INITIATIVE: TOO AUSTERE, TOO LITTLE AND TOO LATE!

In October 1996, as a result of many years of persistent campaigning by a global coalition of NGOs and civil society organizations, the Bretton Woods institutions finally conceded the need to address the issue of poor country debt owed to them and approved the HIPC Initiative.

The ostensible aim of the programme is to make the debt burden of the poorest and most indebted countries 'sustainable'. Once a country is deemed eligible, it must demonstrate a commitment to 'sound economic policies' – the IFIs' usual euphemism for SAPs – to receive debt relief.[4]

The IMF and the World Bank initially identified forty-one countries as possible candidates for debt relief under the HIPC Initiative. In total they owed $221 billion in 1998, about $61 billion of which (roughly 26 per cent of the total debt stock) was owed to multilateral financial institutions (US Government General Accounting Office 1998; United Nations 1998: 165). Under the original HIPC programme, a country could not obtain benefits until it completed six consecutive years of implementation of the Fund's ESAF. The first stage entails a rescheduling of debt-servicing obligations to Paris Club countries on Naples Terms. At the end of that period, the debtor may be accorded up to two-thirds reduction of debt. At this point, a decision can be made on whether the second stage is needed.

Eligibility criteria for the second stage of the initiatives, which could reduce debt-servicing obligation by up to 80 per cent (13 percentage points beyond that accorded under Naples Terms), is much higher and relief is granted on a case-by-case basis. Eligible countries are required to establish a second three-year track record under a Bank/IMF-supported structural adjustment programme. For countries in desperate need of debt relief in order that they can begin to direct resources to social sectors, this type of provisional debt relief is a cruel paradox. To obtain relief, debtor nations are first required to demonstrate their willingness to make socio-economic, and perhaps political, conditions worse by adopting programmes that starve people of health care, food subsidies and education.

Few indebted countries chose to apply for HIPC relief because of the stringent qualification criteria that came with debt relief. By the spring of 1999, only three countries had become eligible for actual debt relief: Uganda and Bolivia, in April and September 1998 respectively, and Mozambique in mid-1999. Although eight others – Mali, Côte d'Ivoire, Benin, Honduras, Senegal, Tanzania, Guyana and Burkina Faso – had reached their 'decision point' and had assistance committed to them by the end of 1999, they represented only a small proportion of the total initially targeted (IMF 1998: 68, table 8).

Moreover, the original HIPC Initiative simply did not take into account human development and poverty eradication issues in the debt sustainability analysis. Nor did the initiative take into account the special circumstances of many poor countries that are confronted with wide-scale humanitarian crisis due to the effects of war and genocide (for example, Sierra Leone, Rwanda); natural disasters (such as Hurricane Mitch in Honduras and Nicaragua; Cheru and Figueredo 2000); and health emergencies such as the HIV/AIDS pandemic in Africa (Nyamugasira 1999). These disasters are wiping out decades of development advances.

## THE ENHANCED HIPC INITIATIVE

Barely two years has passed since the introduction of the HIPC Initiative. The IMF and the World Bank conceded in the spring of 1999 that the

**Table 3.1** Total debt stock reduction under HIPC I (millions of US dollars)

| Country | Total nominal debt relief | % reduction in debt stock (NPV terms) | Total debt relief (NPV terms) |
| --- | --- | --- | --- |
| Uganda | 650 | 20 % | 347 |
| Bolivia | 760 | 13 % | 448 |
| Burkina Faso | 200 | 14 % | 115 |
| Guyana | 410 | 25 % | 256 |
| Côte d'Ivoire | 800 | 6 % | 345 |
| Mozambique | 3,700 | 57 % | 1,700 |
| Mali | 250 | 10 % | 128 |

Source: HIPC Initiative Consultation Meeting: Background Materials, IMF/World Bank, March 1999. Updates on Guyana and Mozambique from IMF press releases dated 14 May 1999 and 30 June 1999 respectively.

HIPC Initiative had major shortcomings and that there was a need for more substantive steps to address the debt problem of low-income countries. Reacting to this, the G7 leaders announced from Cologne in June 1999 a major debt reduction initiative aimed at improving the HIPC Initiative. A total of $90 billion was promised for thirty-three countries, with the cost to creditors (NPV) of $27 billion, primarily due to heavy discounting of the loans and the advantage of purchasing the debt now as opposed to having it accrue interest over its lifetime. Shortly thereafter the original HIPC Initiative was revamped to provide three key enhancements:

1 *Deeper and broader relief*   Debt sustainability thresholds were lowered from 250 per cent in the original framework to 150 per cent, thus providing more debt relief (table 3.1). Also, more countries have become eligible for debt relief as a result of the relaxation of the stringent qualification criteria.
2 *Faster relief*   A number of creditors began to provide interim debt relief immediately so that countries could reach the completion point faster; Britain, Norway, Sweden and Australia announced the cancellation of 100 per cent of their bilateral debts while Canada announced that it will apply a moratorium on debt repayments from eleven countries in Africa and Latin America (Jubilee 2000-UK).
3 *Stronger link between debt relief and poverty reduction*   The new version of HIPC (see table 3.2) seeks to ensure that debt relief will effectively reduce poverty. Countries wishing to apply for debt relief are required to prepare a poverty reduction strategy paper (PRSP). The PRSPs are to be country-driven; prepared and developed transparently with the broad participation of civil society, key donors and other relevant international financial institutions; and linked clearly with agreed international development goals. The PRSP, which would be updated regularly, would in essence become the basic framework that would be used to guide Bank/Fund lending operations to poor countries in the future.

**Table 3.2** HIPC's changing criteria

|  | HIPC-1 1996 | HIPC-2 1999 |
| --- | --- | --- |
| **Debt sustainability ratios:** | | |
| Debt/exports | 200–250% | 150% |
| Debt/revenues | 280% | 250% |
| **GDP-related ratios:** | | |
| Exports/GDP | 40% | 30% |
| Revenues/GDP | 20% | 15% |
| **Time until actual relief** | 6 years | uncertain |

*Source*: IMF/World Bank 2002b.

Countries start out initially by preparing an interim poverty reduction strategy paper (I-PRSP). The I-PRSP is intended as a road map to preparing a full PRSP and as a bridge between the long-term PRSP objectives and a country's short-term needs for financing and debt relief. The I-PRSP paves the way for the country to qualify for its 'decision point', which is followed by an interim support (or a loan) to the government from the IMF's Poverty Reduction and Growth Facility, formerly called the Enhanced Structural Adjustment Facility (ESAF).

While the emphasis on strengthening the link between debt relief and poverty reduction represents a tremendous intentional step forward in the tortured history of debt relief for poor countries, the Enhanced HIPC, like its predecessor, is caught up in a complex web of IMF and World Bank eligibility conditions. Among other factors, eligibility for debt relief is conditioned upon 'good performance' in the implementation of an IMF PRGF (formerly ESAF) programme for a period of three years. Having reached the 'decision point' after the first three years of good economic performance each country must then demonstrate that its debt servicing is unsustainable, following designated threshold values with respect to the ratio of debt to exports, as well as debt to fiscal revenues. If the country finally qualifies for relief after reaching the 'completion point', its debt servicing is brought down to what is deemed within the terms of the initiative to be a sustainable level, but only after reaching the 'completion point', or after a further three-year waiting period. So far, only seven countries have completed the process: Uganda, Bolivia, Burkina Faso, Guyana, Mauritania, Tanzania and Mozambique (Statement by the Group of Eight). This less than generous arrangement still leaves the country deflecting a sizeable portion of its scarce foreign exchange earnings into debt-servicing for an indefinite period of time.

## THE LIMITATIONS OF THE HIPC INITIATIVE

As of July 2002, twenty-six countries are benefiting from debt relief under the enhanced HIPC Initiative, of which seven have reached completion point. The seven include Bolivia, Guyana, Burkina Faso, Mauritania, Mozambique, Tanzania and Uganda. These seven have received debt relief amounting to $7.5 billion in NPV terms (equivalent to $13 billion in nominal terms). The remaining twenty countries have received interim relief when they reached decision points in the amount of $17 billion in NPV terms ($27 billion in nominal terms). Twelve countries with substantial arrears problems and in need of significant relief are yet to be considered, as these countries are mostly conflict-affected. To provide the opportunity for these countries to qualify for HIPC relief, it is proposed to extend the sunset clause of the Initiative by another two years to the end of 2004 (IMF/World Bank 2002a: 3). The $24 billion debt cancellation delivered so far is no small change by any stretch of imagination, but it is not enough. Debt relief is making a real difference to the lives of ordinary people. Two-thirds of resources released are being spent on health and education, with most of the remainder being used for HIV/AIDS, water supply, roads and governance reforms. For example, the Ugandan government has disbursed resources released from debt relief to its districts to improve education. School management committees monitor expenditure, the quality of education and student test results. In concrete terms, the programme to provide free primary education has in a short period doubled the school enrolment rate  (Cheru 2001). In Mozambique, resources released through debt relief have been channelled into various areas, all vital to sustaining development. The budgets for health, education, agriculture, infrastructure and employment training have all benefited.

Despite evidence that debt relief can save lives, neither the original HIPC Initiative, nor the 'enhanced' version introduced in 1999, has succeeded in resolving Africa's debt crisis. While the $24 billion released so far is no small change, the envisioned debt relief has been neither sufficiently deep nor sufficiently broad (Cheru 2000).Furthermore, the first twenty-six countries to qualify for relief are still spending more on debt-servicing than on health care. For those that have begun to get relief as of the end of 2000, the average overall reduction amounts to 27 per cent, not a trivial decrease but hardly the kind of sweeping cancellation needed to transform economies and to make them sustainable. These qualifying debtor countries continue to spend $1.3 billion a year on debt service.

In a surprisingly candid admission, both the World Bank and the IMF released two documents in time for the spring 2002 meeting that admitted that the HIPC Initiative is failing (The Kananaskis Summit Chair's Summary 2002).

■ Of the five countries already at *completion point*, at least two of these do not have sustainable levels of debt according to the HIPC criteria. This will bring to thirteen the number of countries expected to face unsustainable debt burdens at completion point.

■ In one case, *Burkina Faso*, the joint board of the IMF/World Bank approved topping-up assistance to bring that country's NPV debt to 150 per cent of exports at completion point. Although this was considered an exceptional measure by the IFIs, other countries who had gone through the completion point and still show NPV of debt-to-export ratios in excess of the sustainability threshold might be granted topping-up assistance. A case in point is Uganda, whose NPV of debt-to-exports ratio has risen since reaching the completion point in 2000 mainly due to the collapse in coffee prices.

■ Of the twenty countries that are currently between decision point and completion point under the Initiative, at least eight to ten (60 per cent) countries will not have sustainable levels of debt at completion point: Benin, Chad, Ethiopia, the Gambia, Guinea-Bissau, Malawi, Niger, Rwanda, Senegal and Zambia (ibid.: 25). Thirteen of the twenty countries had their PRGF programme suspended due to failure to stay on track with IMF programs. The suspension delays debt cancellation and denies them interim service relief. Among the countries in this group was Ghana, once the darling of the IMF.

■ There have even been delays in providing interim debt-service relief for some countries which are entitled to this relief and are 'on track' with IMF programmes. HIPC appears to be working only for seven to ten countries out of the forty-two included within the Initiative. Part of the reason for the delay in granting relief has to do with the inadequacy of the HIPC Trust Fund. It is currently estimated that the financing required to support debt relief for the thirty-four HIPCs that have already reached their decision points will fully exhaust the resources mobilized to date and will leave a potential funding gap of up to $800 million (IMF/World Bank 2002: 14). In this context, in June 2002, the G8 members agreed to fund their share of the shortfall, recognizing that it will be up $1 billion.

One of the principal reasons why the HIPC Initiative is failing is the unrealistic projections of debt sustainability, which is calculated by comparing total debt in net present value (NPV) terms to a country's total exports. If a country can pay its debt from its export earnings without going broke, then it is assumed to have 'sustainable' debt. When the total stock of debt is more than one and a half times the value of exports, the country is deemed to have an 'unsustainable' level of debt.

The very optimistic export projection by the World Bank and the IMF has actually not materialized (see table 3.3). For example, for the first twenty-four HIPCs to reach decision point, the average growth in exports for 2001 was projected to be 11.6 per cent. This is an extremely high figure, and bears little resemblance to the historical trend of the HIPCs. In fact, since 1965, annual export growth for low-income countries has been less than one-third of this level. It therefore comes as no surprise to learn that the actual export growth for these twenty-four countries during 2001 was less than half the World Bank's projected level, at 5.1 per cent (IMF/World Bank 2002: 21). For those countries that had worsened NPV of debt-to-export ratios, lower exports accounted for about 56 per cent of the deterioration in the NPV of debt-to-export ratios (ibid.: table 9). A similar conclusion was made by an independent evaluation undertaken by the General Accounting Office (GAO), whose report analysing debt sustainability for ten African countries, found out that only two of the ten countries would be debt-sustainable if these countries exports were to grow at rates consistent with historical levels (US General Accounting Office 2002: 13).

**Table 3.3** Debt sustainability ratio for selected HIPC (after additional bilateral debt forgiveness)

| | Decision point projection NPV/export ratio (%) | Spring 2002 projections Range for NPV/export ratio (%) | Updated projections Range for NPV/export ratio (%) |
|---|---|---|---|
| Benin | 138 | 148–154 | 158–170 |
| Chad | 188 | 188–219 | 188–224 |
| Ethiopia | 149 | 164–186 | 137–159 |
| The Gambia | 153 | 162–177 | 162–174 |
| Guinea-Bissau | 107 | 147–152 | 147–152 |
| Malawi | 156 | 158–165 | 165–166 |
| Niger | 164 | 144–148 | 159–167 |
| Rwanda | 185 | 161–171 | 180–198 |
| Senegal | 112 | 157–158 | 158–159 |
| Zambia | 106 | 151–154 | 152–154 |
| Cameroon | 101 | 99–112 | 95–113 |
| Ghana | 82 | – | 82–83 |
| Guinea | 123 | 139–141 | 135–140 |
| Guyana | 57 | 68–76 | 69–77 |
| Honduras | 74 | 90–91 | 91–92 |
| Madagascar | 101 | 75–81 | 76–83 |
| Mali | 143 | 139–140 | 128–130 |
| Nicaragua | 93 | 108–117 | 108–117 |
| Sao Tomé e Principe | 139 | 124–140 | 132–143 |
| Sierra Leone | 139 | – | 139–150 |

Source: IMF, World Bank 2002a: 10, table 4.

   Much of the shortfall in exports has been caused by dramatic falls in commodity prices over 2000–1, particularly for coffee and cotton, which fell by 60 per cent and 10 per cent respectively. As a result of this shortfall, the average ratio of debt to exports in 2001 for the twenty-four HIPCs considered is now estimated to have been a staggering 280 per cent, almost twice the levels deemed 'sustainable' by the World Bank and the IMF. Even the four countries that had already passed completion point are estimated to have an NPV of debt-to-export ratio of 156 per cent (IMF/World Bank 2002: 10, table 4).

   A serious commitment to addressing Africa's challenges must begin by releasing the continent from debt bondage. Many of the HIPCs currently service their debts at the cost of widespread malnutrition, premature death, excessive morbidity and reduced prospects for economic growth. If the resources were freed up and successfully redirected towards basic human needs there could be significant improvements in human welfare. Unfortunately, the World Bank and the IMF have taken the position that completely cancelling the debt of HIPCs is too expensive and could also create a moral hazard, thus encouraging other debtor countries not to honour their commitments. However, recent studies indicate that these institutions hold sufficient wealth on their own balance sheets to absorb the full cost of multilateral debt cancellation from their internal resources.

An audit of these institutions by two independent accounting firms in Britain revealed that the World Bank and the IMF could write off all of the debts of the world's poorest countries from their own assets, without negatively impacting their credit rating or their ability to function (Drop the Debt 2001). Despite these studies, the World Bank and the IMF continue to maintain that outright debt cancellation is a financial impossibility because it would critically undermine their future operations.

In a recent article, 'Resolving the debt crisis for low-income countries', economist Jeffrey Sachs argued that debt reduction for the HIPCs should not be based on arbitrary criteria such as a 150 per cent debt-to-exports ratio, but rather on a systematic assessment of each country's needs for debt reduction and increased foreign assistance, measured against explicit development objectives (Sachs 2002). Sachs argued that the right starting point for assessing needs should be the targets enshrined in the Millennium Development Goals (MDGs), a set of eight major goals and eighteen intermediate targets endorsed by all UN members in September 2000. The MDGs are quantified goals for poverty alleviation, reduction of hunger, reduction of disease burden and other targets, mostly for the year 2015.

## CONCLUSIONS

The HIPC Initiative has failed to resolve Africa's debt crisis. The reason for the failure of the initiative is that it is designed by creditors and controlled by creditors. Creditors have the power to define who gets what, and when, and how. Even by its own measure, the HIPC framework is not reducing debt to levels described by the World Bank as 'sustainable'. As shown in table 3.2 above, the majority of countries will find themselves in a worse condition after completion point than when they first entered the process. Moreover, it obfuscates the illegitimacy of most of this debt. Tinkering with HIPC is a shell game. Tying debt relief to conditions determined by creditors undermines African priorities and initiatives and affords creditors an inordinate degree of control over the running of African countries.

The meagre results of the HIPC programme suggest that its promises are hollow ones, made solely to ensure that countries remain on the debt-and-structural-adjustment treadmill. The guiding principle in the creditors' debt relief strategy has been to loosen the chain lightly, but not to break it. Such a strategy prevents debtor countries from defaulting or opting out of the global financial system altogether. The international financial institutions and the G8 governments in particular also have incentives to avert defaults: any gaps in the globalized economy represent reduced control and loss of potential markets. In the post-1990 political environment, debt relief and the accompanying structural adjustment reforms have, therefore, become important vehicles to facilitate the process of globalization through deregulation, liberalization and reducing the role of the state in national development. Preservation of that influence and control is a far more important factor in the G8 approach to debt policy than recovery of the funds loaned. Illustrating this point was US policy in the wake of Hurricane Mitch's devastation in Central America in 1998. Treasury Department officials privately gave 'loss of leverage' as their reason for refusing to consider comprehensive debt cancellation for Nicaragua and Honduras. The value of the leverage associated with multilateral debt and the extent to which the G8 controls the IFIs are evident at times of international crisis. Just as Egyptian and Kenyan debts were cancelled during the Gulf War, so in the wake of the 9/11 attacks Pakistan was induced to assist the fight against al-Qaeda and the Taliban with promises of debt cancellation and new loans from the IMF. Should the crisis persist, Indonesia, with one of the largest debt burdens as well as the largest Muslim population, will probably benefit as well.

Finally, the key weakness in the IFIs' approach to economic reform has been the failure to recognize that structural adjustment at the domestic level is meaningless without a corresponding adjustment at the global level. Efforts to reform economies at the national level have often been derailed by market failures at the global level. Much more effort by the international community will be required to establish a more propitious trading and financial climate within which debtor nations can hope to increase their exports and attract various forms of financing needed to achieve a positive momentum in their economic development. In order for trade to generate sustainable growth, however, there must be a more equitable trading relationship between rich countries and African countries. Specifically, ensuring fair prices for commodities and market access to these products are of dominant importance. This requires structural changes in the field of primary commodity trade, by giving the least developed better access to Northern markets, encouraging more processing of their commodities before export, extending the preferential treatment now accorded them.

## Notes

1 According to Article 22 of the Universal Declaration of Human Rights, everyone is 'entitled to realization through national efforts and international cooperation, of the economic, social and cultural rights indispensable for his dignity'. In poor indebted countries, this condition is often not fulfilled.

2 These included: the Naples Terms, designed to provide 67 per cent debt stock reduction; and the Trinidad Terms, which aimed to reduce debt stock by two-thirds instead of the 50 per cent provided for under the 'enhanced Toronto Terms'.

3 Named after the architects of the plans, US Treasury Secretary James Baker and Nicolas Brady.

4 Sustainability is defined as the ability 'to meet current and future external debt service obligations in full without recourse to debt relief, rescheduling of debt or the accumulation of arrears, and without unduly compromising growth'.

## References and Further Reading

Botchwey, K. et al. 1998: *Report of the Group of Independent Persons Appointed to Conduct an Evaluation of the Enhanced Structural Adjustment Facility.* Washington, D.C.: IMF.

Browne, S. 1999: *Beyond Aid: From Patronage to Partnership.* London: Ashgate Publishers.

Cavanagh, J. et al. 1985: *From Debt to Development: Alternatives to the International Debt Crisis.* Washington, D.C.: Institute for Policy Studies.

Cheru, F. 1990: *The Silent Revolution in Africa: Debt, Development and Democracy.* London: Zed Press.

Cheru, F. 2000: Debt relief and social investment: linking the HIPC Initiative to the HIV/AIDS epidemic in Africa: the case of Zambia. *Review of African Political Economy,* 86, 519–35.

Cheru, F. 2001: *The PRSP Process in Uganda: What is the Secret of its Success?* Addis Ababa: UN Economic Commission for Africa.

Cheru, F. 2002: Debt, adjustment and the politics of effective response to HIV/AIDS in Africa. *Third World Quarterly,* 23 (2), 299–312.

Cheru, F. and Figueredo, R. 2000: *Debt Relief and Social Investment: Linking the HIPC Initiative to HIV/AIDS Epidemic in Africa, Post-Mitch Reconstruction in Honduras and Nicaragua.* UN Commission on Human Rights, Fifty-Six Session, Geneva.

Chossudovsky, M. 1997: *The Globalization of Poverty: Impacts of IMF and World Bank Reforms.* Penang: Third World Network.

Cornia, G. A. et al. 1987: *Adjustment with a Human Face: Protecting the Vulnerable and Promoting Growth.* New York: Oxford University Press.

Drop the Debt 2001: *Reality Check: The Need for Deeper Debt Cancellation and the Fight against HIV/AIDS.* London.

IMF 1998: *Annual Report 1998.* Washington, D.C.

IMF/World Bank 2002a: *Heavily Indebted Poor Countries (HIPC) Initiative: Status of Implementation.* Washington, D.C.: Development Committee.

IMF/World Bank 2002b: *The Enhanced HIPC Initiative and the Achievement of Long-Term External Debt Sustainability.* Washington, D.C., 21.

Jubilee 2000-UK, Twenty-two countries due to gain some debt relief in 2000, at www.jubilee2000uk.org/reports/dropped1200.htm.

Kahn, M. 1990: *The Macroeconomic Effects of Fund-Supported Adjustment Programs.* IMF Staff Paper 37 (2).

Kananaskis Summit Chair's Summary, The 2002 Summit, Kananaskis, Canada, at www.g8.gc.ca/kan_docs/chairsummary-e.asp.

Kanji, N. 1995: Gender, poverty and economic adjustment in Harare, Zimbabwe. *Environment and Urbanization,* 7 (1), 37–55.

Killick, T. 1991: *Problems and Limitations of Adjustment Policies.* Working Paper No. 36, London: Overseas Development Institute.

Mkandawire, T. and Soludo C. 1999: *Our Continent Our Future: African Perspectives on Structural Adjustment.* Trenton, New Jersey: Africa World Press.

Mosley, P. Harrighan, J. and Toye, J. 1991: *Aid and Power: The World Bank and Policy-Based Lending.* London: Macmillan.

Mukherjee, A. 1994: *Structural Adjustment Programs and Food Security.* Aldershot: Avebury.

Nyamugasira, W. 1999: Rwanda and the impact of debt relief on the poor: reconciliation can't wait; children headed households can't wait. An NGO input to the HIPC Review Seminar, Addis Ababa: UNECA.

Sachs, J. 2002: Resolving the Debt Crisis for Low-Income Countries. Brookings Papers on Economic Activity, 1.

Statement by the Group of Eight (G8) countries meeting in Birmingham, UK, on Africa Debt, at www.birmingham.g8summit.gov.uk.

Tomasevski, K. 1995: The influence of the World Bank and IMF on economic and social rights. *Nordic Journal of International Law*, 64, 385–95.

Turshnet, M. 1994: The impact of economic reforms on women's health and health care in sub-Saharan Africa. In N. Aslanbegui, S. Pressmant and G. Sumerfield (eds), *Women in the Age of Economic Transformation*, London: Routledge, 77–93.

United Nations 1998: *World Economic and Social Survey 1998*. New York: Department of Economic and Social Affairs, 165, 171, 172, table A.35.

United Nations 2000: *World Economic and Social Survey 2000*. New York: United Nations, 276–77, tables A.36–38

UNESCO 1996: *Trends and Projections of Enrollment, 1960–2025*. Paris: UNESCO.

US Government General Accounting Office 1998: *Status of the Heavily Indebted Poor Countries Debt Relief Initiative*. Washington, D.C.

US General Accounting Office 2002: *Switching Some Multilateral Loans to Grants Lessens Poor Country Debt Burdens*. Report to Congressional Requesters, Washington, D.C., 13.

Weissman, S. R. 1990: Structural adjustment in Africa: insights from the experience of Ghana and Senegal. *World Development*, 18 (12), 1623.

World Bank 1992: *Adjustment Lending and Economic Performance in Sub-Saharan Africa in the 1980s: A Comparison with Other Low-Income Countries*. Washington, D.C.: World Bank.

World Bank 1996: *Adjustment in Africa: Reform, Results, and the Road Ahead*. Washington, D.C.: World Bank.

World Health Organization 2001: *Macroeconmics and Health: Investing in Health for Economic Development*. Report of the Commmission on Maroeconomics and Health, Geneva: WHO.

Ziegler, J. 2001: *Economic, Social and Cultural Rights: The Right to Food*. Report by the Special Rapporteur on the Right to Food, Commission on Human Rights, Fifty-Seven Session, Economic and Social Council, E/CN.4/2001/53.

# 4 Globalization and Democracy in the Developing World

Jeffrey Haynes

*Democracy, it is often argued, has become an almost universal standard of governance. Some associate globalization with the diffusion of democratic values and institutions whilst others consider it a limit upon substantive democracy. This chapter explores the relationship between globalization and the spread of democracy across the global South, assessing whether it defines the new political paradigm of development. The discussion commences with an analysis of the theoretical linkages between globalization and the Third Wave of democratization drawing upon the theoretical literature in international relations and comparative politics. It then surveys the sources of political change in the Third World, comparing and contrasting the different regional trends towards democratization and seeking to explain the significant differences in patterns and outcomes. The analysis concludes by emphasizing some of the significant tensions between globalization and transitions to democratic rule, most especially its consolidation, and argues for the integration of insights from international relations, comparative politics, and development studies to a fuller understanding of the transformed political context of development.*

## INTRODUCTION

The aim of this chapter is to examine how transnational and international actors ('globalization') interact with domestic agents to affect democratization and democracy outcomes in developing countries. I start from the premise that *all* developing countries' domestic political arrangements are, to some degree, affected by globalization, but that the precise impact will vary from country to country. For the purposes of this chapter, I define 'democratization' as the *process* of putting in place a democratic political system. I understand the concept of 'democracy' minimally: it involves the holding of relatively free and fair elections, following which a victorious party or parties take power.

I need to set the scene for our discussion by examining (1) the circumstances in which globalization has had a significant political impact in developing countries and (2) how globalization informs contemporary comparative political analysis. A starting point is that pressures on authoritarian regimes to democratize have increased in recent years, with a growth in numbers of countries in the 1990s, following a breakdown of 'existing states and the birth of new ones'. This was especially apparent among both developing countries and those of the former European communist bloc (formerly, the 'Second World'). This trend affected not only 'rock solid ones, as in the case of the Soviet Union' but also 'flimsy reeds, such as Somalia, Liberia, and Afghanistan' (Migdal 1997: 210). During the 1990s, numerous new states were created. Several dozen emanated from the disintegration of the Soviet Union (such as Ukraine, Georgia, Estonia, Latvia and Lithuania), and the Federal Republic of Yugoslavia (such as Croatia and Bosnia-Herzegovina). Others resulted from the fracturing of existing countries, in Africa (Eritrea, Somaliland) and the Middle East (Palestine). Under such circumstances, it seems entirely plausible that both international and transnational actors might have a significant impact on the political arrangements of these new states, not least because many of them have not yet completed the formation of their political systems. In particular, small, weak and vulnerable countries seem especially open to external influences. For example, following a denial of demands both for democracy and for better human rights, the government of Haiti was subjected to European Union sanctions in 1991. This was followed, in the mid-1990s, by US actions to depose the authoritarian government, followed by US-sponsored elections.

However, as we shall see, political arrangements in virtually all developing countries, almost regardless of their age, size, geographical position, type of political system or level of economic development, are influenced – to some degree – by what international and transnational actors do. On the other hand, few if any have their domestic political arrangements dictated for long by extrinsic forces. The question is, how precisely do external actors influence domestic political outcomes in developing countries? The question is contextualized by the fact that, like their counterparts in long-established states, leaders of new ones claim the full panoply of sovereignty: territoriality, autonomy and independence from outside actors. However, many – especially a large number of politically unstable, economically undeveloped countries in the developing world – do not empirically have full control of domestic environments. While part of the reason for this is typically due to domestic instability, it should not lead us to overlook the influence that international and transnational actors may have. In sum, influential transnational and international actors – which I shall refer to in this chapter, for reasons of brevity and conciseness, as 'globalization' – have interactive, dynamic relationships with states in virtually all developing countries. This interaction involves both costs and benefits for *all* such states, although the precise balance will differ from country to country (see, for example, Gillespie and Youngs 2002b on North Africa; Grugel 2000 and Lowenthal 2001 on Latin America; and Yilmaz 2002 on Turkey).

## GLOBALIZATION AND POLITICAL CHANGE IN THE DEVELOPING WORLD

The recent impact of globalization on domestic political environments in developing countries is underpinned by three key developments. First, in the early 1990s, there was *the collapse of European communist governments*. During the Cold War, in the name of fighting communism, Western governments had tended to turn a blind eye to the poor human rights records and denial of democracy of many allies in the developing world. However, once communism in Europe was 'defeated', both democracy and human rights concerns increased in importance. In addition, the emblematic – and sudden – failure of the Soviet Union and its regional communist allies served to encourage many people in the developing world living under authoritarian regimes to demand both democracy and better human rights.

Second, there was *pressure to democratize from transnational civil society*. This refers to the encouragement from both human rights-orientated transnational civil society groups – such as Amnesty International and Human Rights Watch – and from democracy-promotion organizations, including Freedom House. Their goal was to invite authoritarian developing country governments to reform via adoption and implementation of international democratic and human rights norms.

Third, there was *increased international economic integration*. Moves towards a globalized economic system not only facilitated the movement of capital, labour and goods across national boundaries but also increased international economic competition. This led to growing dominance of market forces that, while sometimes producing greater economic efficiency, also had the effect of diminishing the already weak economic position of millions of poor people in developing countries. A consequential result was a demand for more economic justice, expressed in 'anti-globalization' demonstrations in Seattle and elsewhere from the late 1990s. Such outbreaks were novel expressions of contention and often involved groups organized transnationally. Such economic changes were also reflected in a transformation of many production systems and labour markets, and a general weakening of the power of organized labour to pressurize governments to enforce labour standards, such as minimum wage legislation. In addition, adoption of structural adjustment programmes in numerous developing and former communist countries resulted in diminution or destruction of already inadequate welfare programmes. In sum, the socio-political impact of international economic integration led to growing demands in numerous developing countries for democracy.

In sum, three recent events both contextualize and inform the recent political impact of globalization in the developing world:

- the end of the Cold War and the consequential collapse of European state communism;

- the apparently universal triumph of capitalism;

■ 'the emergence of the dialectical anti-thesis to the triumph of capitalism' (Sen 1999: 56), widely expressed in demands for democracy.

However, while there is much agreement that globalization has an impact on domestic political environments in developing countries, there is no consensus about what precisely 'globalization' is. I understand 'globalization' to be a multifaceted concept involving (technological, economic, cultural and political) phenomena that link multiple (domestic, transnational and international) levels of analysis. The technological dimension is largely concerned with recent developments in communications technology. There was development – and gradual speeding up – of technological advances during the latter part of the nineteenth century, and a particular spurt of growth after 1945. While the role of technology, especially communications technology, is widely agreed to be very important to the progress of globalization, we should note that it is a facilitative or enabling component. That is, technology per se is not the determining factor: it is necessary, but not sufficient on its own to propel globalization forward. Technology is essentially neutral, and can be both beneficial *and* hostile to globalization. For example, some governments, for example, those of China, Iran and Saudi Arabia, have recently sought to demonstrate 'that technology is an important source of governmental control over its citizenry . . . It can be used to enhance the autarchic isolation of people from wider international currents. In this way, technology made its own sinister contribution to the totalitarian fragmentation of the inter-war period' (Clark 1997: 21). On the other hand, the enhanced ability of peoples, states and organizations to communicate is much greater than before, enabling the transmission of ideas, ideologies and capital around the world quicker than ever before.

It would be incorrect to claim that the second – but by no means secondary – dimension of globalization, economic globalization, has a uniform impact in and on all regions (Hay 2002: 252–3). On the other hand, it would be appropriate to understand economic globalization in terms of a worldwide trend towards economic liberalization, involving 'changed attitudes towards (neoliberal) economic development' (Schulz et al. 2001: 3). Economic globalization is also concerned with (1) 'the spatial reorganisation of production', (2) 'the interpenetration of industries across borders', and (3) 'the spread of financial markets' (Mittelman 1994: 429). This does not imply that economic globalization is simply a technical development as it has led not only to 'recurrent fears over the stability of the multilateral trading order' but also to domestic concerns about sales of national assets to foreigners as a result of privatizations of formerly state-owned assets.

We can note a further dimension of economic globalization in numerous developing countries: under the auspices of IMF-imposed structural adjustment programmes (SAPs), a loss of control of national economic policy and programmes. Since the 1980s, the adoption of SAPs in dozens of African, Asian and Latin American countries has led to three outcomes. First, the situation enabled both the IMF and its sister organization, the World Bank, to acquire and retain much economic influence in many developing countries. Second, these IFIs continued to champion SAP-based development strategies long after many analysts pointed out their fundamental flaws. Another result was further integration of SAP-ped developing country economies into the Western-dominated global economy.

Third, cultural globalization is a central facet in many sociological interpretations of globalization. Much early theorizing about globalization focused on cultural changes stimulated by the global spread of identical consumer goods and an American(ized) culture. Disseminated primarily by US-based transnational corporations, Americanization was believed to subvert local cultures, encouraging people not only to become 'consumers' but also to buy American goods and services. Together, the 'media revolution' and the growth of consumerism were thought to help erode particularistic cultures and values, replacing them with an Americanized 'global culture' of Disney, McDonald's, Coca-Cola and Starbucks.

Saurin argues that culture has become a potent political force threatening the basis of the current fragmented state system and its structures of supporting nationalism. This is because, he argues, 'culture avoids being located and tied down to any definable physical space' (Saurin 1995: 256). However, and somewhat paradoxically, nationalism and ethnic awareness are also cultural components transmitted around the globe, becoming both a globalized *and* a globalizing phenomenon. One of the main causes of contemporary ethnic and religious conflict in many countries is said to be such groups' awareness of what other groups around the world are doing, and with this knowledge seeking to emulate counterparts' struggles for greater power.

A further result of the spread around much of the world of an Americanized culture is a growing adherence to its key component: individualistic, as opposed to communal, values. This development is apparent not only in the global clamour for more and better (individualistic) human rights but also in the demand for liberal democracy. Although certain 'anti-American' entities, such as Islamists and some Asian governments, fight this, there is no denying that both democracy and human rights are now widely perceived as worldwide issues, necessitating global solutions. This perception helped stimulate development of international organizations and global institutions to address such issues.

The final dimension of globalization is what concerns us most in the current chapter: political globalization. This centres on what Mittelman (1994: 429) has called an 'emerging worldwide preference for democracy'. Since the 1980s, dozens of authoritarian regimes in developing countries have collapsed and, in most cases, democratically elected governments have replaced them. While occasionally such political changes eventuated almost solely because of domestic upheavals, more frequently they were the result of interaction of both domestic and external factors.

To what extent is democratization and its potential outcome, democratic consolidation, influenced in the developing world by extraneous actors and factors? It seems obvious that democratization requires that no foreign power hostile to this development interfere in the political life of a country with the intention of subverting the political system. Whitehead (1993) argues that, in virtually all recent democratization attempts, the influence of international actors was secondary to those of domestic factors. Further, Huntington (1991) suggests that foreign actors may hasten or retard – but not fundamentally influence – democratic outcomes. However, he also notes that foreign encouragement to democratize can actually hinder overall chances of democratic consolidation. This is because such encouragement can, on the one hand, lead to democratization *before* countries reach what he suggests is a 'suitable' economic and social level while, on the other, it might retard or prevent democratization in countries where chances of democratization seem more plausible. In general, international support for democratization grew in the 1980s and 1990s, but its impact was not necessarily clear (Carothers 1999).

The United States has long been a key pro-democracy international actor: not only successive governments but also various state-linked bodies, such as the National Endowment for Democracy, have actively supported democratization. Such a development is not new: in the 1950s, newly democratic governments, for example, those in Costa Rica, Venezuela and Colombia, received support from the USA for democratization. More recently, the evolution of US foreign policy – from President Carter's human rights policy in the late 1970s, through President Reagan's promotion of democracy as a counter to perceived communist expansionism in the 1980s, to President Clinton's less ideologically linked support for democracy in the 1990s – supported democratically elected governments.

Since the late 1980s, the US government has provided more than $700 million to over 100 countries to aid democratization (Carothers 1999). Carothers argues that such assistance was focused in 'a standard democracy template', involving financial support to underpin the electoral process and democratic structures: constitutions, political parties, state institutions, the rule of law, legislatures, local government structures, better civil–military relations and civil society organizations. Leftwich (1993: 612) points out that it takes more than money to develop democracy, as it is not easy to create and embed concrete manifestations of what he calls 'good governance'. Such an outcome is 'not simply available on order', but requires 'a particular kind of politics . . . to institute and sustain it'. This raises an important issue: external funding for democracy will be insufficient to achieve its aims if target regimes are content to 'acquire democratic legitimacy internationally *without substantially changing their mode of operation*' (Lawson 1999: 23; emphasis added). It might be that only superficial democratization is encouraged when external actors limit their perusal of the democratic process to elections alone; often, critics argue, the international observation of elections seemed to be the only meaningful test to judge a shift from authoritarianism to democracy. However, when elections are complete, and the attention of the corpus of international observers shifts, then 'democracy' may be little more than rhetorically achieved, as elite hegemony resurfaces with a narrow base of political systems and 'authoritarian clientelism and coercion' (Karl 1995: 74).

Some external actors, like the US government, possess huge financial resources that can be used to encourage democratization, especially during the transition stage. They tend, however, to be less central to later efforts to institutionalize and sustain democracy. This is because democratic consolidation is always a long-term project, primarily dependent for success on an array of domestic, especially political and economic, developments. These include the spread of a pro-democracy political culture, the building of democratically accountable institutions and, ideally, sustained economic growth and society-wide welfare provision. However, especially in the early stages, democratic consolidation is fraught with obstacles, constantly threatened with reversal.

In sum, globalization consists in changing economic, political and cultural arrangements and configurations within developing countries. One result is an erosion of formerly 'hard' boundaries and a consequential diminution of many states' ability to control their domestic environments. Globalization is said to be reducing the power of the nation-state to make definitive decisions regarding its own future. On the other hand, this 'globalization thesis' – with its emphasis on 'the hollowed out state' and 'a borderless world' – is at odds with several traditional, embedded assumptions of political analysis. These include an understanding that the world comprises: (1) confined political territories governed by national – sovereign – states; (2) nation-states; and (3) national economies. These have long been regarded, respectively, as the 'natural' units of political and political economic analysis. The globalization thesis implies that these long-standing arrangements are in the process of being transcended.

## GLOBALIZATION, COMPARATIVE POLITICS AND INTERNATIONAL RELATIONS

What does globalization imply for comparative political analysis of the developing countries? Traditionally, comparative politics and international relations (IR) are separate spheres of endeavour. While each is a sub-discipline of political science, they have developed dichotomously, separate bodies of analysis exhibiting certain core assumptions about domestic and international realms: each is seen to be inhabited by discrete actors, with specific rules of the game. IR is of course fundamentally concerned with international and, to a lesser extent, transnational actors. Comparative political analysis, on the other hand, is solidly grounded in assessment of what goes on – politically – within states. Traditionally, such analysis has either overlooked non-domestic factors or, at best, seen them merely as an aspect of the analytical context, analysed under such semi-autonomous 'rubrics as intervention, dependency, subversion and foreign aid' (Yilmaz 2002: 68).

Unlike the realm of comparative politics, students of IR have long been cognizant of the argument that the 'nation-state is in retreat'. In the late 1960s and the 1970s, a primary debate in the field of IR was about the status of the state in the international system. The key question was: 'Is the state obsolete?' Coming up with no clear, definitive answer, this turned out to be a recurring question. On the one hand, there was the state-centric (or billiard ball) model of the international system while, on the other, the 'cobweb' model was informed by the idea that the state was being tied down and increasingly incapacitated by growth of countless transnational connections. Later, in the 1980s, the state made a comeback. Most IR specialists accepted (once again) that it still represented the most significant actor by far in the international system. Later, in the 1990s, as globalization entered the conceptual fray, IR, like other social sciences, was encouraged, once again, to survey the putative extinction of the nation-state.

There has been little progress towards an amalgam of the two analytically separate universes of IR and comparative politics, not much in the way of substantive attempts to developing understanding of how the two – domestic and international – universes interrelate with and feed off each other. For example, a well-established comparative politics textbook – Rod Hague and Martin Harrop's *Comparative Government and Politics. An Introduction* (the fifth edition was published in 2001, twenty years after its first appearance) – devotes only limited attention to what the authors call 'the state in a global context'. This is notwithstanding the fact that the book claims to examine 'how relations between countries impinge on politics within them' (p. 47). As a result, it is surprising that the sole chapter devoted to this theme is a mere fifteen pages (that is, 5 per cent of the book's nearly 300 pages). Moreover, this chapter is not well integrated with the remainder of the book. The other sixteen chapters concentrate on comparative assessments of domestic structures and processes in a limited number of countries – such as, how 'democratic' and 'authoritarian' governments work, and what is the role of the 'big three': the executive, legislature and judiciary. However, the almost exclusively domestic focus neglects important categories of international and transnational actors that impact, sometimes significantly, upon domestic political (and economic) outcomes.

The traditionally domestic-orientated focus of comparative political analysis has two key limitations: (1) a lack of analytical concern with international and transnational actors, and (2) too much concern with formal, top-down power structures. The problem is that a limited outlook not only significantly inhibits and constrains the scope of analysis but also, as a result, seriously undermines the possibility of a well-rounded understanding of the contemporary political universe.

The main general shortcoming of conventional comparative politics analysis is an underestimation of the importance of external factors in the analysis of domestic political change. To be relevant and authoritative, comparative political analysis must go beyond a narrow concern with (top-down) domestic power, fully to take into account the impact of external factors. Conventionally, comparative political analysis employs a certain conceptual framework that 'downplays . . . necessary and logical transnational connections between domestic political and economic structures and international politics' (Smith 2000: 4–5). Most comparativists start, sensibly enough, from the assumption that to acquire information we must compare things that, demonstrably, have clear similarities. From there attention shifts to investigate reasons for any differences discovered. Traditionally, as already noted, the central intellectual question in the comparative politics tradition is how best to explain and account for the nature and processes of social and political change in discrete units: states.

Comparative analysis tends to look no farther than domestic factors to seek its explanations. This is especially pronounced in the case of Western democracies, with national political environments characterized by democratic systems, whereby nearly all adults are eligible to take part via periodic, regular, 'free and fair', elections. Many comparativists seem intuitively to believe, however, that democratic outcomes are not strongly influenced by external actors. Europe provides a good example of this tendency. As the editors of a new (2002) journal, *Comparative European Politics*, note in an introductory flyer, Europe is the 'most regionally integrated political and economic space within the global system'. Among its constituent countries, they note, 'dynamic relationships between transnational, international and domestic processes and practices' interact and, it seems entirely plausible, have an impact upon domestic political outcomes. Within European countries – especially among the fifteen current European Union members – processes of government and governance involve inputs not only from a supranational institution – the EU itself – but also from various – economic, religious, ethnic, subnationalist and so on – transnational actors. What does this imply for the study of comparative politics in Europe? At the least, it suggests that the traditional analytical focus of comparative politics needs to be amended to include international and transnational actors. This is because processes of governance and structures of national governments form only a part of the explanation for political and political economic outcomes within countries.

Another example is provided by recent comparative political focus on democratization in developing countries. Earlier, as Gillespie and Youngs (2002a: 1) note: 'the complexities of the international dimension to political change had been inadequately factored into studies of democratization'. During the 1960s and 1970s comparative work on democratization was concerned with the first and second wave democracies, clustered in North America, Western Europe and Japan, and was overwhelmingly domestic-orientated. At this time, the dominant focus was on the manner in which – primarily economic – modernization and its outcome, associated restructuring of social and class alliances, portended certain changes in political structures. Later, in the 1980s, as dozens of countries in Eastern Europe, Latin America, sub-Saharan Africa and Asia made transitions from authoritarian to elected governments, the comparative political approach shifted focus. Attempting to respond to the new global trend – democratization – and, in some cases, democratic consolidation, comparative political analysis sought to fashion a distinct and distinctive body of literature. It sought to comprehend what was happening by focusing on causation and outcomes:

consolidation of democracy would, theoretically, follow democratic transition. Seeking to explain democratization, analysis focused upon domestic political actors, seen as sovereign agencies whose successful tactical strategies led not only to the demise of authoritarian regimes but also to successful democratic transitions. In this process, the role of external actors – including states, intergovernmental organizations and international non-governmental organizations – was either ignored or, at best, consigned to a marginal role.

When we turn to the democratizing regions themselves, we see that what external actors do is sometimes not only not marginal but in fact central to understanding outcomes. For example, it is widely acknowledged that, in the 1980s and 1990s, external actors were crucial to processes of democratization in Central and Eastern Europe (CEE). Not only were intergovernmental organizations, most notably the EU, heavily involved in transitions from communist rule, but so also were transnational civil society networks. Similarly, such external actors were also involved in democratization in other regions, notably sub-Saharan Africa, during the same period (Haynes 2001). Overall, these examples highlight key international and transnational dimensions to political change in democratizing regions. In sum, the impact of both international and transnational actors – in shorthand, globalization – on political outcomes poses analysis of democratization (and by extension comparative political analysis more generally) a significant challenge.

Traditionally, then, the comparative politics literature devoted to the developing world has ignored or, at best, only cursorily referred to external factors as a supplementary add-on. However, attention has recently begun to turn to the impact of international and transnational actors on democratization (see for example, Compton 2002, Gillespie and Youngs 2002b, Grugel 2000, Lowenthal 2001 and Yilmaz 2002). This development has its roots in a branch of international relations: foreign policy analysis. It reflects the fact that both Western governments and international organizations not only proclaim commitment to encouraging democracy in developing regions but also claim, as we saw earlier, to 'put their money where their mouth is' through political and economic 'conditionality' strategies.

A second general limitation of conventional comparative politics analysis is the lack of attention paid to the notion of *governance* as distinct from the more parsimonious idea of *government*. Whereas *government* comprises the formal *institutions* that make the collective decisions for society, *governance* 'refers to the *process* of making collective decisions' (Hague and Harrop 2001: 5; emphasis added). Not only the formal institutions of government but also other organizations, such as business interests, play their part. As Smith (2000: 4–5) notes, although comparativists often stray into the territory of party politics in their discussions of political systems, they tend to overlook influential sectors of society outside formal state institutions. These include religious bodies, the media and business organizations. Unsurprisingly, comparativists also tend to overlook any transnational counterparts. In sum, in order to pay appropriate attention to the notion of governance in comparative political analysis and to present fuller, more rounded, inquiries, comparative political analysis could introduce into analysis previously ignored or under-analysed concern, such as ethnicity, religion, gender, the natural environment, human rights and so on.

Of recent attempts to bridge the gap between the two universes of comparative politics and international relations, Douglas Chalmers's (1993) is not only one of the most developed but also offers pointers to further research. Chalmers seeks to explain what external actors do in relation to domestic politics and political economy in Latin America. He calls this process the 'internationalization of domestic politics' because, he suggests, certain 'internationally based actors' (IBAs) are a significant presence in the domestic political (and economic) environments in many Latin American countries. Chalmers discusses the idea of an 'internationalized domestic politics' in Latin America, and sees this as the result of two factors: (1) 'the tremendous increase in the numbers, types, scope and resources of internationally based actors', and (2) 'the post-Cold War trend of globalisation' (Yilmaz 2002: 70). Among Latin American countries, Chalmers contends, not only are IBAs 'normal parts of the system' but also this development is a recent, although not a novel, phenomenon. It can be traced back three decades: to Latin America's shift to democracy in the 1970s and 1980s. In Latin American contexts, IBAs have three main characteristics:

- they remain, over a period of time, involved in a country's domestic politics;

- they become embedded in national political institutions;

- they are identified with international and transnational sources of power.

However, while Chalmers' analysis of IBAs in Latin America is undoubtedly welcome, there remains an urgent need to understand more widely what happens when the purposive policies of international and transnational actors interact and intertwine with domestic factors regarding democratization in the developing countries. However, this is not a simple task. Hay (2002: 259–60) ends his recent book, *Political Analysis*, with a cautionary statement. The features of 'social and political processes [are] inherently contingent, indeterminant and ultimately unpredictable. . . .[E]ven globalisation, seemingly the most inevitable and inexorable of processes is, in the end, revealed to be complex, contested and contingent'. Not least among the problems is that, to understand why political and social outcomes are as they are, we need to take into account not only what actors do but also under what conditions they act. This is a reference to overarching structural features, factors that can be important in conditioning political outcomes within countries. For example, for most developing countries there are colonial legacies; many Middle Eastern countries and other oil producing nations have political economy factors that derive from that state of affairs; in addition, 'cultural factors', such as 'Islam' and 'Asian values', are said to inform outcomes in large swathes of the non-Western world.

What all this points to is the necessity of developing new analytical tools to explain political and political economic outcomes within developing countries. While both Chalmers (1993) and Yilmaz (2002: 82) suggest that 'the net result of the process of globalization has been the internationalization of domestic politics', Webber and Smith (2002) examine such issues via a focus on foreign policy. They note the emergence of what they call a 'globalist' approach to foreign policy analysis, a modus operandi rooted in a 'post-Cold War logic of globalisation'. They suggest that contemporary foreign policy-making occurs in 'a very indeterminate world of shifting power structures and a multiplicity of external influences'. Because these forces can influence the relationship between states and their populations, analysts should seek to factor them into analysis of democratization in the developing world. In the face of these forces, individual states' foreign policies – in all but the most powerful states – are increasingly of little effect. As Migdal (1997: 211) puts it, states are 'battered by global economic and information systems, [and] by the challenges of virulent ethnic and tribal forces'. Such an analytical framework could usefully be developed in relation to the domestic realm of the state, to identify how the various aspects of what I have called 'globalization' impact upon countries' domestic political and economic arrangements. Let's turn next to a survey of democratization in the developing world.

## DEMOCRATIZATION AND THE DEVELOPING WORLD

During the 1980s and 1990s, numerous developing countries installed democratically elected governments. This starkly contrasted with the situation in the 1960s and 1970s. Then, various kinds of unelected regimes – such as military, one-party, no-party and personalist dictatorships – were the norm in most countries of the developing world. Why did democratization occur? It was the result, many observers agree, of interaction between various domestic and external factors, with the former normally most important. At the domestic level, a shift to democracy – that is, 'democratization' – was typically linked to expressions of popular dissatisfaction with the often abysmal development and political records of unelected governments. Internationally, Western 'political conditionality' was an important factor in the shift to elected regimes in many developing countries. Aid-donating governments, such as those of the USA and Britain, sought to promote democracy by linking moves in that direction to the granting of foreign aid. Political conditionality has two dimensions: 'positive' assistance to encourage democratic development and 'negative' aid sanctions to leverage reform in recipient countries. Overall, four key points, relating to both external and domestic actors, are often made in the literature on democratization and democracy in the developing world.

1 Western pressure – known as political conditionality – encouraged the shift from authoritarian to elected governments in many developing countries.

2  While democratization produced a large number of elected
   governments, many do not have strong democratic credentials.
3  Despite democratization, power often remains broadly in the hands of
   the same groups of elites that held it during authoritarian rule.
4  Strong civil societies are crucial to healthy democracies, but developing
   countries often lack them.

Reflecting such concerns, the structure of the remainder of the chapter
is as follows: first, we investigate the circumstances surrounding the third
wave of democracy in the developing world. Second, we assess the regional
picture, among developing countries, in relation to democracy. In the
conclusion, we sum up the relative importance of domestic and external
factors to democratic outcomes.

## THE 'THIRD WAVE' OF DEMOCRACY

So widespread was the move to democracy in the developing world in the
1980s and 1990s that an American academic and commentator, Samuel
Huntington (1991), gave it a name: the 'third wave of democracy'. The
third wave, which followed two earlier waves (the first was in the late
nineteenth century and the second directly after the Second World War),
began with the shift from authoritarian to democratically elected
governments in Greece, Portugal and Spain in the mid-1970s. In the 1980s
and 1990s democracy spread to Latin America, Eastern Europe, Asia and
sub-Saharan Africa. The extent of the changes in this regard can be
gauged from the fact that in 1973 only a quarter of countries had
democratically elected governments. Twenty years later the proportion of
democracies had grown to more than half and, in the early 2000s, it
reached about 75 per cent, that is 140 or so countries.

While dozens of developing countries held at least one relatively free
and fair national-level election in the 1990s, there were significant regional
differences. Latin America had a comprehensive shift to elected
governments: in 2000, all 23 Latin American countries, with the exception
of Cuba, had elected governments. Several Asian countries – including
Bangladesh, Mongolia, Nepal, the Philippines, South Korea and Taiwan –
registered a shift to democracy in the 1990s, as did a large number of sub-
Saharan African states: the result is that now over half the region's nearly
50 countries have democratically elected governments. In contrast, few
Middle Eastern countries – with the exceptions of Turkey, Jordan, Morocco
and Kuwait – made the shift from authoritarian to popularly elected
governments during the period of the third wave.

There were 45 new democracies in the developing world in 2000.
Regionally, the breakdown was as follows: Asia had 7 new democracies,
Latin America 16, Africa 18, and the Middle East 4. Of the 7 in Asia, the US
organization Freedom House (FH) classified 4 (57%) as 'free' (Mongolia,
the Philippines, South Korea, Taiwan and Thailand), and 3 (43%) –
Bangladesh, Nepal and Indonesia – as 'partly free'. Of the 16 in Latin
America, FH judged 7 (44%) 'free' and 9 (56%) 'partly free'. Africa had 5
(28%) new democracies rated 'free', 13 (72%) 'partly free'. All 4 of the

**Table 4.1**  Regional breakdown of 'free' and 'partly free' countries in the developing world, 2000

| Region | Total 'free' new democracies | % 'free' | Total 'partly free' new democracies | % 'partly free' | Overall total: 'free' and 'partly free' new democracies |
|---|---|---|---|---|---|
| Asia | 4 | 57 | 3 | 43 | 7 |
| Latin America | 7 | 44 | 9 | 56 | 16 |
| Africa | 5 | 28 | 13 | 72 | 18 |
| Middle East | 0 | 0 | 4 | 100 | 4 |
| Total | 16 | | 29 | | 45 |

*Source*: Based on Freedom House survey data available at www.freedomhouse.org/survey00/method/

democracies in the Middle East were 'partly free'. (See the Freedom House website for details at www.freedomhouse.org/survey00/method.) In sum, as table 4.1 shows, in 2000 FH rated 16 of the 45 new developing world democracies (36%) 'free' and the remaining 29 (64%), 'partly free'. Table 4.1 also indicates that the percentage of 'free' states (57%) among new Asian democracies was higher than in Latin America (44%) and considerably better than in Africa (28%) or the Middle East (0%).

## DEMOCRACY IN THE DEVELOPING WORLD: THE REGIONAL PICTURE

Why were democratic outcomes patchy? Why, for example, were there proportionately more 'free' states in Asia than in Latin America or sub-Saharan Africa? It is difficult to argue that time is the main factor as shifts to democracy in all three regions occurred at the same time, the 1980s and 1990s. However, it should be noted that, historically, democratic consolidation is a slow process. Most first and second wave democracies – such as Britain, the United States and Japan – took decades or longer to achieve it. This is because to develop and embed democratic institutions takes both time and continuous effort, while eventual success depends upon a variety of factors. To explain and account for the variable democratic picture in the developing world we turn next to a regional survey.

### Sub-Saharan Africa

Sub-Saharan Africa is a culturally and religiously diverse, politically complex, region of nearly fifty countries. The impetus for political reforms came from a combination of domestic and international sources. However, the background to the region's recent democratic transitions was an array of unpropitious structural characteristics, which, according to many observers, made it surprising that the region has democratized to the extent it has. That is, beset by endemic economic problems and growing societal strife, as Villalón put it, most sub-Saharan African countries seemed 'somehow [to have] "gone wrong" since independence' (1998: 3). Although, currently,

**Table 4. 2** Democracy in sub-Saharan Africa, 2000

| Country | Political rights | Civil liberties | 'Freedom status' |
|---|---|---|---|
| Cape Verde | 1 | 2 | free |
| Sao Tomé e Principe | 1 | 2 | free |
| South Africa | 1 | 2 | free |
| Benin | 2 | 3 | free |
| Namibia | 2 | 3 | free |
| Mali | 3 | 3 | partly free |
| Malawi | 3 | 3 | partly free |
| Seychelles | 3 | 3 | partly free |
| Ghana | 3 | 3 | partly free |
| Mozambique | 3 | 4 | partly free |
| Central African Republic | 3 | 4 | partly free |
| Burkina Faso | 4 | 4 | partly free |
| Guinea-Bissau | 3 | 5 | partly free |
| Lesotho | 4 | 4 | partly free |
| Tanzania | 4 | 4 | partly free |
| Madagascar | 5 | 3 | partly free |
| Gabon | 5 | 4 | partly free |
| Zambia | 5 | 4 | partly free |

1 = most free, 7 = least free; 'free' = combined political rights and civil liberties total of 2–5; 'partly free' = 6–9; 'not free' = 10–17.
*Source*: www.freedomhouse.org/research/freeworld/2000/countryratings/

there are many democratically elected governments in the region, it remains to be seen how many of them will endure (see table 4.2).

## South Asia

South Asian countries differ greatly in terms of size, geography, economic structures, political traditions, forms of rule, relations with external powers, and cultures. Following independence from colonial rule in the late 1940s, the region had a history of political diversity. For example, there was undemocratic monarchical rule in Nepal; a civil war since the early 1980s in Sri Lanka between the majority Sinhalese and the minority Tamils; a democratic system in India since independence in 1947; and alternating military and civilian regimes in Bangladesh and Pakistan. However, both Bangladesh and Nepal democratized in the early 1990s. This followed an earlier move to democratic from military rule in Pakistan in 1988, following pressure from the American government. Later, however, in October 1999, a military government returned to power following a coup d'état.

Despite this setback, regional democratic progress was clear: in the late 1990s, South Asia witnessed over twenty governments and, most unusually, all (except the military regime in Pakistan) came to power via democratic processes. But, like sub-Saharan Africa, the region's countries had many factors unpropitious for democracy, including poverty and underdevelopment and widespread ethnic and religious strife. The overall regional picture regarding new democracies is given in table 4.3. Note that only countries rated by FH as 'free' or 'partly free' are included. Those judged 'not free' are omitted.

**Table 4.3** New democracies in South Asia, 2000

| Country | Political rights | Civil liberties | 'Freedom status' |
|---------|------------------|-----------------|-------------------|
| Bangladesh | 3 | 4 | partly free |
| Nepal | 3 | 4 | partly free |

1 = most free, 7 = least free; 'free' = combined political rights and civil liberties total of 2–5; 'partly free' = 6–9; 'not free' = 10–17
*Source*: www.freedomhouse.org/research/freeworld/2000/countryratings/

## East and South-East Asia

In the 1980s and 1990s, there were shifts to democracy in several regional countries, including South Korea, Taiwan, Thailand, the Philippines and Indonesia. In the Philippines, a 'People Power' movement forced President Ferdinand Marcos and his government from power in 1986 while, almost simultaneously, South Korea and Taiwan moved from unelected to elected rulers. Popular pressure was also notable in two other recent regional examples of democratization: (1) the 'May 1992 events' in Thailand which led to the ousting of the government of Suchinda Kraprayoon and replacement by a new regime, and (2) student-led protests in Indonesia in 1998 which helped catalyse wide societal unrest culminating in the downfall of President Suharto and his regime. Generally, across the region, pro-democracy campaigners – focused in a variety of civil society groups and encouraged by external actors including the government of the United States – helped undermine the legitimacy of unelected governments. The overall regional picture regarding new democracies is given in table 4.4. Note that only countries rated by FH as 'free' or 'partly free' are included. Those judged 'not free' are omitted.

## Latin America

The background to the recent regional wave of democratization in Latin America was the widespread assumption of power by military rulers in most regional countries in the 1960s and 1970s, which took on a particular form, known as bureaucratic authoritarianism. While specific characteristics of military rule differed from country to country, what they all had in common was a political scene where civil and political societies were comprehensively repressed. Prior to the recent regional wave of democracy, regime legitimacy had plummeted in many Latin American countries, consequential to political repression and poor economic performances. Encouraged by the government of the United States, and pressurized by rejuvenated civil and political societies, democratically elected leaders came to power proclaiming a willingness to try to make democracy work. Allegations of fraud in the June 2000 presidential poll in Peru, which led to the ousting of President Fujimori, coup attempts in Ecuador and Paraguay, declaration of martial law to quell a popular uprising in Bolivia, and Colombia's continuing civil war all combined to suggest that overall regional progress towards democracy was

**Table 4.4** New democracies in East and South-East Asia, 2000

| Country | Political rights | Civil liberties | 'Freedom status' |
|---------|------------------|-----------------|------------------|
| South Korea | 2 | 2 | free |
| Taiwan | 2 | 2 | free |
| The Philippines | 2 | 2 | free |
| Thailand | 2 | 3 | free |
| Indonesia | 4 | 4 | partly free |

1 = most free, 7 = least free. 'free' = combined political rights and civil liberties total of 2–5;
'partly free' = 6–9; 'not free' = 10–17
*Source:* www.freedomhouse.org/research/freeworld/2000/countryratings/

**Table 4.5** New democracies in Latin America, 2000

| Country | Political rights | Civil liberties | 'Freedom status' |
|---------|------------------|-----------------|------------------|
| Uruguay | 1 | 2 | free |
| Panama | 1 | 2 | free |
| Bolivia | 1 | 3 | free |
| Chile | 2 | 2 | free |
| Argentina | 2 | 3 | free |
| Dominican Republic | 2 | 3 | free |
| Ecuador | 2 | 3 | free |
| El Salvador | 3 | 3 | partly free |
| Honduras | 3 | 3 | partly free |
| Nicaragua | 3 | 3 | partly free |
| Brazil | 3 | 4 | partly free |
| Guatemala | 3 | 4 | partly free |
| Mexico | 3 | 4 | partly free |
| Paraguay | 4 | 3 | partly free |
| Colombia | 3 | 4 | partly free |
| Peru | 5 | 4 | partly free |

1 = most free, 7 = least free; 'free' = combined political rights and civil liberties total of 2–5;
'partly free' = 6–9; 'not free' = 10–17
*Source:* www.freedomhouse.org/research/freeworld/2000/countryratings/

problematic. Nevertheless, in 2001, popularly elected leaders ruled all thirty-five members of the Organization of American States, except Cuba. The regional democratic picture in 2000 is given in table 4.5. Note that only regional countries rated by FH in 2000 as 'free' or 'partly free' are included. Those judged 'not free' are omitted.

## ACCOUNTING FOR DEMOCRACY: THE COMPARATIVE IMPORTANCE OF DOMESTIC AND EXTERNAL FACTORS

Our regional surveys suggest that we need to take into account a range of domestic and external factors when seeking to account for democratization and democracy in the countries of the developing world. We have seen that while external encouragement can be important, domestic circumstances and factors are of primary importance.

## Domestic factors

Democratic advances are likely to be facilitated when three sets of domestic factors are in place:

■ comparatively unfragmented civil societies;

■ a reasonable amount of social capital;

■ cohesive party systems.

(Lack of space means that I cannot discuss these three factors further here. Anyone seeking further discussion of these factors should see Haynes 2002: 94–9.)

## External factors

Three sets of external factors are of general importance in explaining recent shifts to democracy in the developing world:

■ background factors;

■ state actors;

■ non-state actors.

Because of their importance to the concerns of this chapter, I examine each of them in more detail.

*Background factors*    Background factors, including favourable or unfavourable geostrategic circumstances, can be important to the chances of both democratization and democracy. This can be seen in relation to earlier periods of attempted democratization in the developing world. For example, in the 1930s, tentative democratization in Latin America could not make headway against a background of regional – and global – economic depression. And, in the 1960s and 1970s, fears of the Cuban revolution spreading led to a regional crackdown on calls for democracy.

In the 1980s, global circumstances became more advantageous for democracy, with the unforeseen collapse of European communist states of particular significance. However, as we have seen, not all developing regions moved to democracy at the same pace and with the same enthusiasm. For example, in the Middle East, where the influence of the USSR had long facilitated the continuity of the region's centralized control models of government, there was no shift to widespread democracy (Nonneman 2001). Part of the reason was that many nondemocratic Middle Eastern countries are major oil producers – for example, Saudi Arabia, the Gulf Emirates and Libya. State control of oil wealth helped such governments to ignore any popular demands for democracy while, in addition, Western calls for political reforms in the Middle East were muted. This was due both to the already destabilizing effect of the continuing Arab–Israeli conflict and to the desire not to encourage Islamic 'fundamentalism'.

*State actors*    Western governments, including the largest aid donors in quantitative terms – the USA, Japan, France and Britain – encouraged prospects for democracy, already improved with the collapse of the European communist systems. They did this by introducing political and/or economic conditionalities – linked to the provision of foreign aid. There were two sides to this policy: 'positive' assistance, to encourage democratic development with promises of increased aid, and 'negative' aid sanctions to leverage reform from unwilling recipient governments. However, as Crawford (2001) discovered, aid sanctions undertaken by Sweden, Britain, the US and the EU in the early 1990s helped promote political reform in only eleven of the twenty-nine cases where they were applied. Crawford finds that aid penalties were most effective where they added to pressure on governments from internal pressures for reform. He also found that aid penalties failed where they have met strong resistance from recipient governments or where they threatened the strategic or commercial interests of donors.

*Non-state actors*    Cross-border, non-state actors make up transnational civil society, a concept with three main components. First, like domestic civil society, the term encompasses neither governmental groups nor profit-seeking private entities, like transnational corporations (TNCs). Second, such groups are transnational – that is, they interact across state boundaries, often beyond the control of governments. Third, transnational civil society can take a variety of forms, for example, a single international non-governmental organization (INGO) with individual members or chapters in several countries, such as Transparency International. Or it can be a more ad hoc border-crossing coalition of organizations and associations, such as the International Campaign to Ban Landmines (ICBL), formed to campaign on a certain issue. Several questions are commonly asked in relation to transnational civil society.

*Why* does transnational civil society exist? *How* does it manage to influence powerful states and rich TNCs? *Why* should people scattered around the globe bother to use their unpaid time and energy to work together with other individuals and groups with whom they share neither history nor culture?

To answer such questions we must note, first, that transnational civil society differs from both states and TNCs in key respects. For example, states have sovereignty: they (1) exist within clearly defined physical territories; (2) have power to elicit resources from the territory and populations they control; (3) command legal recognition from other states; and at least theoretically (4) can appeal to citizens' patriotism to cement loyalties to the state. Transnational civil society also differs from transnational corporations, whose constituent parts are linked by common economic interests and legal obligations. Why then does it exist? Transnational civil society networks – which some contend are an emerging 'third force' in international politics – typically aim for broader goals based on their conceptions of the public good. Consequently, such groups are bound together not primarily by self-interest but by shared values. However, the values they embrace differ considerably, ranging from a belief in animal rights, through conviction that democracy is a global right of all peoples, to the inherent superiority of some ethnic groups over others.

## CONCLUSION

I suggested in this chapter that recent attempts in the developing world to introduce and then consolidate democratic systems were informed by a number of domestic and external factors. On the one hand, there is the nature of a ruling elite's control over society and the strength and effectiveness of civil society as a counterweight to state power while, on the other, there is the impact of both international and transnational agents. We saw that while, at least to some degree, many formerly authoritarian developing countries recently installed democratically elected governments, the overall impact of the third wave of democracy was patchy. In some countries, democratically dubious governments managed to stay in power – for example, those in Côte d'Ivoire, Cameroon and Burkina Faso – by transforming themselves, via the ballot box in tightly controlled elections, into 'democratic' governments. Elsewhere, some unelected rulers simply refused to budge and did not allow meaningful elections. We should not overlook that among developing countries in the early 2000s, more than forty – concentrated in the Middle East and Africa – were still devoid of most democratic characteristics.

We also saw that both democratization and the embedding and consolidation of democracy, once perceived as a fairly straightforward set of processes and structures, is actually highly complex. There is not only the question of the relationship between economic and democratic progress – does the latter depend on the former? – but also the issue of the nature of interactions between a state and domestic civil society: how much political space does the former allow the latter? To what extent can civil society organizations collectively pressurize the state to deliver democracy?

To be democratically relevant, civil society will not merely be an ordering of elite groups, but will actively encourage involvement from those traditionally lacking political influence: the poor, women, the young, certain minority ethnic and religious groups. But, because such an extension and deepening of democracy will normally be resisted by those in power, then legal guarantees and extensive protections for individual and group freedoms and associational life are crucial, to be secured by and through an independent, impartial judiciary. To increase welfare to those that need it, redistribution of scarce resources is both politically necessary and economically appropriate, while the military must be neutralized as a political actor. Put another way, the consolidation of democracy necessarily implies a conscious effort to redress past imbalances, a course of action necessary so that the mass of ordinary people come to believe that democracy is a better system than alternative ones, such as benign dictatorship.

External actors, especially those in possession of large financial resources to encourage democracy, like the US government, are often important at the transition stage of democratization. However, they are often less central to efforts to institutionalize and sustain – that is, consolidate – democracy. The point is that democratic consolidation is always a long-term project. It is dependent for success not only on an array of domestic developments – such as building a 'pro-democracy' political culture and a set of appropriate political institutions – but also on a favourable external climate, facilitated by proactive support from both international and transnational actors.

## References and Further Reading

Carothers, T. 1999: *Aiding Democracy Abroad: The Learning Curve*. Washington, D.C.: Carnegie Endowment for International Peace.

Chalmers, D. 1993: Internationalized domestic politics in Latin America, the institutional role of internationally based actors. Unpublished paper, Department of Political Science, Columbia University.

Clark, I. 1997: *Globalisation and Fragmentation, International Relations in the Twentieth Century*. Oxford: Oxford University Press.

*Comparative European Politics* 2002: Flyer for new journal, published by Palgrave from March 2003.

Compton, R., Jr. (ed.) 2002: *Transforming East Asian Domestic and International Politics. The Impact of Economy and Globalization*. Aldershot and Burlington: Ashgate.

Crawford, G. 2001: *Foreign Aid and Political Reform: A Comparative Analysis of Democracy Assistance and Political Conditionality*. Basingstoke: Palgrave.

Gillespie, R. and Youngs, R. 2002a: Themes in European democracy promotion. *The European Union and Democracy Promotion: The Case of North Africa*, special issue of *Democratization*, 9 (1), 1–16.

Gillespie, R. and Youngs, R. (eds) 2002b: *The European Union and Democracy Promotion: The Case of North Africa*, special issue of *Democratization*, 9 (1).

Grugel, J. 2000: State and business in neo-liberal democracies in Latin America. In H. Smith (ed.), *Democracy and International Relations*, Basingstoke: Macmillan, 108–25.

Hague, R. and Harrop, M. 2001: *Comparative Government and Politics. An Introduction*, 5th edn. Basingstoke: Palgrave.

Hay, C. 2002: *Political Analysis. A Critical Introduction*. Basingstoke: Palgrave.

Haynes, J. 2001: *Democracy in the Developing World. Asia, Africa, Latin America and the Middle East*. Cambridge: Polity.

Haynes, J. 2002: *Politics in the Developing World. A Concise Introduction*. Oxford: Blackwell.

Huntington, S. 1991: *The Third Wave. Democratization in the Late Twentieth Century*. Norman: University of Oklahoma Press.

Karl, T. L. 1995: The hybrid regimes of Central America. *Journal of Democracy*, 6 (3), 72–86.

Lawson, L. 1999: External democracy promotion in Africa: another false start? *The Journal of Commonwealth and Comparative Politics*, 37 (1), 1–30.

Leftwich, A. 1993: Governance, democracy and development in the Third World. *Third World Quarterly*, 14 (3), 605–24.

Lowenthal, A. 2001: Latin America at the century's turn. In L. Diamond and M. F. Plattner (eds), *The Global Divergence of Democracies*,

Baltimore/London: The Johns Hopkins University Press and the National Endowment for Democracy, 312–26.

Migdal, J. 1997: Studying the state. In M. Irving Lichbach and A. S. Zuckerman (eds), *Comparative Politics. Rationality, Culture and Structure*, Cambridge: Cambridge University Press, 208–35.

Mittelman, J. 1994: The globalisation challenge surviving at the margins. *Third World Quarterly*, 15 (3), 427–41.

Nonneman, G. 2001: The Middle East between globalization, human 'agency' and Europe. *International Affairs*, 77 (1), 141–62.

Saurin, J. 1995: 'The end of international relations? In J. Macmillan and A. Linklater (eds), *Boundaries in Question. New Directions in International Relations*, London: Pinter, 244–61.

Schulz, M., Söderbaum, F. and Öjendal, J. 2001: Introduction. In M. Schulz, F. Söderbaum and J. Öjendal (eds), *Regionalization in a Globalizing World. A Comparative Perspective on Forms, Actors and Processes*, London: Zed Books, 1–21.

Sen, G. 1999: Developing states and the end of the Cold War. In L. Fawcett and Y. Sayigh (eds), *The Third World Beyond the Cold War. Continuity and Change*, Oxford: Oxford University Press, 56–77.

Smith, H. 2000: Why is there no international democratic theory? In H. Smith (ed.), *Democracy and International Relations*, Basingstoke: Macmillan, 1–30.

Villalón, L. 1998: The African state at the end of the twentieth century: parameters of the critical juncture. In L.Villallón and P. Huxtable (eds), *The African State at a Critical Juncture. Between Disintegration and Reconfiguration*, Boulder, Colo., and London: Lynne Rienner, 3–26.

Webber, M. and Smith, M. 2002: *Foreign Policy in a Transformed World*. Harlow: Pearson Education.

Whitehead, L. 1993: The alternatives to 'liberal democracy'. A Latin American Perspective. In D. Held (ed.), *Prospects for Democracy*, Cambridge: Polity, 312–29.

Yilmaz, H. 2002: External-internal linkages in democratization: developing an open model of democratic change. *Democratization*, 9 (2), 67–84.

Part II

# Globalization, Development and Human Security

# 5 Globalization and Human Security

*Caroline Thomas*

*Caroline Thomas here explores security from a human – rather than a state –
perspective, offering a conceptual approach to the subject, and contextualizing
the notion of human security within a framework of the evolving global
economy. Against a backdrop of increasing inequality between and within
states, and also between corporations in the 1980s and 1990s, she examines
dominant ideas about development and marginalization in contemporary
global politics. She concludes by building on the general acceptance that the
future of globalization as a political project ultimately rests on the extent to
which it can be made commensurate with human security.*

## INTRODUCTION

The chapter uses a human security lens to explore and evaluate some of
the impacts of globalization on developing societies. The adoption of this
perspective is based on two premises. The first is that a state-centric
analysis masks important social consequences of globalization below and
above the level of the state, and that an analysis undertaken at the level of
individual human beings in their communities can offset some of these
shortcomings and offer valuable new insights. The second premise is that
*people matter* and are an appropriate focus of concern for the international
relations community. Importantly, linking back to the first premise,
globalization is affecting security not only at the state level, but at the
level of individuals' day-to-day lived experience. While this is true across
the globe, in specific ways it may be particularly significant for the people
of the South, where the twin challenges of freedom from want and
freedom from fear are the most pervasive. Moreover, given the mandate of
states to provide for the security of their citizens, their mediation between
global processes and local outcomes is crucial. Hence a human security
analysis has the potential both to capture some of the important
consequences of globalization for global citizens, and to support
evaluation of the role of states in attending to their citizens' security
needs. The knowledge generated can help inform policy debates about
how to make globalization work better for everyone, and in so doing
enhance security from the local to the global.

The chapter is divided into three parts. The first part explores in some
detail *what* is meant by human security, as this is a relatively new term in
international relations literature and diplomatic parlance. It explains the

two main strands of human security thinking, in terms of freedom from want and freedom from fear, and suggests the common values that underpin them. Protection of the vulnerable via the reduction of risk is identified as the common core, along with a holistic understanding of the constitution of vulnerability in a globalizing world.

The second part focuses on *why* the human security approach is useful for furthering our understanding of the outcomes of globalization, especially for the non-Western world which is the focus of this collection. In particular it suggests that the *disaggregation of data* required by a human security approach, in terms of both *level and scope of analysis*, offers the opportunity for a deep understanding of the complex results of globalization. Such information is crucial for the development of *transformative policies* to decrease the risks borne by the vulnerable.

The third part illustrates *how* a human security approach can expand our understanding of the impact of globalization on the South. It suggests that while globalization is multifaceted, and driven by a range of different factors, it is corporate-led economic globalization through free trade that is of most obvious and immediate concern for the majority of humankind because of the *assumption* that it is the best route to deliver economic growth and employment opportunities for all. A human security approach demands consideration of the *evidence*. To what extent is trade liberalization enhancing or undermining human security as freedom from want at various levels:

- entire world-regions;

- sub-state regions;

- economic sectors (e.g. agricultural, non-agricultural);

- specific social groupings (e.g. gendered, ethnic, racial, age-based);

- community;

- household.

Thus, a human security lens brings forth important insights regarding the impact of globalization, which would be lost by an exclusively state-level analysis. These insights are important for an evaluation of globalization as currently constituted, and for policy prescriptions to reduce the vulnerability of people.

## CONCEPTUALIZING HUMAN SECURITY

Currently, most analysts, following Kofi Annan (2000), agree that human security encompasses both freedom from want and freedom from fear. Broadly speaking, human security as freedom from want describes a condition of existence in which basic material needs are met, and in which there is a reasonable expectation that protection will be afforded during any crisis or downturn – natural or man-made – so that survival is not threatened. Human security as freedom from fear describes a condition of existence in which human dignity is realized, embracing not only physical safety but going beyond that to include meaningful participation in the life of the community, control over one's life and so forth. This suggests a radical account of politics as freedom from domination/exploitation, not simply the freedom to choose as advocated by the liberal tradition. Thus, while material sufficiency lies at the core of human security, in addition the concept encompasses non-material dimensions to form a qualitative whole. In other words, human security embraces the whole gamut of rights, civil and political, economic and social, and cultural.

By contrast, human insecurity refers to a condition of vulnerability, in which human beings' physical or material well-being is threatened. Such threats may be due to natural disasters, such as cyclones, or volcanic eruptions; or man-made disasters such as rising sea levels, mudslides, oil spillages and nuclear and chemical explosions. They may be due to political conflict within or between states. Also they may arise from the fundamental structure of the global economy in which decision-making power is concentrated in the core capitalist states, commodity producers are continually disadvantaged, and billions of people live precariously on the edge where life is structured by lack of reliable access to material resources. Particular events arising within the global economy (e.g. financial crises due to poor management, at levels from the global to the national) can cause instant havoc to the livelihoods of millions.

A more comprehensive understanding of human security can be achieved by a brief examination of the differences between human security and the orthodox state-centric analysis which has long dominated international relations. (For a full exploration, see Wilkin 2002.) These are illustrated in table 5.1, and their significance becomes clear below. Where has 'human security' come from and who are its advocates?

While human security represents a relatively new approach in the lexicon of politicians, diplomats and international relations scholars, its core concern – protection of the vulnerable – and core expression – freedom from want and freedom from fear – have a long lineage. Concern with individuals and communities – not simply states – has been growing on the international agenda since the Second World War. However, it was in the mid-1990s that use of the term 'human security' took hold, in the context of the political space which opened post-Cold War. Significant humanitarian crises, especially the genocide in Bosnia in 1992–5 (200,000 people killed), and in Rwanda in 1994 (500,000 deaths), coupled with growing acknowledgement of the uneven distribution of the benefits of economic globalization, drew attention to human insecurity. The downside associated with particular aspects of globalization, such as rapid liberalization of financial flows, hit the headlines with the East Asian crisis in 1997. During the 1990s, therefore, protection of the vulnerable – whether physical or material – gained attention from several important constituencies, ranging from NGOs, to middle-ranking powers, the G7 states, the international financial institutions (IFIs) and the UN.

As is usual for a newly emerging approach, human security has taken on different nuances with various policy makers and writers. The two core strands of interest in human security have found different champions. The

**Table 5.1** Key elements of orthodox security and human security

|  | Orthodox, state-centric security | Human security |
|---|---|---|
| Referent object | The state | Humanity |
| Operating principle | The state and national security | Global holism, connectivity |
| Agenda | Justification and status quo Military power and national defence | Explanation and transformation (economic and social welfare) |
| Means | Self-help by states | Collective, integrated, multifaceted response at multiple levels |
| Input | Military expenditure and arms | Redistribution, structural reform |
| Output | Secure borders | Enjoyment of economic, social, civil and political and cultural human rights |
| Outcome | Interstate stability Order | Global social justice |
| Future? | Intrastate conflict International instability Unsustainable resource use | Sustainable peace |

*Source:* Thomas 2000.

Canadian government, for example, building on long-standing Canadian interests, has paid most attention to protection of individuals from acts of violence – humanitarian intervention, the landmines treaty, the International Criminal Court (see below). The Japanese government, on the other hand, heavily influenced by the effects of the Asian currency crisis at the end of the 1990s, has paid more attention to the economic aspects of human insecurity and threats to survival, and the need to protect people from sudden economic downturns. These two core strands of human security are outlined below. Importantly, they are not mutually exclusive; quite the contrary – they represent two integral and interrelated components of the condition of human security and of the emerging human security approach, based on the common value of all human beings. On its own, each aspect represents a necessary but insufficient ingredient for human security.

## Freedom from want

The challenge of poverty and inequality is long-standing. In the mid-1970s the developing countries, through the UN system, had called for a New International Economic Order. This call had fallen on deaf ears, and from the late 1970s onwards the discursive UN system gave way to the less democratic international financial institutions, the IMF and the World Bank, under the direction of the G7. While some limited progress was made over the next twenty years to address specific social concerns, such as increasing the number of people with access to clean water, in general inequality grew within and between states as the IFIs sought to promote debt repayment by governments and peoples of the South, and global economic integration, via economic and political restructuring.

From the late 1980s, with the end of the Cold War, there was the hope that a peace dividend would follow which would divert resources from the arms race into the development challenge. It soon became apparent that this would not happen, and the dwindling pot of resources available as aid during the 1990s was shared amongst a larger group of countries, with the former Eastern bloc competing for finance.

During this period, the influence of the UNDP's then Director, development economist Mahbub ul Haq, was significant in placing human beings and their perceptions of security on the global political agenda. Ul Haq pioneered the use of the concept of 'human development', with the UNDP publishing a Human Development Index in 1990.[1] Dissatisfied with mainstream development economists' measurements of poverty around income/expenditure, he championed efforts to incorporate an evaluation of literacy and life expectancy alongside income. Annual Human Development Reports have produced rankings of countries based on this broader set of criteria. In 1994, the UNDP's annual report went a step further, and focused specifically on human security, arguing that:

> For too long, the concept of security has been shaped by the potential for conflict between states. For too long, security has been equated with threats to a country's borders. For too long, nations have sought arms to protect their security. For most people today, a feeling of insecurity arises more from worries about daily life than from the dread of a cataclysmic world event. Job security, income security, health security, environmental security, security from crime, these are the emerging concerns of human security all over the world. (UNDP 1994: 3)

The UNDP hoped that its 1994 report would influence the 1995 Copenhagen UN World Summit for Social Development. Yet while that summit put the global spotlight briefly on key questions of unemployment and poverty eradication, it did not bring forth concrete results in terms of a reassessment of the basic development model by the G7 and IFIs, or greater flows of aid. Instead, it continued in the tradition of the 1992 Rio UN Conference on Environment and Development, which had legitimated rather than undermined the neoliberal development model: poverty eradication and environmental protection as integral parts of sustainable development were to result from the free play of market forces.

Through the 1990s, the OECD countries were happy to set new targets for the reduction of global poverty and associated indicators in education, health and so forth, but this was not matched either by additional resources in terms of increased aid, or by attempts to tackle structural inequalities, or by debt write-off. Indeed over this period aid flows continued to decline, while private flows of capital increased enormously and very destructively. The private capital was concentrated in a dozen or so states, while the rest received nothing; and it was highly volatile, moving in and out of countries rapidly. These rapid flows contributed to the East Asian crisis of the late 1990s, which threw millions of people back below the poverty line. This indicated just how insecure were the lives of millions of people who had been enjoying improved satisfaction of material needs. Also it showed just how interconnected the world had become. For example, British employees of Asian companies in South Wales, UK, lost their jobs.

The mid- to late 1990s witnessed growing dissatisfaction with the performance of neoliberal economic development policies throughout the South and former Eastern bloc, within specific constituencies in the G7 countries such as church groups and social justice NGOs, and even some individuals within the World Bank. The failure of structural adjustment, coupled with the social reversals brought about by specific currency crises in the late 1990s, further eroded confidence in the model and added fuel to this protest movement. The Jubilee 2000 campaign to write off Third World debt was highly effective in mobilizing a transnational alliance of global citizens who could not easily be dismissed by G7 governments as anarchists and troublemakers. Demonstrations at Seattle, Genoa and other meeting locations led some within G7 governments and the IMF and World Bank to question the political expediency of continued application of neoliberal development without modification. Indeed there was the concern amongst such groups that the global economic integration project might be derailed if the benefits of the project were not more evenly distributed, and if civil society groups could not be made to understand the benefits of globalization.

With the rise of political protest against the uneven distribution of the benefits of globalization, James Wolfensohn, then President of the World Bank, noted in 2000 that: 'When we think about security, we need to think beyond battalions and borders. We need to think about human security, about winning a different war, the fight against poverty' (cited in Thomas 2000: 5). Similarly, Michel Camdessus, then President of the IMF, remarked in 2000 that 'Poverty is the ultimate threat facing humanity. The gap between rich and poor nations . . . [is] . . . potentially socially explosive. . . If the poor are left hopeless, poverty will undermine societies through confrontation, violence and civil disorder' (cited in Thomas 2000: 3).

The need to promote growth with equity began to be taken seriously within the international financial institutions, and poverty-centred development became the buzzword of the World Bank, which repackaged its lending products in terms of nationally owned poverty reduction strategies ostensibly designed by countries and their people themselves.

At the UN General Assembly's Millennium Assembly in 2000, specific targets were set for development – the Millennium Development Goals (UN/OECD/IMF/World Bank 2000: 5). The notion of freedom from want as integral to global justice was gaining ground, as was the recognition that global problems require global solutions. The events of 9/11 lent weight to this analysis. However, the route to its achievement remains a topic that incites deep divisions. For the G7 and the IFIs, a slightly modified version of the economic neoliberalism of the last twenty years is the assumed road to development, with free trade as the motor for pro-poor growth.

For many social justice groups, the market can never deliver human security, and in fact is seen as a cause of insecurity. These different approaches were evident in competing assessments of the 2002 Johannesburg Social Summit. The route to human security as freedom from want remains contested, even as the notion of human security becomes more embedded in the language of the UN agencies.

## Freedom from fear

In the mid-1990s there was growing attention on the part of middle-ranking states, particularly Norway and Canada, to the notion of *human security rather than simply state security*. In addition to the safeguarding of states, leaders of these countries were especially interested in the protection of individual human beings and communities in terms of their freedom from fear (Heinbecker 1999: 6). Canadian Foreign Minister Lloyd Axworthy was deeply affected by his perception that in the aftermath of the Cold War, intrastate conflicts had become more prevalent than interstate conflicts. Indeed, the number of people killed in the 1990s compared with the 1980s in interstate wars dropped by two-thirds, to 220,000. By contrast, the numbers killed in intrastate conflicts in the 1990s stood at 3.6 million (UNDP 2002). Often linked to these conflicts, the numbers of refugees and displaced people grew over this period by 50 per cent to 18 million. The use of low technology to fight such wars resulted in very high percentages of civilian casualties, and women and children were often disproportionately the victims. Axworthy was mindful of the importance of human security as freedom from want, but chose to focus Canadian efforts on the aspect of human security on which he felt Canada could make greatest impact – freedom from fear.

Human security as freedom from fear has been pursued via two main channels (Osler Hampson 2002): a rights-based approach anchored in the rule of law and treaty-based solutions; and a humanitarian conception with safety of peoples/freedom from fear as the objective behind international interventions, humanitarian relief and post-conflict peace-building. While tangible achievements in the development of both channels has been influenced significantly by the bottom-up political activities of NGOs and key individuals, it could be argued that the opportunity for this resulted from the general post-Cold War international environment. This provided the context in which top-down particularistic interests of certain middle-ranking states, keen to gain global influence via the power of ideas, were able to articulate, progress and institutionalize a broadly humanitarian agenda (see Suhrke 1999).

The first major achievement was the negotiation of the Ottawa Convention on Antipersonnel Landmines and its signing in December 1997 (Osler Hampson 2002; Gwozdecky and Sinclair 2001). Canada and Norway forged a strong partnership on this issue, and there was the hope that this momentum and partnership could be carried over into other areas. In 1998 those two countries signed the Lysoen Declaration, which pledged them to work in partnership on a human security agenda. The agenda, while wide-ranging, focused on freedom from fear issues (see box 5.1).

Box 5.1    The Lysoen Partnership agenda

Landmines
International Criminal Court
Human rights
International humanitarian law
Gender dimensions in peace-building
Small arms proliferation
Children in armed conflict, including child soldiers
Child labour
Arctic and Northern cooperation

*Source*: Adapted from Small 2001: 232.

The establishment of the Human Security Network took this partnership a stage further, embracing a collection of over twelve Northern and Southern states. This informal network identifies areas for collective action, and aims to act as a catalyst by bringing international attention to new and emerging issues. For example, it has been instrumental in attempting to get non-state actors, such as armed groups, to comply with international humanitarian and human rights law (www.humansecuritynetwork. org/menu-e.php). The network has also discussed the development of a Human Security Index which could be used to measure achievements of states, but the precise content of the index remains under discussion. While the desire to have an impact has led the network to narrow its focus (for example, on training police forces in human rights law), members have discussed broader ideas which encompass freedom from want as well as freedom from fear. In this context the work of the Latin American Faculty of Social Sciences (FLACSO) is significant: it emphasizes five dimensions of human security – economical, social, environmental, political and cultural. The network is still at a relatively early stage, feeling its way (see www.humansecuritynetwork.org).

The human rights/rule of law approach has as its most noteworthy recent success the establishment of the International Criminal Court in 1998 (Osler Hampson 2002). Spyros Economides (2003: 29–30) comments that: '. . .the ICC is intended to pursue, prosecute and punish those individuals who have ordered, induced, assisted, abetted or committed crimes which are deemed to be of international "concern" in that they violate the rights and conscience, not of nation-states or the international system, but of particular victims or humanity as a whole'. This is a potentially significant development in the pursuit of human security as freedom from fear, though the jury is out on how far national interest will get in the way of its operation.

## Freedom from want and freedom from fear: common values

The emerging streams of human security thinking share the simple belief that people everywhere matter and they are thus a legitimate focus for our attention; and our actions should be directed towards decreasing their vulnerability and, in particular, protecting the most vulnerable. For Kofi Annan (2001), 'No shift in the way we think or act is more crucial than that of putting people at the centre of everything we do. That is the essence of human security.' Other institutions – whether local or state governments, international institutions, private corporations or NGOs – are there ultimately to serve people, to contribute to the well-being of society as a whole, not a selective and exclusive strand of it at the expense of the rest and future generations. But the common ground of the emerging streams of human security go beyond this, since by different degrees these approaches all accept, to paraphrase Mark Duffield (2001: 10), 'a shift from the study of objects to the study of interconnections'. In a similar vein, Kofi Annan (2001) comments that the 'pillars of what we now understand as the people-centred concept of "human security" are interrelated and mutually reinforcing'.

Following in this vein, human security represents a paradigmatic shift from mechanical to complex analyses of the political world, or, in its most far-reaching formulation, 'the difference between seeing the world as a machine and seeing it as a living system or organism' (Duffield 2001: 9–10). What happens in one part affects the condition of other parts. In a globalizing world, understanding these interconnections is essential for understanding human vulnerability and for designing policies to ameliorate it. *The two key aspects of human security are not mutually exclusive; indeed, neither aspect is sufficient for the enjoyment of human security, and each depends on the existence of the other for its own full realization. An individual and his/her community must be free from fear to reliably enjoy freedom from want; and without freedom from want there can be no freedom from fear.*

Consider for example the immense threat to millions of people posed by HIV/AIDS, not only in Africa but increasingly elsewhere – notably India, China and Russia. We cannot understand and tackle this crisis simply in terms of freedom from want. Of course we must understand its intimate relationship with poverty and access to medicines, in terms of the global rules governing development policy and access to medicine, and their national transmission. But we must also understand the role of conflict and armies in promoting its transmission, gender relations, governments' attitudes, spending priorities, and prejudices, cultural practices and so forth. A holistic understanding of the problem and its place in cultural, social, economic, military and political structures, local to global, is necessary to the development of policies to decrease human vulnerability and thereby increase human security.

The importance of highlighting the common values underlying the two main strands of human security thinking has not been lost on key personnel in the UN system. The concept of human security was formally recognized in the UN in the context of the UN Security Council's first debate on AIDS, in January 2000 (Piot 2001). Then in the autumn of 2001 the Human Security Commission was established. One of the key tasks of this Japanese-funded, UN-affiliated Commission was to bridge the two aspects – freedom from want and freedom from fear, or broadly development and conflict, and to develop the concept of human security as an operational tool for policy formulation and implementation geared toward protection of the vulnerable (Ogata 2001: 7). Both have an important role to play in promoting a transformative agenda and this of course was the task of the Human Security Commission. Each is making a contribution to putting the human experience at the centre of policy, rather than an abstract state which serves the interest of elite groups. The Commission, jointly directed by Nobel Prize winner Amartya Sen and former UNHCR Sadako Ogata, released its report 'Human security now' in 2003 (see www.humansecurity-chs.org).

The human security approach has come in for much criticism. It has been derided by academic adherents of the traditional security orthodoxy (e.g. Paris 2001) who continue to prioritize the state and national security, and by some commentators in the South who see it as serving Western interests. Some have argued that the champions of freedom from fear are aiming at little more than 'the transformation of societies to fit liberal norms and expectations' (Duffield 2001: 22). Currently we are still at an early stage in the embedding of the approach in global discourse. The precise manner in which the discourse evolves, the ideas that gain legitimacy, will be crucial in determining the potential of the approach to help deliver transformation in the lives of the majority of humanity.

## WHY IS A HUMAN SECURITY APPROACH USEFUL IN THE CONTEXT OF GLOBALIZATION?

Horst Kohler (2002: 1), until 2004 the Managing Director of the IMF, has defined globalization as '. . .the process through which an increasingly free flow of ideas, people, goods, services and capital leads to the integration of economies and societies. . .'. Yet while there may be broad agreement on what globalization *is*, as noted earlier there is less agreement on its impact and value.

Under the current conditions of corporate globalization, a human security approach – particularly the emphasis on basic needs and its link to political voice – has great potential to critique globalization and to inform policy debates. Given current global inequality and widespread poverty, and given projected trends in the global system across a range of indicators such as demography and sustainable resource use to name but two, the pursuit of sustainable human development is both urgent and multifaceted. Even Kohler, who believes that integration into the global economy has huge potential for improving human welfare, concedes that 'there is clear evidence that far too many of the world's people have been left behind. The disparities between the world's richest and poorest nations are wider than ever. Nearly three billion people who are trying to survive on less than $2 a day deserve the chance for a better future' (Kohler 2002: 2). The continuation of these socio-economic divisions is a very clear indication that globalization to date is not delivering the human security needs of the mass of humanity; but to what extent is it exacerbating them?

Just as globalization involves an intensification of global–local linkages, human security involves a broadening and deepening of our understanding of the political and social worlds. In a sense, human security maps onto globalization. Thus the concept has resonance for those scholars, global citizens and policy makers who are trying to make sense of the political world at the beginning of the twenty-first century and to devise appropriate policies for dealing with global challenges. A human security approach requires us to explore issues relating to level and scope of analysis, and transformative agendas.

## Issues relating to level of analysis

In contrast to a state-based analysis, human security requires a disaggregated and therefore richer, more sophisticated, exploration of the very complex and sometimes contradictory impacts of globalization on actual human experience across the globe. Mechanistic state level analyses of security are based on zero-sum games, assumptions of governmental legitimacy and impermeable borders. A human security analysis, in disaggregating the idea of the nation-state, which in the South is not strong in many places, focuses on the perceptions and lived experience of real people and their communities rather than abstract states.

Similarly, regarding development, in contrast to orthodox state-based analyses based on national income and expenditure data, the human security approach invites far greater disaggregation of data, and a consideration of additional criteria, thus potentially offering a fuller, richer, more meaningful picture. While we are all well aware of the shortcomings of national averages, measurements of development, poverty, water and food availability and a host of other indicators have for too long relied on national per capita averages. These often paint a very partial picture, and can be very misleading.

Take the World Bank's very positive categorization of a handful of countries as 'the new globalizers' (see below). Yet when we scratch below the surface, national averages can mask huge intranational disparities and hide deep and growing social problems. For example, in China global economic integration has been accompanied by more acute rural–urban polarization; and also by unemployment for previously secure workers in restructured state-owned enterprises (Cook and Jolly 2003). Likewise, national figures for growth in India in the 1990s look positive, but a deeper investigation reveals a very complex picture. Growth is geographically and sectorally imbalanced, and thus it is not being translated into needed impact on poverty reduction in terms of either national or state statistics (Datt and Ravallion 2002). It has been accompanied by an intensification of the political and economic divide between the four southern states – Karnataka, Tamil Nadu, Andhra Pradesh and Kerala – which are home to India's technical institutes and industries, and the Northern states such as Bihar, Madhya Pradesh, Orissa and Uttar Pradesh (Kripalani 2002). Sectorally, agriculture is lagging behind other sectors, and even within the agricultural sector, higher growth in yields is not occurring within the states where a pro-poor result is most urgently needed. There has been a failure in terms of organized employment generation, a failure to redress inequalities between urban and rural areas, increased vulnerability of the hundreds of millions of poor in the north and also south (especially landless labourers and women dependent on the agricultural sector for livelihoods and food security), and a failure of the central or state governments to attend to ensuing micro-social problems (Samuel 2002). A very general conclusion that can be drawn is that individuals and communities are best able to take advantage of potential opportunities of global economic integration if their governments have prioritized literacy; hence the relative achievements of people in Kerala.

Development economist Ravi Kanbur (2001) has highlighted the importance of disaggregation, using the example of Ghana to show that while national data indicate a decrease in the poverty index over the period 1987–91, disaggregation reveals that the poverty index for entire regions of the country worsened. He suggests further that disaggregation undertaken along lines of gender, ethnicity or race, etc, would reveal a complex picture.

The same point is made by Swatuk in relation to the concrete example of access to potable water in southern Africa. He remarks that: '. . . national trends . . . mask the facts of intranational disparities. Moreover, there are rural/urban, sex, class and race aspects to inequalities of access, with poor, black females in rural areas, for example, being most likely to lack access both to potable water and to adequate sanitation' (Swatuk 2000: 509).

A human security approach forces us to think about how global, national and local structures/forces interrelate, and their cumulative impacts on individuals and communities. It requires us to ask: to what extent does the current form of globalization impact on the experience of human vulnerability across the globe, and how do governments at various levels mediate outcomes? What is the lived experience of globalization, and who is responsible for it? What does it look like to most of humanity? What does it feel like? Consider not politicians in Washington or Brussels, nor members of the core workforce of highly skilled people integrated into the global economy; but rather the majority of citizens, precarious workers or the rest, the expanding pool of people in First and Third World states excluded from international production (Cox 1999). What of those hopelessly marginalized by the globalization process, such as the over 1 billion people who are unemployed? How do the 1.2 billion people (probably much more – the figures are contested; Wade and Wolf 2002) people living on $1 or less a day feel about the current order? How do the HIV/AIDS infected in Africa feel, knowing that medication exists but they cannot afford it, and that their governments at best can only provide treatment to a few of those in need? How do poor women feel in Ghana and all over the developing world, giving their children water infected with guinea worm or other threats because they are faced with the bitter choice of either paying for clean water or paying for food? How do northern Indians perceive their situation, knowing that the disparities between them and southern Indians are becoming increasingly significant, as southern India integrates more rapidly into the global economy? How do the 12 million refugees, and 6 million internally displaced people, feel, living often permanently in conditions of total insecurity (UNDP 2002)? In contrast, how do the super-rich 1 per cent of global population – earning annually as much as the poorest 57 per cent of humanity, and growing worldwide in relative wealth – experience the current form of globalization, living behind high walls and electronic fences, and with private security forces?

## Scope of analysis

Human security provides a useful starting point for thinking about the *interrelated* nature of many current and future global political challenges. It requires us to investigate and reflect holistically on matters that affect the security of real people and their communities, and where appropriate to make connections in a way that traditional state-based analysis – whether in terms of the security debate or of the development debate – has failed to do. Thus it invites a consideration of whatever factors affect the security of human beings, ranging from state-sponsored repression, to international hostilities, to the weather, to environmental degradation or resource depletion, to the unregulated activities of multinationals, to fluctuating commodity prices, or to capital market volatility. Human security requires an analysis of the *interconnections* between these factors, as a necessary step to addressing the security concerns of human beings. For example, if mining companies fail to respect the local environment and render insecure the lives of local people, then an understanding of the vulnerability of those communities requires an analysis not only of the company, but of the national government, which has failed to regulate the company in the public interest, and of the complicity of the global institutions, which are promoting trade and investment liberalization via conditional loans without due regard to local impact.

## Policy response: transformative agenda

A consideration of the values underpinning human security suggests that policies devised in support of its achievement must be geared towards social transformation, not in the sense proposed by the neoliberal agenda, but rather the radical politics of equality, solidarity, sustainability, and so forth. The human security approach offers a conceptual shift, which is necessary to meet the changed conditions of *mutual vulnerability* that increasingly characterize the globalized world. An analysis based on simple 'one size fits all' national security or national development indicators is limited. A human security analysis by contrast is more in tune with lived experience on the ground, where 'multiple factors affect the existence of concrete people' (Nef 1999: 23). It charges us to identify causes of insecurity wherever we find them – including within the structure and functioning of the global whole – and to work to overcome them at multiple levels.

This contrasts sharply with the largely business-as-usual approaches that hang onto the state as the primary referent, whether emanating from the security community (such as the securitization of issues such as disease, environmental change, etc., discussed in Buzan et al. 1998) or the development community (for example voices calling for a reassessment of rational choice, and standard national development and poverty indicators, such as Kanbur 2002 and Stiglitz 2002). For Jorge Nef (1999), adherence to such modified orthodoxies is limiting because it fails to engage with the most important question: '. . . whose security and whose interests are at stake, or more specifically, of what the connection is between the abstract public, or "national" interest and the specific and concrete interests of diverse national and international constituencies'.

Wilkin (2002) argues that adherence to a modified orthodoxy will do nothing to help us address global social crises of poverty, social polarization, unemployment, etc. The global social problems arising today and the trends predicted for future decades are not amenable to grand solutions, nor can they be tackled by discrete, bounded sovereign states. The latter do not exist in practice, and even if they did, they could not use the old security frame of referents to tackle the increasing range of transboundary problems that confront humanity. In a globalized world, environmental problems and disease recognize neither social nor political boundaries. While we may regard HIV/AIDS as being primarily a problem in Africa, it has global implications (Singer 2002). Consequently, if the rich world helps address the problem in Africa, it is helping secure not just 'them' but 'us'. In a global economy, financial stability and instability are systemic not state-bounded characteristics: crises in Argentina impact on the US; crises in East Asia affect jobs in the UK; consumer preferences locally affect livelihoods globally.

A modified orthodoxy privileges the West, by dealing with/adding to the standard security agenda issues with which the West is uncomfortable, such as refugees/migration/immigration, while sidelining others of wider significance, such as the constitution of global poverty. This latter example is important. Wilkin (2001) argues that while currently dominant liberal thinking rejects a direct link between the generation of wealth and poverty, increasingly active social justice groups, campaigning on for example the issue of debt and trade, maintain the centrality of this mechanism. In so doing, they echo the position of early dependency theorists who argued that the North/South divide was systemically, mutually and directly constituted, with the economic security of the centre being sustained at the expense of the economic insecurity of the periphery.

## GLOBALIZATION AS GLOBAL DEVELOPMENT POLICY: ENHANCING OR UNDERMINING HUMAN SECURITY IN THE SOUTH?

While acknowledging the importance of human security as both freedom from want and freedom from fear – and indeed the intimate interconnections between these two – constraints of space suggest a narrower focus at this point. Freedom from want has been selected for further study for several reasons:

1 because in the human security literature this has received relatively little attention;
2 because corporate-led globalization through free trade has been substituted for development policy, as the best route to achieve freedom from want;

3 given the enormity of the challenge – almost half of the world's 6 billion people live on $2 a day or less (UNDP 2005), and the global population is set to increase to perhaps 8 billion by 2025 (UN/DESA 2005) – the appropriateness of trade liberalization for delivering human security must come under scrutiny.

Hence the case study which follows examines the contribution of globalization via trade liberalization to meeting the challenge of freedom from want for the world's poorest people and communities. It begins with a brief overview of globalization as development policy, highlighting the key actors involved and the key policies being promoted. Then, drawing on a growing body of evidence, an indicative assessment is made of the potential of unadulterated trade liberalization to contribute to human security.

## Trade liberalization as a blueprint for development

Over the past two decades, the liberal governance network under US hegemony has promoted a *neoliberal development blueprint* which it claims offers the greatest hope to humanity. The network identifies the causes of underdevelopment as lying squarely within countries, rather than resulting mainly or at least in part from the structure of the global economy. Hence the remedy lies not in large-scale redistribution of wealth or structural transformation of trade and finance, but rather in domestic reform. The desperate need of countries outside of the core capitalist states for aid has provided the context in which the liberal governance network can effect policy changes in the South through conditional aid. Given the neoliberal assumption that trade liberalization is the best way to promote growth and therefore development, a key policy reform required of Southern states is trade liberalization. This has been and continues to be promoted through an ever more coordinated set of trade-related policies and conditions emanating from the IMF, the World Bank, the WTO and bilateral donors (Wilks and Lefrancois 2002: 26–7). Alternative understandings of the causes of underdevelopment, and alternative policies, have been marginalized in the mainstream global development discourse.

The theory of comparative advantage from which the trade blueprint derives was developed for a world of separate nation-states, in which investment of national capital took place largely within the domestic economy. Today's world is characterized more by footloose global capital, roaming the world in search of the biggest, fastest profit, rather than by loyal national capital. Whether the assumptions about trade, growth and development still hold true in practice is an important question.

## Does trade liberalization amount to development? From assumptions to evidence-based evaluation

While Washington Consensus stalwarts continue to put great store by the potential contribution of trade liberalization to development, some other analysts are less convinced (e.g. Weisbrot and Baker 2002). A UNDP study, for example, notes that 'There is no convincing evidence that trade liberalization is always associated with economic growth. Thus there is no evidence that trade liberalization is inevitably good for human development' (UNDP 2003: 28).

Moreover, even if growth occurs, it doesn't necessarily and inevitably translate into development for people in general, even if it does for their states or select interests within them (see box 5.2). Indeed recent evidence by World Bank researcher Milanovic (2002) questions long-held assumptions of international trade theory, which say increased openness will result in more equal income distribution within poor countries. Milanovic found that in countries with a low per capita income level, such as sub-Saharan Africa, it is the rich who benefit from trade openness, while in countries where average income has risen, such as Chile or the Czech Republic, openness seems to be related to the rise in the relative income of the poor and middle class relative to the rich. This reinforces the crucial importance of disaggregating data, highlighted above.

---

Box 5.2    Economic growth and human development

'Economic growth is necessary but insufficient for human development. And the quality of growth, not just its quantity, is crucial for human well-being. Growth can be jobless, rather than job creating; ruthless, rather than poverty reducing; voiceless, rather than participatory; rootless, rather than culturally enshrined; and futureless, rather than environmentally friendly. Growth that is jobless, ruthless, voiceless, rootless and futureless is not conducive to human development.'

Source: Selim Jahan 2000; reproduced in UNDP 2003: 23.

---

What are we to make of these differing views on the contribution of trade liberalization to development? After all, the human security of billions of people hangs in the balance. Let us consider a number of key issues.

(1) First, let us consider the experience of the core countries. Looking back in history, the modern industrial economies developed in the context of protected trade, not free trade, and so did the East Asian tigers more recently. They pursued trade liberalization *after* they had become strong, not before. And even today, their degree of trade openness lags far behind the countries of the Third and former Second Worlds on whom they continue to impose deeper liberalization irrespective of their particular local circumstances and history.

Indeed, the double standards practised by the core countries are a major concern for those who believe in the power of trade liberalization to deliver human security as freedom from want. Horst Kohler, the former head of the IMF, has drawn attention to this problem which is costing developing countries dear (see box 5.3). The IMF promotes trade liberalization throughout the South, yet is ineffective in getting the core capitalist states to implement similar policies and play by the same rules.

Box 5.3    Horst Kohler, former IMF Director, on trade double standards

'It is unconscionable for the United States, Japan, and the European Union to spend hundreds of billions of dollars on agricultural subsidies to maintain marginal activities for the benefit of a small segment of their population, while undermining agricultural sectors that are central to peace and development in poor countries. Yet this is exactly what is happening now.

'For example, in the US, price support payments for cotton cost more than $2 billion a year. This is larger than the annual cotton production of all sub-Saharan Africa. Subsidized US production has taken over 30% of world cotton exports, while cotton sectors that are crucial for economic life in some of the world's poorest countries, like Benin, Chad, Mali and Togo, are devastated.'

'In the EU, governments spend over $2 billion a year to buy up excess domestic sugar production, and the resulting surplus is dumped on world markets. A few developing countries get preferential access to the EU market, under a quota system, but this just means that other sugar producers in Latin America, Asia and southern Africa lose even more.'

'Japan's agricultural subsidies are the highest of any advanced country, so that rice prices, for instance, are 8 times as high as the world market price. This means that developing countries – especially in Asia – lose major trading opportunities.'

*Source:* Kohler 2002: 7.

The assault on the agricultural sector of the South is particularly vicious because three-quarters of poor people live in rural areas, yet job opportunities in agriculture are declining, and they are not being replaced by opportunities in urban areas. In West Africa, for example, the livelihoods of 11 million cotton farmers and their families have been undermined, and there is no prospect of shifting into alternative export production quickly. Also, food security is being eroded globally. While the impact of subsidized rice from the US may mean cheaper food in Ghana or Haiti for example, without alternative employment for rice farmers (and there is none) then vulnerable people are left without the means to buy the imported rice – indeed they are left without adequate means to survive.

The problem is not limited to agriculture: the very manufactures in which developing countries can have a competitive edge, such as textiles and clothing, are the very ones which the developed countries are least willing to liberalize, thus denying the opportunity for growth of exports from developing countries and the growth of employment opportunities for their people. While some progress has been made to increase opportunities for exports from the developing world, far more must be done. For example, the EU's gesture of duty- and quota-free access for 'everything but arms' from the least developed countries is a step in the right direction, but its value is limited by the weak capacity of these countries to generate exports due to the shortage of investment among other things. In the case of the US's Africa Growth and Opportunity Act, the possible benefits of increased clothing exports are severely limited by the very restrictive 'rules of origin' (Mattoo et al. 2000).

The question we must ask is: why do the core capitalist states practise these double standards? Why do they not apply unadulterated trade liberalization at home, whilst promoting it in the South? The answer is not difficult to deduce. The governments of the core states are well aware that such policies would cause significant damage to their domestic societies, and they are unwilling to risk the political price of this. It is for this very reason that the post-Second World War order was founded on embedded rather than pure liberal principles; governments understood the political importance of attending to social requirements such as employment matters.

(2) Second, let us consider the experience of Southern states that the World Bank regards as successful, and probe just how confident we can be that this result is due to trade liberalization. In support of the achievements of free trade, the World Bank has pointed to the success of the 'new globalizers': a group of about twenty-four developing countries like India, China, Brazil, Hungary, Mexico, Vietnam and Bangladesh, which have integrated in the global economy and which export not only commodities but manufactures and services (Collier and Dollar 2002). Yet other sources have cast doubt on whether the success of countries like India and China has really derived from trade liberalization as the engine of growth and development.

For example, a UNDP study suggests that the picture is very complicated:

> China and India implemented their main trade reforms about a decade after the onset of higher growth. Moreover, their trade restrictions remain among the highest in the world. The increase in China's growth started in the late 1970s. Trade liberalization did not start in earnest until much later, in the second half of the 1980s and especially in the 1990s – once the trend growth rate had already increased substantially. India's growth rate increased substantially in the early 1980s, while serious trade reform did not start until 1991–93. (UNDP 2003: 31)

These findings are extremely important, for they suggest that the unadulterated free trade mantra which still dominates IMF, World Bank and WTO policy may well be misplaced. The study is not suggesting that states should never liberalize trade. Rather it is suggesting that *the sequencing and intensity of trade liberalization policies may well be crucial for growth, and for human security.*

A further problem of course has already been referred to earlier: the asocial nature of national statistics. This should be borne in mind here – 'national' success tells us very little about the development impact on people, communities or regions. So even if the 'national' success of India, for example, is due to trade liberalization – a claim that is highly questionable – we still need to consider what this means for people and communities within the country.

(3) Third, let us consider the trade characteristics of the states and 2 billion people of Africa and the former Soviet Union, which have been excluded from the benefits of trade openness even whilst practising it. The World Bank cites several reasons as contributing to this exclusionary outcome, but none refers to the structure of the global economy or the structure of global trade, or indeed its governance; rather the problem is still seen to rest with domestic policies, local institutions and local governance, geography, disease or civil war (Collier and Dollar 2002).

But surely the structure of the global economy plays a role? Detailed evidence from UNCTAD studies (2002a and 2002b) suggests that this is the case. The Trade and Development Report (2002b) points out that developing countries, despite a massive increase in their openness to trade over the last twenty years, are earning less, and this will have an obvious impact on human security. This result is attributed to a number of reasons, such as their continued concentration on production of primary commodities that (with the exception of oil) have been characterized by stagnant markets and declining prices over the last two decades; and also the failure of most developing countries to shift their production into technology-intensive products. They lack the necessary finance and technological expertise, as well as human capacity, and they are unable to attract direct foreign investment to remedy this. Where they have moved from primary commodities into manufactured exports, the latter have been resource-based and labour-intensive, thus adding little value. Moreover, the export drives undertaken simultaneously by so many developing countries contribute to price decreases (see the coffee example, below).

These findings are reinforced by the UNCTAD study (2002a) on the forty-nine least developed countries, which shows that action is urgently needed at the international level to deal with excessive price instability which threatens the human security of millions of poor people. Coffee provides an excellent illustration. Worldwide, 25 million peasant smallholder coffee farmers in countries as diverse as Vietnam and Ethiopia produce 70 per cent of global coffee exports. Between 1998 and 2002, the price plummeted, and the lives of the coffee farmers, plus those of their extended families, were in ruins. Yet the major coffee companies, such as Nestlé, continued to make a significant profit from coffee. In the absence of a solution from the public global governance institutions most intimately involved with either trade or development, it was left to NGOs to suggest a Coffee Rescue Plan (Oxfam 2003). The coffee prices have since recovered somewhat. However, while the coffee crisis provoked extensive discussion of alternative approaches to slow or reverse the long-run fall and short-run variability in prices, the recovery in price had its origin in the same market mechanisms of supply and demand as did the price collapse (FAO 2005). Coffee farmers are therefore still vulnerable to price fluctuations. Looking to the future, given the surfeit of labour in these poor countries the picture grows even more worrying, as we can foresee a race to the bottom with low wages being used as an enticement in the highly competitive market to attract foreign direct investment (Salfield 2002). This point is evidenced in the experience of the more developed region of South-East Asia, where foreign investment has solved some problems for some people at some points only to create others at a later date. This example also shows that trade cannot be divorced from issues of finance and attendant instabilities of global financial markets. This contributed to millions being thrown below the poverty line in 1997. A UN Economic and Social Commission for Asia and the Pacific (ESCAP) study of 2002 suggests that another financial crisis could result in severe hardship for millions of people there. Investors continually seek out the location where they can make the greatest profit, and this results in capital and export production being moved from one location to another, with all the attendant difficulties for local populations in terms of insecure employment opportunities.

(4) Fourth, let us consider the governance of world trade. The liberal global governance network which determines the rules of the world trading system is essentially undemocratic, unaccountable and lacking in transparency (McGrew 1999). The IMF, World Bank and WTO are of course heavily influenced by the states that exercise most power within them, and they of course are the core capitalist states. Indeed some analysts have identified the structural embedding of US power and interests via these institutions (George 1994). The structure of global trade directly impacts on human security of the vulnerable billions, and their governments and the people themselves have no voice to affect this. All too often corporate actors have had a hand in setting the global trade agenda, in drafting WTO agreements, and generally exercising a role that is not open to most developing countries because of their low level of financial and human resources. The WTO's Agreement on Agriculture and also its Trade-Related Aspects of Intellectual Property Rights Agreement (TRIPS) provide pertinent illustrations of this phenomenon. Also, while the WTO in theory operates on the basis of one country, one vote, it is the exclusive 'green room' process that really matters.

The ever greater institutionalization of the trading system makes it increasingly difficult for developing countries to argue politically against it. At the WTO's Doha Conference in November 2001, it was decided through undemocratic means (for example, the exclusive green room process) that the WTO, instead of redressing existing, profound imbalances in its rules and the structure of trade, would henceforth expand its power and remit. Despite the opposition of many developing countries and social movements, the WTO would negotiate agreements on four areas: investment, competition, transparency in government procurement and trade facilitation (Khor 2001: 11–14). More than 100 NGOs from North and South joined together in December to declare the Doha Declaration, which is touted by supporters as a development agenda 'Everything but development' (Joint Statement by NGOs 2001: 15–17).

Without more extensive representation in the governance of trade, it is unlikely that all-important job creation will be prioritized, and this is one of the mandates of the WTO Charter. Yet in human security terms, this is imperative, and demands action. Without employment opportunities, individuals, households, communities, sub-state regions, countries and entire world-regions are denied the chance to fulfil basic needs within the market place. Juan Somavia, head of the International Labour Organization (ILO), has suggested of the failure to create jobs that 'This is probably globalization's biggest failure' (*Tehran Times* 2002). More than 1 billion people are classified as unemployed by the ILO, and this is a push factor in migration, with the majority of migrants being unskilled. Somavia estimated that about 500 million new jobs need to be created over the next decade to cope with the numbers of women and young people entering the labour market, but 'no-one is producing a scenario for the next decade based on the need to fill this yawning deficit'.

The main aim of this case study was to explore the contribution of trade liberalization to attending to human security as freedom from want. A number of conclusions can be drawn.

1  Trade liberalization has been promoted beyond the core capitalist states by the G7 and by unrepresentative, undemocratic global governance institutions which they dominate.
2  It is difficult to test the validity of the assumption that free trade promotes growth and development, when politically motivated, self-interested protectionism characterizes the trade policies of core states, thus denying export opportunities to the rest, while simultaneously forcing them to liberalize and dumping on them heavily subsidized products, thus crippling local production outside of the core.
3  The fact that core capitalist states are unwilling to play by free-market rules must prompt us to reflect on the reason for this reluctance. The answer is that to go down this road would be hugely destructive of sections of their domestic societies. In other words, G7 governments are well aware that capitalist markets based purely on profit do not work well for societies, and hence their unwillingness to implement them.
4  This suggests that attempts by well-intentioned groups such as Oxfam to get a more genuine commitment to free trade by the core capitalist states may well be misguided.

The evidence to date suggests that free-market capitalism does not and cannot achieve its stated goals and it must be replaced by an approach to trade that prioritizes human need rather than private profit. Trade must be a means to an end, not an end in itself: it must be people-centred, and decrease rather than increase the vulnerability of the poor. Finally, it seems reasonable to conclude that reform of the process of governance of trade itself is a necessary condition for recasting the structure of trading relationships in a manner which respects human security. Thus both aspects of human security – freedom from fear (civil and political) and freedom from want (economic and social) – are integral to each other and to lasting progress.

## CONCLUSION

This chapter has explored how a human security approach can enrich our understanding of the complex impacts of globalization. First, it reveals the different ways in which globalization impacts on the relative vulnerability of real human beings and communities, rather than abstract states. It does so by requiring disaggregation of data. Thereby, it unmasks official, state-level statistics, national positions, explanations and power structures – which obscure as much if not more than they reveal – be they the product of international organizations, governments or companies. Second, in a world facing enormous, complex, interconnected challenges, not least *mutual vulnerability involving not simply weapons but diseases and financial instability*, the concept of human security provides us with a starting point to think about *global social crises* and to construct *appropriate policy responses*.

In addition to human security's explanatory power, the approach has normative power, based as it is on an inherently radical, transformative agenda. Human security is essentially a political project, distinguished by its commitment to the interests of a broad, rather than narrow, band of humanity. This is of special importance for analysis of the less developed areas of the world, where the power of the state to regulate the globalization process is limited, and where the state itself may obstruct secure livelihoods. Yet it is also a powerful vehicle for normative analysis of more developed societies, for inherent in the globalization process is the transmission of consequences of events in one part of the globe to another.

An essential component of human security as a political project is the reform of global governance, to make it more representative of the majority of humanity. We have seen above in relation to trade that without this, global governance and the globalization process it oversees will remain distorted and fail to attend to the needs and concerns of ordinary human beings in their communities.

There is a sense in which the future of globalization as a political project ultimately rests on the extent to which it can be made commensurate with human security. The current scope and depth of impoverishment of the majority of humanity, amidst such great but concentrated wealth and opportunity, is staggering. It will take far more than a tweaking of the prevailing process and policy to put the global house in order, thereby ensuring human security for a broad band of humanity. Reform within developing countries is a necessary but insufficient condition to achieve these goals; it must extend outside the borders of developing countries to encompass global economic and financial structures, and the process of governance itself. Necessary ingredients include significant additional and more effective aid to meet basic human needs and develop infrastructures, the writing-off of debt, and the reform of global trade and finance in a manner that prioritizes the needs of human beings rather than capital. Only when both parts of the equation – the domestic and the structural/external – are addressed, will there be a chance for globalization to deliver sustainable results – human security – for the vast majority of humankind.

**Note**

1  See for example the 1994 Human Development Report, which focused
   specifically on human security.

**References and Further Reading**

Alkire, S. 2002: Conceptual framework for human security (16 February), at
   www.humansecurity-chs.org/doc/frame.html.

Annan, K. 2000: We the peoples: the role of the UN in the 21st Century.
   Millennium report of the Secretary-General at the Millennium Assembly,
   A/54/2000, at www.un.org/millennium/sg/report/summ.htm.

Annan, K. 2001: Foreword. In R. McRae and D. Hubert (eds), *Human Security
   and the New Diplomacy*, Montreal: McGill-Queen's University Press.

Axworthy, L. 2001: Human security and global governance: putting people
   first. *Global Governance*, 7 (1), January/March, 19–23.

Buzan, B., Waever, O. and Wilde, J. de (eds) 1998: *Security: A New Framework
   for Analysis*. Boulder, Colo.: Lynne Rienner.

Collier, P. and Dollar, D. 2002: *Globalization, Growth and Poverty*. Washington,
   D.C.: World Bank.

Commission on Global Governance 1995: *Our Global Neighbourhood*. Oxford:
   Oxford University Press.

Cook, S. and Jolly, S. 2003: A new revolution: experiences of poverty for
   urban China's laid-off workers. ID21 *Society and Economy*, 3 February
   2003, at www.id21.org/society/s5bsj1g1.html.

Cox, R. 1999: Civil society at the turn of the millennium: prospects for an
   alternative world order. *Review of International Studies*, 25 (1), 3–28.

Datt, G. and Ravallion, M. 2002: Is India's economic growth leaving the
   poor behind? *Journal of Economic Perspectives*, 2.

Duffield, M. 2001: *Global Governance and the New Wars*. London: Zed Press.

Economides, S. 2003: The International Criminal Court: Reforming the
   politics of international justice. *Government and Opposition*, 38 (1), winter,
   29–51.

ESCAP 2002: *Reducing Poverty and Promoting Social Protection*. ESCAP/2168
   Report.

FAO 2005: Food outlook. Global information and early warning system on
   food and agriculture (GIEWS), 2 (June), Rome: Food and Agriculture
   Organization of the United Nations.

George, J. 1994: *Discourses of Global Politics*. Boulder, Colo.: Lynne Rienner.

Gwozdecky, M. and Sinclair, J. 2001: Case study: landmines and human
   security. In R. McRae and D. Hubert (eds), *Human Security and the New
   Diplomacy*, Montreal: McGill-Queens University Press, 28–40.

Heinbecker, P. 1999: human security. *Canadian Foreign Policy*, 7 (1), fall,
   19–25.

Joint Statement by NGOs 2001: International Civil Society Rejects WTO
   Doha Outcome and Manipulative Process (December). Reprinted in
   *Third World Resurgence*, November/December, 135–36, 15–17.

Jordan, L. 1999: The death of development: the converging policy agendas
   of the World Bank and the World Trade Organisation. BIC (November),
   at www.bicusa.org/publications/deathdev.htm.

Kanbur, R. 2001: Economic policy, distribution and poverty: the nature of disagreements, at www.people.cornell.edu/pages/sk145/papers/Disagreements.pdf.

Kanbur, R. 2002: Conceptual challenges in poverty and inequality: one development economist's view, at www.arts.cornell.du/poverty/kanbur/CCPI.pdf.

Khor, M. 2001: *Rethinking Globalization*. London: Zed Books.

Kohler, H. 2002: Working for a better globalization (28 January), at www.imf.org/external/np/speeches/2002/012802.htm.

Kripalani, M. 2002: A tale of two Indias. Can the North ever catch the South? *Business Week*, 15 April, at www.businessweek.com/magazine/content/02_15/b3778126.htm.

Mattoo, A., Devesh Roy, D. and Subramaniam A. 2000: The Africa Growth and Opportunity Act and its rules of origin: generosity undermined? IMF Working paper, Africa Department, WP/021158, September, at www.imf.org/external/pubs/ft/wp/2002/wp02158.pdf.

McGrew, A. 1999: The WTO: technocracy or banana republic? In A. Taylor and C. Thomas (eds), *Global Trade and Global Social Issues*. London: Routledge.

McGrew, A. 2002: From global governance to good governance. In M. Ougaard and R. Higgott (eds), *The Global Polity*, London: Routledge.

McRae, R. and Hubert, D. (eds) 2001: *Human Security and the New Diplomacy*. Montreal: McGill-Queen's University Press.

Milanovic, B. 2002: Can we discern the effect of globalization on income distribution? Evidence from household budgetary surveys. World Bank Policy Research Working paper 2876 (April), at http://econ.worldbank.org/files/17877_wp2876.pdf.

Nef, J. 1999: *Human Security and Mutual Vulnerability*, 2nd edn. Ottawa: IDRC.

Ogata, S. 2001: Overview for the Commission on Human Security, at www.humansecurity-chs.org/past/first/overview.html.

Ogata, S. 2002: Globalization and human security. Weatherhead Policy Forum, Columbia University; at www.humansecurity-chs.org/doc/columbia.html.

Osler Hampson, Fen 2002: *Madness in the Multitude: Human Security and World Disorder*. Ontario: Oxford University Press.

Oxfam 2002a: Cultivating poverty: the impact of US cotton subsidies on Africa. September, Briefing paper 30, at www.oxfam.org/policy/papers/30cotoon/index.htm.

Oxfam 2002b: Boxing match in agricultural trade: will WTO negotiations knock out the world's poorest farmers? November, Briefing paper 32, at www.oxfam.org/policy/papers/32.

Oxfam 2003: Make trade fair in the Americas. February, Briefing paper, at www.oxfam.org.uk/policy/papers/37ftaa/37ftaa.html.

Paris, Roland 2001: Human security: paradigm shift or hot air? *International Security*, 26 (2).

Piot, P. 2001: Aids and human security. Speech, United Nations University, Japan, at www.unaids.org/whatsnew/speech/eng/piot021001tokyo.html.

Salfield, T. 2002: New UNCTAD trade and development report throws Washington consensus into doubt (May), email information, New Economics Foundation, London.

Samuel, J. 2002: Growth sans Development: India, at
   www.infochangeindia.org/features (accessed 9 October 2002).

Singer, P. W. 2002: AIDS and international security. *Survival*, 44 (1), spring,
   145–58.

Stiglitz, J. E. 2002: *Globalization and its Discontents*: New York: W. W. Norton.

Suhrke, A. 1999: Human security and the interests of the state. *Security
   Dialogue*, 30 (3), September, 265–76.

Swatuk, L. A. 2000: *Swimming upstream – Water and the Discourses of Security*.
   Johannesburg: University of the Western Cape.

*Tehran Times* 2002: Globalization's inability to create jobs fuels mass
   migration: ILO chief, at www.globalpolicy.org/globaliz/econ/
   2002/0613ILO.

Thomas, C. 2000: *Global Governance, Development and Human Security*.
   London: Pluto Press.

UN/DESA 2005: *World Population Prospects, the 2004 Revision. Highlights*.
   New York: United Nations Department for Economic and Social Affairs,
   Population Division.

UN OECD IMF World Bank 2000: *A Better World for All*. New York: United
   Nations.

UNCTAD 2002a: *The Least Developed Countries' Report: Escaping the Poverty Trap*,
   Geneva, at www.unctad.org/en/pub/ps11dc02.en.htm.

UNCTAD 2002b: *Trade and Development Report 2002*, Geneva.

UNDP 1994: *Human Development Report*. Oxford: Oxford University Press.

UNDP 2002: *Human Development Report*. Oxford: Oxford University Press.

UNDP 2003: *Making Global Trade Work for People*. London: Earthscan, at
   www.undp.org/mainundp/propoor/docs.trade-jan2003.pdf.

UNDP 2005: *Fast Facts: The Faces of Poverty*. New York: UN Millennium
   Project.

UNESCAP 2002: Protecting marginalized groups during economic
   downturn: lessons from the Asian experience. Bangkok: United Nations
   Economic and Social Commission for Asia and the Pacific.

UNGA 2000: Resolution 55/2: United Nations Millennium Declaration
   (18 September), A/RES/55/2.

Wade, R. and Wolf, M. 2002: Are global poverty and inequality getting
   worse? *Prospect*, March, 16–20.

Weisbrot, M. and Baker, D. 2002: The relative impact of trade liberalization
   on developing countries, 11 June, at www.cepr.net.

Wilkin, P. 2001: *The Political Economy of Global Communication*. London: Pluto
   Press.

Wilkin, P. 2002: Global poverty and orthodox security. *Third World Quarterly*, 3.

Wilks, A. and Lefrancois, F. 2002: Blinding with science of encouraging
   debate? How the World Bank's analysis determines PRSP policies, at
   www.brettonwoodsproject.org/topic/adjustment/blinding/blinding.pdf.

Wolfensohn, J. 2002: President's revised note to the development
   committee of the IMF and World Bank. DC2002-0007/Rev1, annex on
   Multilateral Development Bank Collaboration and Reform, Washington,
   D.C.: World Bank.

# 6 Health in Development

*Sandra J. MacLean*

In this chapter Sandra J. MacLean explores the evolution of the present multilateral system of international health, arguing that the health of poor people in poor countries has been inadequately served by a regime in which the predominant focus has been clinical issues. She maintains that international health cannot be treated outside of broader social contexts and that health research and policy cannot be separated from the forces and constraints of the global political economy. This implies that the recent trend towards the collapse of disciplinary borders is salient with respect to health as in other areas of development. She concludes with the recognition that a system of global health governance is emerging in which transnational coalitions of state and non-state actors play central roles.

The world's biggest killer and the greatest cause of ill health and suffering across the globe is listed almost at the end of the international Classification of Diseases. It is given the code Z59.5 – extreme poverty. Poverty is the main reason why babies are not vaccinated, why clean water and sanitation are not provided, why curative drugs and other treatments are unavailable and why mothers die in childbirth. It is the underlying cause of reduced life expectancy, handicap, disability and starvation. Poverty is a major contributor to mental illness, stress, suicide, family disintegration and substance abuse. (Sreenivasan and Grinspun 2002: 1)

## INTRODUCTION

There is compelling evidence that social standing is one of the strongest determinants of health. On a population basis, poor people have higher levels of disease and they die earlier than wealthier members of society. Moreover, the greater the difference in social standing between the poor and the rich in a society, the greater are the differentials in health. Given then that one of the changes attributed to globalization is increasing disparities in wealth and power in the world, we can expect the impacts on health to be significant. We can also expect that the burdens of health will be disproportionately held, with poorer people, countries and regions being the most negatively affected.

Yet, despite considerable evidence that health is strongly determined by social conditions, most of the emphasis to date in health research and policy at the international as well as national level has been on clinical determinants – access to health-care services, availability of drugs and vaccines for the treatment and prevention of diseases, etc. Few would deny that progress in these areas has been important for improving the health of many people around the world. However, not only do social disparities, in themselves, determine health, but they also influence who has access to services and to technical treatments and innovations.

This chapter explores the evolution of the present multilateral system of international health, arguing that the health of poor people in poor countries has been inadequately served by a regime in which the predominant focus has been clinical issues. I maintain that international health cannot be treated outside of broader social contexts and that health research and policy cannot be separated from the forces and constraints of the global political economy. This implies that the recent trend towards the collapse of disciplinary borders is salient with respect to health as in other areas of development. This chapter, therefore, attempts to bring research on the social determinants of health together with recent work in the sub-fields of international relations, political economy and/or development on inequalities and human (in)security. It begins with a description of the international health regime that emerged in conjunction with the developments in multilateralism that emerged from the First and Second World Wars and proceeds to discuss the limitations of that system for the governance of health in the era of globalization. It concludes by examining the possibility that a system of global health governance is emerging in which transnational coalitions of state and non-state actors play central roles.

## THE CONSTRUCTION OF AN INTERNATIONAL HEALTH REGIME

## Health and multilateralism

The study of international relations (IR) in the West emerged as a separate discipline in the early part of the last century while the sub-field of international development became established following the Second World War. Until very recently, health has not figured prominently in the *theoretical* constructions of international relations or its sub-fields, as compared with conflict, for instance, where the activities of war have been examined for insights into the motivations, interests and relations of the various stakeholders. In other words, the field of health has not been regarded as a particularly interesting political terrain for furthering the advancement of knowledge for international relations specialists. Rather, health issues have been regarded mainly as technical problems, requiring pragmatic solutions decided by highly specialized health experts and practitioners.

This is not to say, however, that there have not been important international developments in health. Indeed, within a largely technical paradigm, international health has evolved over the past century into an established, mature discipline. And, interestingly, although health and international relations/security/development have developed largely as separate silos of research, the evolution of international health has, in several respects, mirrored the patterns of change observed in these fields.

## League of Nations Health Organization

Some of the early initiatives in international health coincided with advances in multilateralism and especially the emergence of the League of Nations. Cooperation among states in various functional areas had begun by the mid-nineteenth century, and in the second half of the century international conferences were held to foster cooperation in various areas such as postal and telegraphic communications; weights and measures; patents, trademarks; transportation; navigation, the slave trade; and labour legislation (WHO 1958: 6). By the beginning of the twentieth century, aspects of health also were being seen as an international issue and several international organizations and agreements were established to deal with these concerns.[1] The most significant of these organizations was the League of Nations Health Organization, which came into being in 1923 (WHO 1931).

The spread of infectious disease was the main concern of the new organization. A number of diseases such as plague, cholera, yellow fever, smallpox, typhus, poliomyelitis, typhoid, dysentery and scarlet fever had spread rapidly in Europe during the First World War because of refugee and troop movements. Disease was also being spread throughout the world because of advances in travel and transport. In response to the escalating rates of disease transmission, states were responding unilaterally by imposing strict, often brutal, quarantines on sailors and travellers from abroad.[2] Such restrictions were very costly to industry, and shippers began to press their governments to establish terms and conditions for international cooperation on quarantines (Brockington 1985: 30). It was largely as a result of this pressure that the League of Nations Health Organization was formed with the mandate 'to take steps in matters of international concern for the prevention and control of disease' (p. 31).

Although it began with the singular preoccupation to control disease transmission – especially from the developing to industrialized worlds – the Health Organization soon broadened its list of concerns to include issues such as nutrition. Also, early on, it began to facilitate greater international cooperation in the development and dissemination of research. As a result, major advancements were made in the 1920s and 1930s, both in the development of vaccines to control or eradicate certain diseases and in their distribution throughout the world. As well, there were considerable improvements in the preparation and sharing of the systematic documentation of diseases and related bibliographies and in the coordination of laboratory work and epidemiological surveys. Significant advances were also made in the international standardization of statistical methods and measurements (Brockington 1985: 30–1; WHO 1931). Finally, various initiatives on infectious disease contributed to the elaboration of the network of multilateral organizations through commissions on various diseases set up during the 1920s and international conferences in the 1930s.[3] Combined, these initiatives were major developments in the construction of a modern, technically-oriented, international public health system.

The positive impact of these initiatives on human health around the world was significant, even if, as Fraser Brockington (1985: 30) argues, international public health originated from the 'mundane consideration of how to protect trade, and not human feeling about how to prevent disease'. And, although 'human feeling' did not perhaps figure significantly in the Organization's calculations, several NGOs motivated primarily by humanitarianism had by now become part of the international health scene. The International Committee of the Red Cross/Red Crescent, which had been formed in 1863, was already a well-established player in international health. Other NGOs had also become involved in health; for instance, in 1913, the Rockefeller Foundation had held mass campaigns against hookworm and yellow fever (Brockington 1985: 32). But the First World War, in particular, had created the need for concerted humanitarian action (Clark 1991: 34) and NGOs had proliferated during the war years, thus establishing non-state as well as state actors as part of the international health regime.

## The World Health Organization

This regime had been established as a part of the multilateral system that had emerged after the First World War, and following the Second World War, the new developments in multilateralism brought major changes to international health governance. Yet, interestingly, at the 1945 San Francisco Conference at which the UN came into being, neither health nor the establishment of an international health organization were on the agenda. Indeed, it seems that the World Health Organization (WHO), which replaced the League's Health Organization, came about quite 'accidentally', and it was only because of the personal efforts of three members of delegations who also happened to be physicians that blueprints for the WHO were drawn at the conference and that 'health' came to be mentioned in the original UN Charter (WHO 1988).[4]

Presumably, 'health' was not featured on the conference agenda because it was not deemed to be an important topic for international relations specialists and diplomats. However, international relations specialists were not the only ones who were clear on which issues were relevant, or not, to their field; social scientists from other fields and health specialists also had definite ideas about the lines that separated their respective disciplines. To illustrate, when one of the three physicians credited with founding the WHO left his country's UN delegation team, his replacement was soon made aware of disciplinary boundaries: 'Karl Evang's replacement was a social scientist who was not interested in health: he wanted to create an organization for social sciences. We [the other two founding members] had to tell him in no uncertain terms that that was not what we had in mind' (WHO 1988).

With the health specialists, political strategists and other social scientists in agreement that health was a 'technical' issue to be left to the experts in the field, there was a relatively seamless transition in terms of the operations mandated by the United Nations and those that had been carried out under the technically-oriented League. As had been the case with its predecessor, however, the range of functions carried out by the new international health organization expanded rapidly. Much of this expansion was due to advances in technology and knowledge, but political events also played a role. Among the most significant of these was the decolonization movement that brought several newly independent African states into the UN system. These new countries possessed distinctly different sets of health issues; they also presented new challenges for devising effective measuring and recording systems for comparative evaluations of conditions and standards (Brockington 1968: 18–35; WHO 1958, 1968). Partly because of the distinctive health problems of Africa and of other regions, pressures increased to decentralize operations, with the result that new regional organizations such as PAHO (Pan American Health Organization) emerged. Internal struggles around regionalization contributed to the politicization of the WHO as did divisions within the organization based on East–West Cold War animosities, intra-regional conflicts, and exclusionary politics involving a few 'pariah states' (Siddiqi 1995).[5] The politicization processes, the introduction of new technologies and knowledges, advances in the field of public health and moderate successes in the control of communicable diseases created considerable changes over time in the functions and philosophy of the WHO (pp. 193–4). But perhaps the strongest force of change was the emerging field of developing studies.

## Health in/and development

Development studies emerged as a distinct field following the Second World War, initially as a feature of the newly established development 'enterprise' – that is, development as project or business venture.[6] An underlying premise of liberal *modernization* theories and policies of the early post-war development period was that it would be possible to 'quick-start' the development process in the poor countries of the South through the transfer of 'modernizing' technologies and practices from the North.[7] This thinking was pervasive in health as it was in other fields. For instance, a public health expert writing at the time (Brockington 1968: 20) assumed that '[t]he picture presented by the developed world is the mirror image of the under-developed world'. In other words, development was assumed to be a unilinear, evolutionary course that all countries could follow; the key was to provide the methods and resources in order for poor countries to emulate their industrialized counterparts.

By the 1970s, however, when it was becoming obvious that modernization theories and policies were not going to achieve the anticipated outcomes, critics began to emerge. The main challenge to modernization theory was from dependency theorists who argued: (1) that stronger North–South ties would deter rather than encourage development in the Third World; (2) that (inter)dependent relations between poor and rich countries increased benefits to the latter while contributing to the underdevelopment of the former; and (3) that the remedy, at least according to the more radical theorists from this group, was collective self-reliance; that is, poor countries would have to disengage from their dependent relations and cooperate with each other in order to prosper.[8]

A few scholars working in the health field were influenced by the dependency perspective. Vincent Navarro, in particular, wrote extensively to call attention to the disparities in health as a function of the international division of labour (see, for example, Navarro 1976, 1986). There were developments within the liberal paradigm as well where greater attention was being paid to health as a human right. This was highlighted in particular by the basic human needs (BHN) strategy launched by the ILO in the mid-1970s and endorsed soon thereafter by powerful international organizations such as the World Bank, the latter having been infused by this time with the philosophy of 'enlightened internationalism'. This approach, which Hoogvelt (1982: 96) has termed 'global Keynesianism', combined moralism with enlightened self-interest; in other words, providing support for basic needs would achieve humanitarian objectives, but also a 'developed' South would contribute to stability in the world and provide a source of materials and markets for the continued growth of Western capitalism.

With dependency theorists promoting disengagement of the developing world from the international economic order, and enlightened liberal internationalists supporting the ideals of basic needs, self-reliance and local development became the major themes in development circles of the 1970s. In international health, they emerged as central objectives in 1978 when they appeared as the cornerstone of a major WHO document. Known as the *Alma Ata Declaration*, this document outlined a clear change in direction for the WHO and the international health regime generally. Of particular significance was the elaboration of a new, 'positive' definition of health which freed the concept from overly technologized connotations. The *Alma Ata Declaration*[9] declared that:

> Health, a state of complete physical, mental and social wellbeing, and not merely the absence of disease or infirmity, is a fundamental human right and . . . the attainment of the highest possible level of health is a most important world-wide social goal whose realization requires the action of many other social and economic sectors in addition to the health sector.

Among the necessary conditions to achieve the state of wellness that the term 'health' implied were that 'people have the right and duty to participate individually and collectively in the planning and implementation of their health care'; that governments 'have a responsibility . . . [to provide] . . . adequate health and social measures', and that 'primary health care is the key to attaining this target as part of development in the spirit of social justice'. With commitment to these principles, the drafters of the document assumed that it would be possible to achieve 'health for all by the year 2000'.

The notion of people-centred, participatory health strategies was institutionalized at Alma Ata, and since then, concepts of participation and primary health care have continued to resonate within the health regime. However, the concepts have proved difficult to put into practice and disappointing results in health, as well as in other sectors, have highlighted the apparent failure of mainstream policies: the so-called 'crisis in development' (Escobar 1995; Crush 1996; Schuurman 1993; Brohman 1997). Theoretical and practical responses to the documented 'crisis' are frequently subsumed under the heading of 'alternative development' (AD). The conceptual changes associated with this new approach for the 'post-development era' are described by Pieterse: 'Structural approaches such as dependency theory and the Keynesian reformism of the new international economic order emphasize structural economic change – just as mainstream modernization thinking does – whereas alternative development emphasizes agency, in the sense of people's capacity to effect social change.' (Pieterse 2001: 74–5). However, rather than being a new, distinct paradigm, AD is 'a series of alternative proposals and methodologies that are loosely inter-connected' (p. 74). With roots in the waning support for state-led development models and the growing strength of grass-roots movements as well as theoretical and methodological advancements – for example, in critical theory, gender analyses, participatory action research (PAR), rapid rural appraisal (RRA) – that explicitly and/or implicitly supported 'bottom-up' emancipatory projects, AD emerged as 'a roving critique of mainstream development' (p. 74). Yet, despite its radical origins, but perhaps because it lacks a clear ideological direction, many AD principles and techniques have been appropriated by mainstream development agencies such as the World Bank and the WHO (p. 78).

In addition to AD's theoretical limitations (e.g. Pieterse 1998), criticism of its associated methodologies has also begun to appear (e.g. Parpart 2000). Much of the criticism, as with previous 'advances' in the field of development, stems from claims that AD strategies have not produced significant improvements. In international health, for instance, the implementation of primary care strategies has been largely disappointing and, certainly, achievements have fallen well short of the Alma Ata target of 'health for all by the year 2000'. Nevertheless, in the last annual *World Health Report* of the twentieth century (WHO 1999), Gro H. Brundtland, the then Director-General of the WHO, points out that there have been overall improvements in the past few decades (for example, increased life expectancy and decreased fertility rates), which she attributes partly to the 'critical role of primary health care'. However, in the same message, Brundtland acknowledges that it has been 'the generation and application of new knowledge about diseases and their control' that has produced the greatest improvements in health. In other words, two decades after the new direction in international health was announced with great optimism and fanfare at Alma Ata, the WHO Director was still maintaining that technical achievements in controlling the transmission of disease are the WHO's greatest achievement.

This is not an insignificant achievement, but it needs to be qualified. When Brundtland wrote the above in 1999, she used 'the eradication of smallpox' as the supreme example of this achievement. Two years later, in the aftermath of the terrorist attack on New York City, alarmed health officials confirmed that the security of the few remaining laboratory stockpiles of the bacterium could not be assured and the world was forced to acknowledge that in fact this disease may not have been eradicated after all but once again might erupt as a deadly epidemic. This and several other problems – the intractable spread of HIV/AIDS, the emergence of new 'superviruses', the re-emergence of old diseases in new virulent forms, and the resurgence of previously well-controlled infectious diseases such as tuberculosis – should quickly erode any sanguinity about the ability of technology to wipe out communicable diseases.

Moreover, such new twists on old issues are not the only problem for the international health regime. Another concern is that the improvements that have occurred in world health, especially increased life expectancy, will be offset to some extent by the effects of the 'demographic transition' that occurs as a result of the gains; that is, increased numbers of middle-aged and elderly who are susceptible to a different set of non-communicable diseases such as cancer and heart disease. The high costs of this transition are already challenging health-care systems in the North and will be an onerous addition indeed to the burden of health in the developing world. For many countries, the situation is one of double jeopardy, in that rapidly expanding middle classes will develop and demand treatment for the diseases of affluence while the poor, often very large, majorities will continue to suffer the health problems associated with underdevelopment.

Overall, social inequality is probably the single most troublesome problem in the contemporary era for international health (and health generally). To recognize that this is the case is to remove health from the isolated, 'scientific' category in which it is usually situated and place it within the arena of political economy. Obviously, such a shift in analysing health matters is problematic. For one thing, it is not easy to convince specialists trained to view health as a technical issue that power relations in society are as important as physical causes in determining human health status. Also, opinions on effective ways to treat the human costs of social inequality are divided on philosophical and ideological grounds. Nevertheless, recent research that correlates health status with relative social standing and access to public goods confirms the need for a political economy of health approach (Black et al. 1982; Frank and Mustard 1995). Studies regarding the social determinants of health present compelling evidence that poverty contributes to higher rates of mortality and morbidity (Mayor, 2001). Moreover, social gradients are correlated inversely with health; in other words, lower relative social standing regardless of absolute social-economic levels produces negative effects on health (Marmot 1986; Marmot et al. 1991; Whitehead 1987; Davey-Smith et al. 1990; Sen 1993; Leon et al. 2001; Wilkinson 1997).[10]

## HEALTH IN THE POST-DEVELOPMENT ERA: GLOBALIZATION AND ITS DISCONTENTS

Awareness about the social determinants of health is growing at a time in world history when major shifts in wealth and power are occurring. As Craig Murphy (2001) observes, new equalities are evident – as the result of the worldwide flourishing of formal democracies, global gender politics, and the reduced power of the state relative to local, national and transnational non-state forces. Yet, although 'formal' equality is increasing, and there may have been 'continued improvement in living standards in the world overall (World Commission 1987), Murphy concludes that 'income inequality is probably rising'. And, even if the evidence for this is not conclusive, it is clear that 'inequality is very high' (Murphy 2001: 19). The UNDP (2001: 19) reports that in 1993 'around 25 per cent of the world's people received 75 per cent of the world's income'; the richest 1 per cent received as much income as the poorest 75 per cent; and the combined income of richest 10 per cent in the US was greater than that of 43 per cent of the world's poorest. Extreme inequalities exist within countries of both the North and the South, although in the 1990s the countries with the greatest divergence in income were in Latin America and the Caribbean and in Africa. Extreme inequalities also exist between countries and between regions, with the poorest countries tending to be in the poorest regions of South Asia and sub-Saharan Africa.

The research discussed at the end of the last section indicates that the more extreme the social gradients, the more adverse are the effects on health. And, with income and social status being the most significant determinant of health, statistics on mortality and morbidity for the poorest regions are predictably dismal. In some countries, they appear to be getting worse. For example, the UNDP's *Human Development Report 2001* (pp. 168–9) shows life expectancy at birth in 1995–2000 had decreased from 1970–5 in several African countries, including Uganda, Malawi, Rwanda, Mozambique and Burundi. The gravity of this becomes even more apparent when it is observed that, in the earlier period, the highest life expectancy at birth in any of these countries (Rwanda) was only 46.4 years. Also, although some of the least developed countries of Africa did show some improvement in life expectancy for the same period, the statistics were discouraging nonetheless. In Sierra Leone, for instance, life expectancy increased by 2.3 years, but from 35.0 to 37.3 years.

These statistics reflect deaths that are due to several different causes, such as childbirth problems, food shortage, accidents, communicable and non-communicable diseases and conflict. All are exacerbated by poverty. Moreover, improvements due to some effective interventions – immunization for certain diseases, for example – have, in many cases, been offset by alarming increases in deaths from other sources. New communicable diseases – HIV/AIDS, in particular – are among the most devastating, and long-standing communicable diseases such as malaria have resurged in recent years with disturbing virulence.[11] With cures not yet in sight and with a lack of political will to provide the resources necessary to deal with the issues (see opening quote by Lewis; also see below), these diseases will continue to kill people – especially poor people – in excessively high numbers for some time to come. Even more worrisome, however, are predictions that the overall burden to health from these diseases will decline over the next two decades, not so much because of advances in controlling them, but because other causes of death (e.g. cardiovascular disease, road accidents and war) will increase disproportionately (GFHR 1999: 29).

These health issues are also development issues. The social determinants of health literature provides compelling evidence to support the claim that health is impaired by poverty and income inequality and that the burden of health is more onerous for poor people and poor countries. Logic suggests that part of the solution is to implement policies that create more even income redistribution. Yet, with neoliberal ideology currently dominant, there appears to be little support for this strategy. While mainstream agencies such as the World Bank have begun to urge governments to place more investments in health (see, for example, World Bank 1993), it is not as a rejection of neoliberalism but because of recent research establishing that poor health standards in societies impede economic growth. Furthermore, there is an inherent contradiction in the Bank's advocating more governmental spending in one sector (health) while systematically reducing the state's role overall. But perhaps the main problem is that the Bank continues to focus on the health sector as if it were responsive to remedial treatment as an isolated domain disconnected from larger social issues. Yet, ultimately, as is argued above, inequality and the underlying structures that produce it are the major determinants of health.

## Health, human security and the new inequalities

Ronnie Lipschutz (2001: 328) points out that the beneficiaries of global neoliberalism appear to have little interest in reducing the new inequalities. According to Lipschutz, these beneficiaries constitute a 'CosmoCapitalClass' of 'new First World' for whom 'there is really One World, with shared methodologies, epistemologies, and ontologies' (p. 328). At the same time, a new Second World is emerging which consists of 'symbolic analysts' – a new productive class of 'language workers' in the service of the First World, many of whom are 'inscribing and tasting of the good consumer life without ever fully making it, while a fair number will discover that they have become redundant and that their services are no longer required' (p. 328). Finally, 'the new Third World is everyone else, including those who work in services, mass production, gray markets, and black markets . . . [and who have] few, if any, economic rights and almost no security of livelihood' (pp. 328–9).

The lines between these worlds are not entirely fixed. But, while the recent precipitous declines in stock markets and the arrests recently of several top executives of large American conglomerates have highlighted the instability within the new First World, they have also underscored the sharp divide that exists between the majority of people and those who have become extremely wealthy as members of the new 'CosmoCapitalClass'. Robert Cox, for one, has written extensively on the implications of this 'polarization of rich people and poor people [that] is becoming increasingly accentuated throughout the world' (Cox 1999: 3). He has observed that this divergence has produced both constructive and destructive forces. On the positive side, the reaction against the structural inequalities of the new world order has produced a new vitality in civil societies: at the national level, in pressures for greater democratic and human rights in various countries, and transnationally in the emergence of new social movements for human rights, environmental protection, peace, gender equality, etc. On the negative side, it has increased the levels of hardship for many people in the world and in addition has fostered the development of a 'covert world' of crime and violence, a world where 'covert power substitutes for legitimate authority in a totally unregulated market – contracts are enforced by goons with guns' (p. 133).

## Health and human security

The changing conditions and relations that Cox and others have described have important implications for health. Most obviously, the new inequalities are directly negative determinants of health. Moreover, various difficult health problems are associated with contemporary warfare (which, according to some analysts, may be the direct or indirect result of inequality). Numerous injuries, loss of limbs, etc., are resulting from the use of light weapons and landmines and great numbers of people have lost access to lands for growing food or have had their farmlands destroyed by fighting. Also, although the extent of the problem is not yet fully ascertained, it is expected that the mental health problems of those directly involved – child soldiers, ex-combatants and the traumatized victims of rape and other war crimes – are severe. Finally, there are indirect effects of conflict that impact on health: drug addiction and the socialization of violence, for example.

Against such obstacles to achieving 'health for all' any time soon, however, a number of advancements toward a new world order offer some hope for the construction of an effective global regime in health. One of these is the new energy in civil society (see reference to Cox, above), which, especially in partnership with government and sometimes business, has led to the growth of innovative 'mixed-actor' networks that are bringing new awareness and programming on specific health issues – for instance, HIV/AIDS, malaria, tobacco, small arms, anti-personnel mines – as well as in areas that impact on health indirectly – for example, trade and debt (see below).

Another encouraging development is the recent theoretical shift in security studies toward a new human security agenda, in which *the human* replaces *the state* as the main referent. With this transformation in the meaning of security, health can no longer be treated as an inconsequential subject for international relations, but rather it becomes a central issue. As Lloyd Axworthy (2001: 19) exclaims: 'No longer are we limited to discussions of states' rights and national sovereignty. Protecting civilians, addressing the plight of war-affected children and the threat of terrorism and drugs, managing open borders, and combating infectious diseases are now part of the dialogue.' While the human security agenda brings health issues into clearer focus for analysts and policy makers in international relations, several contemporary health issues and events have also helped to establish the authenticity of the human security agenda. HIV/AIDS in particular has demonstrated that security is threatened as much or more by human vulnerability to biological processes as challenges to national integrity. And, with the spectre of biological warfare looming in the post-9/11 era, and with conflicts erupting over water, even those who argue that human security does not represent a clear ontological shift, but merely extends the list of what is accepted as legitimate security items, are forced to acknowledge that health matters currently hold more interest for security specialists. Also, increasingly, issues related to health challenge other dominant discourses in international relations: (1) threats and potential threats posed by biogenetically engineered foods, chemical additives, etc. have focused critical attention on the WTO agenda to remove national restrictions on trade; (2) recent challenges to patent rules that prevented the sale of generic-brand pharmaceuticals question the fairness of WTO policies and argue that the South is disproportionately disadvantaged by the neoliberal trading regime; and (3) critics charge that hunger and poverty in poor countries are exacerbated by an international trade regime that permits rich Western countries to discriminate against agricultural products from the South (and this at the same time that international financial institutions (IFIs) impose structural adjustment programmes (SAPs) requiring Southern countries to open their economies and to remove subsidies).

## FUTURE PROSPECTS: TOWARDS A NEW GLOBAL HEALTH REGIME?

Given that the Alma Ata objectives fell well short of achievement by the projected 2000 date, given mainstream development and security agencies' limited conceptualizations of the relationship between security and development, and given that there is likely to be a listless response, at best, from the beneficiaries of global neoliberalism to the insecurities produced by the new inequalities, the likelihood of establishing a truly 'human' security agenda seem remote.

Yet, there are signs of progress. In the past, the tendency has been to look to 'political will' as the source of any meaningful action on such issues and to conclude, with fatalistic resignation, that it will always be lacking because governments are constrained by the realistic requirements of the international system and/or because the comfortable minority who control most of the resources have settled into an ennui of greed or self-satisfied complacency. However, with globalization, governance is evolving and 'governance institutions are no longer just state or inter-state actors but now include myriad non-state organizations, from companies to civil societies' (MacLean and Shaw 2001: 17). National governments are looking increasingly to establish 'partnerships' with the other two sectors and new patterns of regionalism and multilateralism that combine state and non-state players are forming. Analyses have begun to appear recently that document new opportunities for (and forms of) agency within civil societies and/or combinations of actors from civil society, state and business sectors (Florini 2000). Many of these combinations have emerged in areas of health, and notably 'health as development and/or human security'. Taken together, these new governance combinations can be seen as features of a nascent global health regime.

Global coalitions have developed over the past decade on several issues that are directly or indirectly related to health. By now, few are unaware of various actions around the 'new' disease of HIV/AIDS (see, for example, 'Special Issue', *Third World Quarterly*, 2002). Many of these have focused on finding treatments or devising education strategies for prevention. In 1999–2001, the North-South dimensions of HIV/AIDS and the health effects of global neoliberalism and the international laws that support it were highlighted by a confrontation between the South African government and the pharmaceutical companies that produce drugs to alleviate symptoms of the disease. The case is interesting because it underscored the relationship between AIDS and inequality; in short, it brought the issue into the realm of political economy (see Laing 1999; Poku 2001), thus raising awareness to the broadening of the dimensions of health in a global era.

Recent action on 'old' diseases that have reappeared with renewed virulence as features of the globalization of disease can also be seen as steps in the construction of a new global health regime. Kelly Lee and Richard Dodgson (2000) document the progress that has been made in dealing with the re-emergence of cholera as a serious health problem. They explore the implications of the strategies employed in treating cholera for global governance and observe that an important feature of the new structures of governance that are emerging (and that need further development) is 'an amalgam of member states, civil society groups, and individuals (p. 232) A similar amalgam is evident in the anti-malaria campaign that brings together academics, NGOs, representatives of the medical community, governments in affected countries and the WHO (e.g. Mons et al. 1998; Abuja Declaration, 2000; MSF 1999; MIM 2001). One of the main thrusts of this campaign is to expose the political economy of malaria: one approach has been to explore the economic costs of malaria (Gallop and Sachs 1998; WHO 2000); another has been to examine the development divide as a reason for the delay in finding solutions to the problem (Desowitz 1991; Dubovsky 2001).

The anti-tobacco campaign is one of the more successful efforts to address a non-communicable disease issue. As Lee and Dodgson (2000: 231) point out, this may prove to be a model for activism in other areas, as plans for a Framework Convention on Tobacco Control bring together shared interests across nations, civil society and the business community (for example, the pharmaceutical sector) for a more comprehensive effort to control the production and consumption of tobacco.[12]

Other important initiatives are being undertaken that explicitly address the issues of health, security and development as integrated issues. Two of the more active of these deal with the issues of anti-personnel mines and small arms. The International Campaign to Ban Landmines (ICBL), which was founded in 1992, grew rapidly from a half-dozen NGOs (at least a couple of which were health-focused)[13] to a membership of 1,300 groups. Measured by growth alone, the coalition has been successful. But, also it has made significant progress in its push to have new legal architecture established; a *Mine Ban Treaty* came into force in March 1999,[14] and by September 2000 had 139 signatories and 107 ratifications (ICBL website). And it has aroused public awareness of the construction of a new international norm on the issue; success in this area was assisted when the ICBL was awarded the Nobel Peace Prize in 1997 (see ICBL website; Mekata 2000; Tomlin 1998; Tomlin et al. 1998).

A growing transnational small arms coalition of state and non-state actors is similarly committed to the goal of reducing the proliferation and use of these weapons. Various organizations with expertise in arms control, human rights and health/trauma have 'conducted groundbreaking research on the trade in light weapons and have begun to lobby governments for vigorous action in this field' (Boutwell and Klare 1999: 218. Health has been a major focus of this campaign. Noting that deaths and injuries from small arms have been classified as a 'scourge', a 'disease' and a 'preventable global health' problem, the *Small Arms Survey* 2001 claims that 'it comes as little surprise that a humanitarian stance on small arms has been embraced by the medical profession' and that 'the public health community has already begun to forge a "neutral bridge" to reconcile highly politicized discussions on firearms and traditional supply-side or militarist theorizing on arms control' (p. 214). It further observes that, while the lead role is shared by the WHO and the ICRC (International Committee of the Red Cross), 'the wider medical community's efforts to recast the problem as a "measurable" public health issue amenable to medical intervention has greatly contributed to sensitizing the international community' (p. 214).

Bringing health, security and development issues together as the small arms coalition has done is an innovative approach to deal with a serious issue of human insecurity. As components of a new global health regime, such initiatives by mixed sets of actors are also representative of the changing nature of governance generally. In the emerging structures of 'global' governance, civil societies play an increasingly responsible role, often in combination (and recombination) with governments and business. The WHO, which was the leading organization of the international regime, seems well aware of the new systems of governance that are emerging and is poised to continue to play a central role in a global health regime. The organization has been involved directly in the various campaigns discussed above, often as an advocate for an approach that addresses these issues from a political economy perspective that recognizes inequality as a health risk. And, although the WHO is impeded, like other UN organizations, by limited resources as well as by internal struggles that are factors of both international politics and institutional competition, it does play a major role in the construction of international norms on health. It may also begin to play a larger role setting norms in the broader area of human security not only through its involvement in the various coalitions discussed above, but also in its recent attempts to bring attention to the relationship between health and trade. Research into issues of political economy – the illegal trade in tobacco, for instance, as well as research on the use of taxation to control the export of tobacco, the implications for health of current patent regulations, the trade regulations on products affecting health, etc. – are now as much, or more, a feature of the WHO mandate as were the technical issues of the last century (see www.who.int). The shift from a predominantly clinical approach to health to one that addresses political economy factors is a major step forward in improving the social determinants of health.

### Notes

1 It is generally agreed that international health cooperation began in 1851 with the first International Sanitary Conference in Paris (WHO 1976: 8). In the second half of the century, several conferences on sanitation and epidemics were held which led to the establishment of several important international institutions such as L'Office Internationale d'Hygiene Publique (OHIP) in 1907 (see, WHO 1968) and regional organizations such as the Pan American Sanitary Bureau, established in 1902 (WHO 1931).

2 This issue was not new to the twentieth century, however. Examples of 'cordons sanitaires' date as far back as AD 630 when armed guards were placed on the road between Provence and Cahers to block the movement of diseased travellers.

3 For example, between 1924 and 1928, commissions were established for malaria, sleeping sickness and tuberculosis, smallpox, leprosy and rabies. This did not apply to infectious diseases alone, as a commission on cancer had been established in 1923 (WHO 1931). The various international conferences on health in the 1930s included the European (1931) and Far Eastern (1937) conferences as well as ones focused on Africa in Cape Town (1932) and Johannesburg (1935; Brockington 1985: 32).

4 The three were Dr Szeming Sze (China), Dr Karl Evang (Norway) and Dr Geraldo de Paula Souza (Brazil).

5 The Arab–Israeli dispute was the most serious of the intra-regional divisions, while the war-related origins and/or governmental policies of China, North Korea, North Vietnam, East Germany, Spain and South Africa had made them very controversial states in the new UN structure.

6 It is widely held that this 'modern' and highly technocratic and politicized development model was established on 20 January 1949, when newly elected US President Harry S. Truman called, in his augural speech, for a 'more vigorous application of modern scientific and technical knowledge' to help the less fortunate in the world and thus to establish the conditions for greater prosperity and peace for all. Promoting 'development' was a new aspect of American foreign policy resulting from the US position as the new dominant power in the post-Second World War world order. With the Cold War brewing, US policy makers were concerned to bring newly independent countries into the emerging Western camp and saw foreign assistance as one way of constructing friendly alliances.

7 There is an extensive literature on modernization theories and policies.

For brief, useful summaries of these (with bibliographies), see Hoogvelt 1982: esp. 116–19 and Pieterse 2001:esp. 20–5.

8  Thirty years later, it is clear that most developing countries are not more self-reliant and interdependence has increased. Nevertheless, the influences of dependency theory were significant, one of the most important being the call by Third World countries for a new international economic order, which resulted in the adoption of the *Declaration of the Establishment of a New International Economic Order* at a special session in 1974 of the UN General Assembly (see Hoogvelt 1982).

9  It can be found at www.who.int/hpr/archive/docs/almaata.html.

10  From such studies, it has been found that the key determinants of health (from more to less determinant) are: (1) income and social status; (2) employment/working conditions; (3) social environments; (4) physical environments; (5) personal health practices and coping skills; (6) healthy child development; (7) biological and genetic endowment; (8) health services; (9) gender; and (10) culture. See list and more on the Social Determinants of Health at Health Canada's *Population Health Approach* website, www.hc-sc.gc.ca/hppb/phdd/determinants/#key_determinants.

11  The WHO (2005:12) reports that child mortality due to malaria doubled during the 1980s and early 1990s, while mortality resulting from other causes decreased over the same period.

12  For a discussion of this framework, see Collin et al. 2002.

13  The founding members included the following NGOs: Handicap International, Human Rights Watch, Medico International, Mines Advisory Group, Physicians for Human Rights and Vietnam Veterans of America Foundation (ICBL website).

14  Convention on the Prohibition of the Use, Stockpiling, Production and Transfer of Anti-Personnel Mines and on their Destruction (Ottawa Convention).

## References and Further Reading

African Heads of State and Government 2000: Abuja declaration on roll back malaria in Africa. African Summit, 25 April, at www.who/int/rbm/RBM/Abuju_declaration.htm.

Axworthy, L. 2001: Human security and global governance: putting people first. *Global Governance*, 7 (1) (January–March), 19–23.

Black, D. J., Smith, C. and Townsend, P. 1982: *Inequalities in Health: The Black Report*. New York: Penguin Books.

Boutwell, J. and Klare, M. 1999: *Light Weapons and Civil Conflicts*. Boston, Mass.: Rowman and Littlefield.

Brockington, F. 1968: *World Health*, 2nd edn. Boston, Mass.: Little, Brown & Company.

Brockington, F. 1985: *The Health of the Developing World*. Lewes, Sussex: The Book Guild Ltd.

Brohman, J. 1997: *Popular Development: Rethinking the Theory and Practice of Development*. Oxford: Blackwell.

Clark, J. 1991: *Democratizing Development: The Role of Voluntary Organizations*. London: Earthscan.

Collin, J., Kelley Lee, K. and Bissell, K. 2002: The Framework Convention on Tobacco Control: The politics of global health governance. *Third World Quarterly*, 23 (2) (April).

Cox, R. 1999: Civil society at the turn of the millennium. *Review of International Studies*, 25 (1) (January), 3–28.

Crush, J. (ed.) 1996: *The Power of Development*. London: Routledge.

Davey-Smith, G., Bartley, M. and Blane, D. 1990: The Black Report on Socio-economic Inequalities in Health 10 years on. *British Medical Journal*, 301, 373–7.

*Declaration of Alma Ata* 1978: International Conference on Primary Health Care, Alma Ata, USSR (6–12 September), at www.who.int/hpr/archive/docs/almaata.html.

Desowitz, R. S. 1991: *The Malaria Capers: More Tales of Parasites and People, Research and Reality*. New York: W. W. Norton & Co.

Dubovsky, F. 2001: Creating a vaccine against malaria. The Malaria Vaccine Initiative, at www.malariavaccine.org.

Escobar, A. 1995: *Encountering Development: The Making and Unmaking of the Third World*. Princeton, N.J.: Princeton University Press.

Florini, A. M. (ed.) 2000: *The Third Force: The Rise of Transnational Civil Society*. Japan and Washington: Japan Centre for International Exchange and Carnegie Endowment for International Peace.

Frank, J. W. and Mustard, J. F. 1995: The determinants of health from a historical perspective. *Daedalus*, 123 (4) (Fall), at http://children.metrotor.on.ca/taskforce/must.html.

Gallop, J. L. and Sachs, J. D. 1998: The economic burden of malaria. Paper prepared for Centre for International Development at Harvard (October).

GFHR (Global Forum for Health Research) 1999: *The 10/90 Report on Health Research 1999*. Geneva: GFHR.

Hampson, F. O. and Hay, J. B. 1992: Human security: a review of the scholarly literature. *Human Security Bulletin*, 1 (2) (July), at www.liucentre.ubc.ca/nsq/_articles/Fen_fulldocument.pdf.

Health Action International 2000: Improving access to essential medicines: confronting the crisis. Drug policy at the 53rd World Health Assembly, at www.haiweb.org/WHA53en.html.

Health Canada 2002: Key determinants. *Population Health Approach* website, www.hc-sc.gc.ca/hppb/phdd/determinants/#key_determinants.

Hoogvelt, A. M. M. 1982: *The Third World in Global Development*. London: Macmillan.

ICBL (International Coalition to Ban Landmines) 2003: A brief history of the ICBL: chronology of the movement, at www.icbl.org/.

ICRC (International Committee of the Red Cross) at www.icrc.org/Web/eng/siteengo.nsf/iwpList288/ FAFDE5C21CBC5ACDC1256B66005B0E39.

Kapoor, I. 2002: The devil's in the theory: a critical assessment of Robert Chambers' work on participatory development. *Third World Quarterly*, 23 (2).

Keck, M. E. and Sikkink, K. 1998: *Activists Beyond Borders: Advocacy Networks in International Politics*. New York: Cornell University Press.

Khong, Y. F. 2001: Human security: a shotgun approach to alleviating human misery? *Global Governance*, 7 (3), 23–36.

Laing, R. 1999: Global issues of access to pharmaceuticals and the effects of patents. Presentation to the AIDS and Essential Medicine Compulsory Licensing Meeting, Geneva (26 March), at www.haiweb.org/campaign/cl/laing.html.

Lee, K. and Dodgson, R. 2000: Globalization and cholera: implications for global governance. *Global Governance*, 6 (2) (April), 213–36.

Leon, D. A., Walt, G. and Gilson, L. 2001: International perspectives on health inequalities and policy. *British Medical Journal*, 322 (March), 591–4.

Lipschutz, R. D. 2001: Because people matter: studying global political economy. *International Studies Perspectives*, 2 (4) (November), 321–39.

Mack, A. 2001: Notes on the creation of a human security report. Paper delivered at the Kennedy School of Government, Harvard University (1–2 December).

Mack, A. and Dewitt, D. 2002: Editorial: CCHS and human security. *Human Security Bulletin* (of the Canadian Consortium on Human Security), 1 (2) (July), at www.liucentre.ubc.ca/hsq/en/hsq010201.htm.

MacLean, S. J. and Shaw, T. M. 2001: Canada and the new 'global' strategic alliances: prospects for human security at the start of the 21st century. *Canadian Foreign Policy*, 8 (3), 17–36.

Marmot, M. G. 1986: Social inequalities in mortality: the social environment in class and health. In R. G. Wilkinson (ed.) *Class and Health*, London: Tavistock Publications, 21–34.

Marmot, M. G., Smith, G. D., Stansfeld, S. et al. 1991: Health inequalities among British civil servants: the Whitehall II Study. *Lancet*, I, 1387–93.

Mayor, S. 2001: Poorest women 20 times more likely to die in childbirth. *British Medical Journal*, 323, 1324.

Mekata, M. 2000: Building partnerships toward a common goal: experiences of the International Campaign to Ban Landmines. In A. M. Florini (ed.), *The Third Force: The Rise of Transnational Civil Society*, Japan and Washington: Japan Centre for International Exchange and Carnegie Endowment for International Peace, 143–77.

MIM (Multilateral Iniative on Malaria 2001: About MIM, at www.mim.nih.gov/english.

Mons, B. et al. 1998: Partnership between South and North crystallizes around malaria. *Science*, 279 (5350), 498–500.

MSF (Medicins Sans Frontières) 1999: Drugs for communicable diseases: stimulating development and securing availability, at www.accessmed-msf.org/.

Murphy, C. 2001: Political consequences of the new inequality. *International Studies Quarterly*, 45 (3), 347–56.

Navarro, V. 1976: *Medicine under Capitalism*. New York: Prodist.

Navarro, V. 1986: *Crisis, Health, and Medicine: A Social Critique*. New York and London: Tavistock Publications.

Parpart, J. L. 2000: Rethinking participation, empowerment and development from a gender perspective. In J. Freedman (ed.), *Transforming Development*, Toronto: University of Toronto Press.

Pieterse, J. N. 1998: My paradigm or yours? Alternative development, post development, reflexive development. *Development and Change*, 29 (2), 343–73.

Pieterse, J. N. 2001: *Development Theory: Deconstructions/Reconstructions*. London: Sage.

Poku, N. K. 2001: Africa's AIDS crisis in context: 'how the poor are dying'. *Third World Quarterly*, 22 (2) (April).

Poku, N. K. and Whiteside, A. (eds) 2002: Special issue: Global health and governance: HIV/AIDS. *Third World Quarterly*, 23 (2) (April).

Schuurman, F. J. (ed.) 1993: *Beyond the Impasse, New Directions in Development Theory*. London: Zed Books.

Sen, A. 1993: The economics of life and death. *Scientific American* (May), 40–7.

Siddiqi, J. 1995: *World Health and World Politics: The World Health Organization and the UN System*. London: Hurst & Company.

Sreenivasan, G. and Grinspun, R. 2002: Trade and health: focus on access to essential medicines. Paper 4 in Canadian Council for International Cooperation Trade and Poverty Series, 'Global Trade/Global Poverty: NGO Perspectives on Key Challenges for Canada' (June).

Thomas, C. 2001: Whatever happened to 'Health for all by the year 2000'? Paper presented at International Studies Association, Annual Meeting (February), Los Angeles.

Thomas, C. 2002: Global governance, development and human security: exploring the links. *Third World Quarterly*, 23 (1) (February).

Tomlin, B. (ed.) 1998: Special issue: The global movement to ban landmines. *Canadian Foreign Policy* 5 (3) (Spring), 1–165.

Tomlin, B. Maxwell, A. C. and Lawson, R. T. (eds) 1998: *To Walk without Fear: The Global Movement to Ban Landmines*. Toronto: Oxford University Press.

UNDP 2000: *Human Development Report 2000*. New York: UNDP.

UNDP 2001: *Human Development Report 2001*. New York: UNDP.

Whitehead, M. 1987: *The Health Divide*. London: Health Education Council, at www.who.int/en/.

WHO n.d. Vingt-cinq ans d'activité de L'Office Internationale d'Hygiène Publique 1909–1933, at http://whqlib.doc.who.int/hist/chronicles/publique_hygiene_1909–1933.pdf.

WHO 1931: League of Nations Health Organization, at http://whqlibdoc.who.int/hist/chronicles/health_org_1931.pdf.

WHO 1958: *The First Ten Years of the World Health Organization*. Geneva: WHO.

WHO 1968: *The Second Ten Years of the World Health Organization*. Geneva: WHO.

WHO 1976: *Introducing WHO*. Geneva: WHO.

WHO 1988: WHO: from small beginnings. Forum interview with Szeming Sze, at http://whqlibdoc.who.int/analytics/WHForum_1988_9(1)_29–34.pdf.

WHO 1996: *The World Health Report, 1995: Bridging the Gaps*. Geneva: WHO.

WHO 1999: *World Health Report*. Geneva: WHO.

WHO 2000: Economic costs of malaria are many times higher than previously estimated (25 April). Geneva.

WHO 2005: *World Malaria Report 2005*. Geneva: WHO.

Wilkinson, R. G. 1997: Health inequalities: relative or absolute material standards? *Education & Debate* (22 February).

World Commission on Environment and Development 1987: *Brundtland Report*. UN General Assembly A43/427 (4 August).

World Bank 1993: *World Development Report 1993: Investing in Health*. Washington, D.C.: Oxford University Press.

# 7 HIV/AIDS in a Globalized World: An Uneven Pandemic in an Unequal World

*Nana K. Poku*

*In this chapter Poku outlines the complex but real relationship between the processes, forces and agents of globalization and the pace, intensity and destruction of HIV/AIDS across the developing world. He argues that the changes in the distribution of income and poverty and the impact of neoliberal economic strategies, which characterize globalization, have a direct impact on human well-being and thus provide the context for the rampant spread of HIV/AIDS. The chapter concludes that multinational corporations, the multilateral institutions of global economic governance and the G8 group of powerful states not only force the pace of globalization but also dictate both the spread of the HIV/AIDS epidemic in the developing world and the treatment that is available for complications of HIV infection.*

## INTRODUCTION

To attempt to narrate the challenges posed by HIV/AIDS in the modern world is to confront a complex topography encompassing a potent mix of sex and death, science and politics and deep-rooted divisions and inequalities between North and South, as well as between rich and poor, men and women, black and white, homosexuals and heterosexuals. In this sense, an account of the pandemic is much more than a gruesome tale of desolation the scale of which humanity has yet to comprehend, but probably the furthermost illustration of the opportunities, challenges and threats posed by globalization. It would certainly be foolish to blame globalization for all the many social challenges that now face the developing world, or indeed to suggest that it is the primary cause of HIV/AIDS. But equally, there is clear evidence that global restructuring has exacerbated many old problems while also introducing new ones of its own, and it is in this context that HIV/AIDS must be placed. Across the world, the dominant drivers of globalization (multinational corporations, the multilateral institutions of global economic governance and the G8 group of powerful states) structure not only the contours of the pandemic in terms of transmission and new infections, but also the outcomes once an individual is sick with complications of HIV infection (Berwick et al. 2002, Cheru 2000, Poku 2002a).

In this chapter, it is our intention to detail the complex, but real, relationship between the processes, forces and agents of globalization and the pace, intensity and destruction of HIV/AIDS. Drawing on examples from Africa, we will argue that the changes in the distribution of income and poverty and the impact of neoliberal economic strategies, which characterize globalization, have a direct impact on human well-being and thus provide the context for the rampant spread of HIV/AIDS. It is, however, with a brief global overview of challenges posed by the pandemic that we begin our analysis.

## AN UNEVEN PANDEMIC

Figure 7.1 confirms the strikingly patterned nature of the HIV epidemic. Despite an estimated 65,000 new infections in 2004, HIV prevalence rate in the high income countries of Western and Central Europe and North America remains relatively low, with infections concentrated principally among injecting drug users and men who have sex with men – although recent studies indicates that this is changing. Across Western Europe, data suggests that a larger proportion of new HIV diagnoses (59 per cent, overall between 1997 and 2001) are taking place among the heterosexual

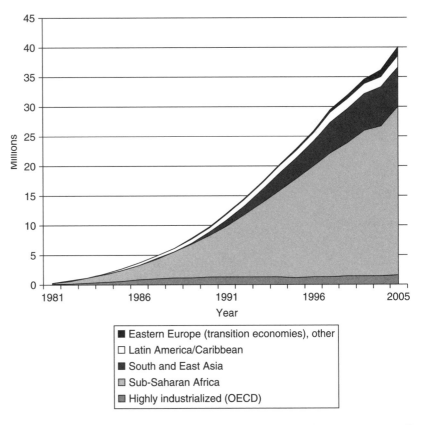

**Figure 7.1** People with HIV/AIDS, cumulative regional total (millions) (UNHCR 1998)

community (UNAIDS 2002). In the case of the United Kingdom, for example, there has been a steep increase in the number of HIV diagnoses since 1999, and the major component of the rapid increase has been in heterosexually acquired infections. Although the majority of these were contracted in countries with high HIV prevalence, infections acquired within the UK have also risen (Avert 2005). In Ireland, a similar trend is visible, with the number of heterosexually transmitted HIV infections increasing four-fold between 1998 and 2001 (UNFPA 2002).

The position is more diverse across the developing world where most transmission occurs through sex between men and women, but there are also very high rates of infection among men who have sex with men and injecting drug users. In much of Latin America, HIV infections are confined largely to these sub-populations. This is also the case in Eastern Europe, the Middle East and North Africa (UNAIDS/WHO 2004). With particular reference to Eastern Europe, where the world's fastest growing epidemic is taking place, the then Director-General of the WHO, Dr Brundtland, puts the risk of contracting HIV associated with injecting drug use in the following way: 'Unsafe injecting drug use [in Eastern Europe] drives very rapid expansion of the epidemic, but it also does not take long before the sexual partners of the injecting drug users become part of the steadily widening epidemic' (WHO/UNAIDS 2003). While in Africa – where two-thirds of the global HIV population resides – the virus is spread primarily through heterosexual and perinatal transmission, with heterosexual activity being the dominant mode of transmission (Hope 2001).

Beyond the differential impact of the pandemic globally, it is possible to make at least three general observations about the unique challenges posed by it. First, HIV/AIDS is at one and the same time both an emergency and chronic condition. It is an emergency because the speed of its spread has proved to be quite overwhelming. In many countries, infection rates have increased from 7 to 25 per cent in adult populations in less than a decade. In South Africa, for example, the level of infections rose roughly ten-fold to more than 20 per cent in just six years (1992–8), and has since risen to 29.4 per cent in 2004 (South Africa Department of Health 2005). Thus, before people are even aware that infected families and friends surround them, their communities have been deeply penetrated. Take the case of India, where the national adult HIV prevalence rate of less than 1 per cent offers little indication of the serious situation facing the country. An estimated 5.1 million people were living with HIV at the end of 2003 – the second-highest figure in the world, after South Africa. HIV prevalence among women attending antenatal clinics was higher than 1 per cent in Andhra Pradesh, Karnataka, Maharashtra, Manipur, Nagaland and Tamil Nadu (UNAIDS/WHO 2004). This figure is expected to more than quadruple in the next decade – thus making the country one of the most infected countries in the world. Indeed, over the same period just five countries in the world – China, India, Russia, Nigeria and Ethiopia – will collectively have the largest number of HIV/AIDS cases on earth (National Intelligence Council 2002). That the pandemic is a chronic condition is demonstrated by the fact that HIV infection moves through a population giving little sign of its presence. It is only later – when substantial numbers are infected

– that AIDS deaths begin to rise. Whiteside puts the position this way; 'people do not leave the infected pool by getting better as there is no cure . . . the effect of life-prolonging ARVs (anti-retroviral drugs) is, ironically, to increase the pool of infected people' (Whiteside 2002).

Second, the pandemic manifests itself as a precise problem but also as an all-encompassing one. Its precision is revealed in its associated morbidity and mortality in increasing numbers of people – mostly otherwise healthy, productive, young people – getting sick and dying (Cohen 2002; Collins and Rau 2000; UNAIDS/WHO 2004). The response of the first two decades of the epidemic addressed this quality of the crisis. It focused on the epidemic as a health crisis and on its ramifications for health service delivery. However, the repercussions of these deaths are beginning to permeate and affect every facet of human life and national development in the regions most affected (Stillwagon 2000; Poku 2001a). Take the case of the agricultural sector. Recent studies suggest that for all types of households in farming communities, AIDS death also brings with it loss of productive resources through the sale of livestock to pay for sickness, mourning and funeral expenses, as well as a sharp decline in crop production (Mutangadura 2000; Engh et al. 2000; CHGA 2004). Sickness also contributes to the scarcity of labour because of both the incapacity of infected workers and the time others have to devote to looking after them. In addition, the scale of the number of people dying from the agricultural communities is threatening to undermine the transmission of vital intergenerational farming knowledge in some communities.

Third, across the world HIV infectivity shows a great gender variance – with women being particularly vulnerable to contracting the virus. Recent figures from UNAIDS/WHO suggests that more women than men are dying of HIV/AIDS, and also that the age pattern is significantly different for the two sexes (UNAIDS/WHO 2004). National population-based surveys carried out in 2001–2 show an HIV prevalence of 3 per cent among Zambian men aged between fifteen and twenty-four, while the figure for women in the same age group is almost four times higher at 11.2 per cent. In Zimbabwe, 5 per cent of men aged between fifteen and twenty-four are HIV-positive, while among women the figure is a staggering 18 per cent (WHO-AFRO 2003). In explaining the vulnerability of women to the pandemic, a combination of factors are clearly involved, reflecting differences in biology (Seidel 1993), sexual behaviour (Orubuloye et al. 1997; Orubuloye et al. 1993; Baylies and Bujra 2000), social attitudes and pressures (Poku 2001b), economic power and vulnerability (Schoepf 1993; Smith and Cohen 2000).

## AN UNEQUAL WORLD

It is largely within the context of globalization that one can make sense of the pandemic's differential patterns of manifestation North/South and the overt vulnerability of the countries in the latter category. Over the past decade or so, the utility of globalization as a concept has been the subject of intense debate and a veritable avalanche of writings (Albrow 1996; Allen and Hammett 1998; Falk 1995; Giddens 1990). Without wishing to traverse the corpus of this literature, it is possible to see the concept as denoting a fundamental process in global politics that exhibits at least three core manifestation: first, the multiplication and intensification of economic, political and cultural linkages among people, organizations and countries at the global level (Dicken 1992); second, the real or perceived tendency towards universalization of some economic, institutional, legal and cultural practices (Falk 1990); third, the compression of both time and space (Albrow 1996). For many observers, even if the eventual picture remains in doubt, the principal agents of these processes are evident enough, such as globalizing corporations emerging from a rapid development of super-mergers, technoscientific networks and the aesthetic architects of mass culture. At the same time, there is also a shrinking of the world brought about by the third technological revolution that has enabled us to travel both vicariously and instantaneously to almost all regions of the world (Allen and Hammett 1998).

Manifestly, the benefits are enormous, as a result of the increased sharing of ideas, cultures, life-saving technologies, and efficient production processes. Yet, the euphoria these developments generate can often serve to disguise the very real social and economic inequalities that are not merely leftovers from the past, but are the results of the globalizing process. Most obviously, global welfare inequalities have mushroomed alongside the noted advancements in technological developments and the rapid expansion of trade and investment. Take, for example, the gap in income and investment patterns over the past decade. According to the United Nations Development Programme (UNDP) the gap between the richest and the poorest 20 per cent of the world has increased to 86:1 and widens every day (UNDP 2004). Similarly, at the beginning of this decade, the OECD countries held over three-quarters of the accumulated stock of foreign direct investment (FDI) and attracted over 60 per cent of new FDI flows. Insofar as FDI went to the developing countries (South), it was concentrated in ten countries, with China alone accounting for more than one-third. Thus foreign-investment resources are being concentrated on those countries – such as Thailand, Indonesia, Colombia, Malaysia, Taiwan – which are performing most strongly in global trade (Sachs 2001). Eight countries that accounted for 30 per cent of developing country GDP absorbed around two-thirds of total FDI (World Bank 2000a). At the other extreme, the forty-eight less developed countries (LDCs) received around $800 million in FDI in 1999 – roughly the same size as flows into Brazil, and less than 1 per cent of the total transfer to developing countries (UNCTAD 2000).

This uneven distribution of global investment patterns with its associated selectivity and polarization of societies has given rise to:

- a growing gap between the rich and poor within and between nations – in particular between North and South (UNDP 2002);

- the destruction of quality jobs and their replacement by casualization and temporary jobs brought by a process of subcontracting of so-called non-core business activities (ADB 2002);

- growing unemployment in particular in the developing countries, which goes hand in hand with poverty, that itself leads to more social problems (Wallace 1999); and

- mass migration in pursuit of adequate standards of living (Allen and Hammett 1998).

As a result, a true process of immiseration is now observable in many parts of the world, particularly within developing countries. The facts of global inequalities are truly staggering: the richest 25 million Americans have an income equal to that of almost 2 billion people, while the assets of the world's three richest men, even after the recent fall in the value of stock markets, is greater than the combined income of the world's LDCs with a population of more than 600 million (UNDP 1999; UNDP 2001).

The living standards of Sierra Leone – ranked bottom of the United Nations Human Development Index – are roughly equivalent to those in the West 600 years ago. The average income per head stands at only $150 a year, less than the $1-a-day level that the World Bank regards as subsistence level (UNDP 2004). Not surprisingly, the resulting inequalities in life outcomes are stark. The average Sierra Leonean can expect to live until the age of forty, a life expectancy level not witnessed in Western Europe since the Industrial Revolution (UN/DESA 2005). Indeed, across the developing world, those living in absolute poverty are five times more likely to die before reaching five years of age than those in higher income groups (Whitehead et al. 2001). Moreover, poverty has a woman's face. Of the 1.3 billion people defined by the WHO as the poorest – that is those surviving on less than $1 per day – only 30 per cent are male. Poor women are often caught in a damaging cycle of cultural bias and gender discrimination that further exposes them to exploitation and disease (Baylies and Bujra 2000). Take the following passage from one woman's experience in South Africa:

> My husband lost his job about five months ago. It was a big shock but we thought we could cope. I was earning a reasonably good wage. We had to cut a few corners though. We had to eat less meat. We had to save on all kinds of things . . . Then two months ago I lost my job. We were desperate. There was no money coming in now . . . Now they've cut off the electricity and we're two months in arrears with rent. They're going to evict us, I'm sure, we just can't pay though. My husband decided to go to Jo'burg . . . I don't know where he is . . . Sometimes (the children) lie awake at night crying. I know they are crying because they are hungry. I feel like feeding them Rattex. When your children cry with hunger, your heart wants to break. It will be better if they were dead. When I think things like that I feel worse . . . I'm sick. I'm sick because of the cold. I can't take my children to the doctor when they are sick because there is no money . . . What can one do? You must start looking. You can also pray to God that he will keep you from killing your children. (Poku 2006)

Notwithstanding decades of domestic economic mismanagement with its associated corruption and violence, the culpability of global forces in shaping this disheartening reality cannot be overlooked. Since the early 1980s, the monetarist notion that the 'invisible hand' of the market mechanism must be allowed to operate unimpeded has been promoted with an almost missionary zeal across the developing world by the dominant institutions of global economic governance – International Monetary Fund (IMF) and the International Bank for Reconstruction and Development (IBRD) commonly referred to as the World Bank. Under structural adjustment programmes (SAPs), government actions and control is seen as the cause of inflation, debt and economic retrogression, while the private sector is promoted as the creator of efficiency and growth. Although there are many variations of SAPs, two broad policy components have come to characterize all of them: short- to medium-term macroeconomic stabilization measures to restore internal and external balances, which falls within the province of the IMF; and SAPs proper, which are designed to 'unleash market forces so that competition can help improve the allocation of resources . . . getting price signals right and creating a climate that allows business to respond to those signals in ways that increase the returns to investment' (World Bank 1994: 61).

Since the mid-1980s over 130 developing countries have been generally found wanting on both counts: they have incurred unsustainable fiscal and external deficits, which in turn has forced them to accept SAPs from the World Bank as a crucial prerequisite to receiving vitally needed loans from the IMF. Today, there are no signs that the policies are achieving their desired objectives: macroeconomic stability and growth. Amid the bitter recriminations between the concerned parties – developing countries, NGOs and the institutions of global economic governance – it is not clear whether the lack of effective implementation results from unwillingness to effect reforms on the part of the developing countries; or from the objective conditions of the economies not permitting the kind of adjustment policies being recommended. Yet, SAPs have led to a radical rationalization of recipient governments' expenditure commitments in mainly – but not exclusively – areas concerned with the provisions of welfare (i.e. the health, education and basic sustenance such as food subsidies). Cuts in government expenditure have forced up the costs of primary education and health care beyond the reach of many ordinary people. Rushed privatization has resulted in the laying off of tens of thousands of workers in many adjusting countries. The removal of price controls and the devaluation of the national currency have led to a spiralling cost of living.

In this sense the combined effects of SAP policies in the developing world has left millions of people already unable to make ends meet. In Africa, for example, Lipumba observes that the dominant 'opinion among African intellectuals is that structural adjustment programs are part of the continent's problems rather than the solution' (Lipumba 1994). It is not difficult to see why: the promotion of exports for debt repayment and the cutting of public expenditure on welfare in a region where 200 million people are undernourished; where there is one doctor for nearly 40,000 people, compared with one for 400 people in industrial countries; and where nine out of the ten HIV-infected people worldwide reside, is a scandal (Poku 2002b). One author has even referred to SAPs as a form of economic genocide:

> Structural adjustment is conducive to a form of economic genocide which is carried out through the deliberate manipulation of market forces. When

compared to genocide in various periods of colonial history (for example, forced labour and slavery), its impact is devastating. Structural adjustment programmes directly affect the livelihood of more than four billion people. (Chossudovsky 1996)

## GLOBALIZATION AND AIDS: THE CONTEXT OF VULNERABILITY

It is largely in this framework of uneven globalization with its associated defencelessness that the HIV/AIDS pandemic can be situated, in terms of the social changes that transnational neoliberalism precipitates, and relates to people's vulnerability to, and capacity to live with, the disease. In the case of Africa, for example, Sisonke Msimang provides this compelling dramatization of the complexly interrelated relationship between history (colonial legacies) and the forces of globalization to outline the intense vulnerability of the continent's people to HIV/AIDS:

> Take some men from rural areas and put them in hostels far away from home in different countries if need be. Build excellent roads. Ensure that the communities surrounding the men are impoverished so that a ring of sex workers develops around each mining town. Add HIV. Now take some miners and send them home for holidays to their rural, uninfected wives. Add a few girlfriends in communities along the road home. Add liberal amounts of patriarchy both home grown and the colonial variety. Ensure that women have no right to determine the conditions under which sex will take place. Make sure that they have no access to credit, education or of any of the measures that would give them options to leave unhappy unions or dream of lives in which men are not the centre of their activities. Shake well and watch an epidemic explode. (Poku 2006)

Three key themes from Sisonke Msimang's dramatization becomes particularly worthy of further attention: (1) spatial changes relating to the migration of people resulting from global inequalities affecting poverty; (2) the role of poverty in both providing the context for the pandemic to spread and retarding the possibility of effective response to it on the part of developing countries; and (3) the gendered nature of global inequalities and its implications for the spread of HIV amongst women.

## Spatial changes

The spread of HIV/AIDS is facilitated by the resultant changes in the spatial dimensions of human relations. Due to globalization, a number of major developments in global migration patterns have placed the phenomenon at the heart of the spread of HIV/AIDS (Poku and Graham 2000). First, the scale of movements has increased exponentially (Cohen 1997). In the 1960s only a handful of countries, mainly the traditional immigration nations of North America and Oceania, were significantly affected by international migration, but by the late 1990s more than 22 per cent of the world's population was living outside of their country of birth, and virtually every nation was influenced in some way by immigration or emigration of various kinds (see Tables 7.1, 7.2, 7.3, 7.4). Second, there

**Table 7.1** Estimated foreign-born population by region, 1965, 1975, 1985 and 1990 (thousands)

|  | 1965 | 1975 | 1985 | 1990 |
|---|---|---|---|---|
| **World total** | 75,214 | 84,494 | 105,194 | 119,761 |
| **Developed countries** | 30,401 | 38,317 | 47,991 | 54,231 |
| **Developing countries** | 44,813 | 46,177 | 57,203 | 65,530 |
| **Africa** | 7,952 | 11,178 | 12,527 | 15,631 |
| Northern Africa | 1,016 | 1,080 | 2,219 | 1,982 |
| Sub-Saharan Africa | 6,936 | 10,099 | 10,308 | 13,649 |
| **Asia** | 31,429 | 29,662 | 38,731 | 43,018 |
| Eastern and South-Eastern Asia | 8,136 | 7,723 | 7,678 | 7,931 |
| China | 266 | 305 | 331 | 346 |
| Other Eastern and South-Eastern Asia | 7,870 | 7,419 | 7,347 | 7,586 |
| South-Central Asia[a] | 18,610 | 15,565 | 19,243 | 20,782 |
| Western Asia | 4,683 | 6,374 | 11,810 | 14,304 |
| **Latin America and the Caribbean** | 5,907 | 5,788 | 6,410 | 7,475 |
| Caribbean | 532 | 665 | 832 | 959 |
| Central America[b] | 445 | 427 | 948 | 2,047 |
| South America | 4,930 | 4,695 | 4,629 | 4,469 |
| **Northern America** | 12,695 | 15,042 | 20,460 | 23,895 |
| **Europe and USSR (former)** | 14,728 | 19,504 | 22,959 | 25,068 |
| Countries with economies in transition[c] | 2,835 | 2,394 | 2,213 | 2,055 |
| USSR (former) | 140 | 148 | 156 | 159 |
| Other Europe | 11,753 | 16,961 | 20,590 | 22,853 |
| **Oceania** | 2,502 | 3,319 | 4,106 | 4,675 |

[a] Excluding Armenia, Azerbaijan, Georgia, Kazakhstan, Kyrgyzstan, Tajikistan, Turkmenistan and Uzbekistan.
[b] Including Mexico.
[c] Including Albania, Bulgaria, the former Czechoslovakia, the former Democratic Republic of Germany, Hungary, Poland, Romania and the former Yugoslavia and excluding the former USSR.
*Source:* UNHCR 1998.

has been an enormous increase in the diversity of international population movement (Hugo 1997). Whereas in the past the bulk of such movement involved permanent, or at least long-term, settlement at the destination, world migration is now characterized not only by increased levels of permanent settlement in foreign countries but also by a myriad of temporary, circular migrations of varying duration with a range of largely economic purposes from mainly rural to urban areas.

The dislocation of so many millions of people from their traditional places of residence stems – in large part – from the gross inequities in global distribution of wealth identified earlier (Chirwa 1998). Across the developing world, the development paradigm imposed through SAP has focused on exporting agricultural products and minerals (Poku 2002b). The plantations,

**Table 7.2** Estimated foreign-born population as percentage of total population by region, 1965, 1975, 1985 and 1997

|  | 1965 | 1975 | 1985 | 1997 |
|---|---|---|---|---|
| **World total** | 2.3 | 2.1 | 2.2 | 2.3 |
| **Developed countries** | 3.1 | 3.5 | 4.1 | 4.5 |
| **Developing countries** | 1.9 | 1.6 | 1.6 | 1.6 |
| **Africa** | 2.5 | 2.7 | 2.3 | 2.5 |
| Northern Africa | 1.4 | 1.1 | 1.8 | 1.4 |
| Sub-Saharan Africa | 2.9 | 3.2 | 2.5 | 2.8 |
| **Asia** | 1.7 | 1.3 | 1.4 | 1.4 |
| Eastern and South-Eastern Asia | 0.7 | 0.5 | 0.5 | 0.4 |
| China | 0.0 | 0.0 | 0.0 | 0.0 |
| Other Eastern and South-Eastern Asia | 1.9 | 1.5 | 1.2 | 1.2 |
| South-Central Asia[a] | 2.8 | 1.9 | 1.8 | 1.8 |
| Western Asia | 7.4 | 7.6 | 10.4 | 10.9 |
| **Latin America and the Caribbean** | 2.4 | 1.8 | 1.6 | 1.7 |
| Caribbean | 2.4 | 2.5 | 2.7 | 2.9 |
| Central America[b] | 0.8 | 0.6 | 1.0 | 1.8 |
| South America | 3.0 | 2.2 | 1.8 | 1.5 |
| **Northern America** | 6.0 | 6.3 | 7.8 | 8.6 |
| **Europe and USSR (former)** | 2.2 | 2.7 | 3.0 | 3.2 |
| Countries with economies in transition[c] | 2.4 | 1.9 | 1.6 | 1.7 |
| USSR (former) | 0.1 | 0.1 | 0.1 | 0.1 |
| Other Europe | 3.6 | 4.9 | 5.8 | 6.1 |
| **Oceania** | 14.4 | 15.6 | 16.9 | 17.8 |

[a] Excluding Armenia, Azerbaijan, Georgia, Kazakhstan, Kyrgyzstan, Tajikistan, Turkmenistan and Uzbekistan.
[b] Including Mexico.
[c] Including Albania, Bulgaria, the former Czechoslovakia, the former Democratic Republic of Germany, Hungary, Poland, Romania and the former Yugoslavia and excluding the former USSR.
*Source:* UNHCR 1998.

mines and industries, though development enclaves from one point of view, have required and attracted massive quantities of labour not only from the traditional rural areas, but also from neighbouring and regional states. Decosas and Adrien note that migrants have higher infection rates than those who do not migrate, independent of the HIV prevalence at the site of departure or the site of destination (Decosas and Adrien 1997).

The mining community in Carletonville, South Africa, is a tragic but powerful reminder of how mobility provides an environment of extraordinary risk for HIV infection. With a mine-working population of 85,000 people, of whom 95 per cent are migrant workers, Carletonville is the biggest gold-mining complex in the world. These migrant workers leave their families behind in rural villages, live in squalid all-male labour

**Table 7.3** Annual percentage rate of change of estimated foreign-born population by region for periods between 1965 and 1997

| | 1965–1975 | 1975–1985 | 1985–1997 | 1965–1997 |
|---|---|---|---|---|
| **World total** | 1.2 | 2.2 | 2.6 | 1.9 |
| **Developed countries** | 2.3 | 2.3 | 2.4 | 2.3 |
| **Developing countries** | 0.3 | 2.1 | 2.7 | 1.5 |
| **Africa** | 3.4 | 1.1 | 4.4 | 2.7 |
| Northern Africa | 0.6 | 7.2 | −2.3 | 2.7 |
| Sub-Saharan Africa | 3.8 | 0.2 | 5.6 | 2.7 |
| **Asia** | −0.6 | 2.7 | 2.1 | 1.3 |
| Eastern and South-Eastern Asia | −0.5 | −0.1 | 0.6 | −0.1 |
| China | 1.4 | 0.8 | 0.9 | 1.0 |
| Other Eastern and South-Eastern Asia | −0.6 | −0.1 | 0.6 | −0.1 |
| South-Central Asia[a] | −1.8 | 2.1 | 1.5 | 0.4 |
| Western Asia | 3.1 | 6.2 | 3.8 | 4.5 |
| **Latin America and the Caribbean** | −0.2 | 1.0 | 3.1 | 0.9 |
| Caribbean | 2.2 | 2.2 | 2.8 | 2.4 |
| Central America[b] | −0.4 | 8.0 | 15.4 | 6.1 |
| South America | −0.5 | −0.1 | −0.7 | −0.4 |
| **Northern America** | 1.7 | 3.1 | 3.1 | 2.5 |
| **Europe and USSR (former)** | 2.8 | 1.6 | 1.8 | 2.1 |
| Countries with economies in transition[c] | −1.7 | −0.8 | −1.5 | −1.3 |
| USSR (former) | 0.6 | 0.5 | 0.5 | 0.5 |
| Other Europe | 3.7 | 1.9 | 2.1 | 2.7 |
| **Oceania** | 2.8 | 2.1 | 2.6 | 2.5 |

[a] Excluding Armenia, Azerbaijan, Georgia, Kazakhstan, Kyrgyzstan, Tajikistan, Turkmenistan and Uzbekistan.
[b] Including Mexico.
[c] Including Albania, Bulgaria, the former Czechoslovakia, the former Democratic Republic of Germany, Hungary, Poland, Romania and the former Yugoslavia and excluding the former USSR.
*Source:* UNHCR 1998.

hostels and return home maybe once a year. Lacking formal education and recreation, these hardworking men rely on little else but home-brewed alcohol and sex for leisure. For these men, there is a 1 in 40 chance of being crushed by falling rock, so the delayed risk of HIV seems comparatively remote. Astonishingly, some 65 per cent of adults in Carletonville were HIV-positive in 1999, a rate higher than any region in the world (Williams et al. 2000). When these men return back to their families, they often carry the virus into their rural communities. A study in a rural area in the South African province of KwaZulu-Natal, for example, showed that 13 per cent of women whose husbands worked away from home two-thirds of the time were infected with HIV (Morar et al. 1998).

**Table 7.4** Percentage distribution by region of estimated foreign-born population, 1965, 1975, 1985 and 1997

|  | 1965 | 1975 | 1985 | 1997 |
|---|---|---|---|---|
| **World total** | 100.0 | 100.0 | 100.0 | 100.0 |
| **Developed countries** | 40.4 | 45.3 | 45.6 | 45.3 |
| **Developing countries** | 59.6 | 54.7 | 54.4 | 54.7 |
| **Africa** | 10.6 | 13.2 | 11.9 | 13.1 |
| Northern Africa | 1.4 | 1.3 | 2.1 | 1.7 |
| Sub-Saharan Africa | 9.2 | 12.0 | 9.8 | 11.4 |
| **Asia** | 41.8 | 35.1 | 36.8 | 35.9 |
| Eastern and South-Eastern Asia | 10.8 | 9.1 | 7.3 | 6.6 |
| China | 0.4 | 0.4 | 0.3 | 0.3 |
| Other Eastern and South-Eastern Asia | 10.5 | 8.8 | 7.0 | 6.3 |
| South-Central Asia[a] | 24.7 | 18.4 | 18.3 | 17.4 |
| Western Asia | 6.2 | 7.5 | 11.2 | 11.9 |
| **Latin America and the Caribbean** | 7.9 | 6.8 | 6.1 | 6.2 |
| Caribbean | 0.7 | 0.8 | 0.8 | 0.8 |
| Central America[b] | 0.6 | 0.5 | 0.9 | 1.7 |
| South America | 6.6 | 5.6 | 4.4 | 3.7 |
| **Northern America** | 16.9 | 17.8 | 19.5 | 20.0 |
| **Europe and USSR (former)** | 19.6 | 23.1 | 21.8 | 20.9 |
| Countries with economies in transition[c] | 3.8 | 2.8 | 2.1 | 1.7 |
| USSR (former) | 0.2 | 0.2 | 0.1 | 0.1 |
| Other Europe | 15.6 | 20.1 | 19.6 | 19.1 |
| **Oceania** | 3.3 | 3.9 | 3.9 | 3.9 |

[a] Excluding Armenia, Azerbaijan, Georgia, Kazakhstan, Kyrgyzstan, Tajikistan, Turkmenistan and Uzbekistan.
[b] Including Mexico.
[c] Including Albania, Bulgaria, the former Czechoslovakia, the former Democratic Republic of Germany, Hungary, Poland, Romania and the former Yugoslavia and excluding the former USSR.
*Source:* UNHCR 1998.

Among women who spent two-thirds of their time or more with their husbands, no HIV infection was recorded (Lurie et al. 2000).

## Poverty and HIV/AIDS

Poverty affects the course of HIV/AIDS in three fundamental ways. The first of these is the existence of undiagnosed and untreated sexually transmitted diseases among many of the poor. Take the case of Africa. Data for 2003 indicate that the continent has the highest incidence of curable sexually transmitted diseases (STDs) at 284 cases per 1,000 people aged between fifteen and forty-nine, compared to the second highest of 160 cases per 1,000 people in South and South-East Asia (WHO-AFRO 2003). There is now growing recognition of the public health implications of curable STDs (especially those causing genital ulcers) by virtue of their frequency of occurrence as well as their ability, when present, to facilitate the transmission of HIV (World Bank 2000b). One study suggests that the presence of an untreated STD can enhance both the acquisition and transmission of HIV by a factor of up to ten (Mutangadura 2000). Such painful bacterial STDs are relatively uncommon in rich countries because of the availability of antibiotics. Yet, in the developing world, even when the poor have access to health care, the clinics may have no antibiotics to treat those bacterial STDs that act as co-factors for the transmission of HIV.

Second, the nature of poverty leads to outcomes that expose the poor to a higher probability of contracting HIV. Poverty, especially rural poverty, and the absence of access to sustainable livelihoods, are factors in labour mobility – a key function of globalization (Whiteside and Sunter 2000). Mobile workers are defined as those workers who work far away from their permanent places of residence and are usually unable to return home at the end of the working day. They therefore have temporary residences in the vicinity of their work sites and return home at various intervals. Such workers include, for example, truck drivers, road/dam/building construction workers, itinerant traders, soldiers, wildlife officers, seafarers, agricultural workers, miners and commercial sex workers. As Hope rightly observes, 'for these workers, being mobile in and of itself is not a risk factor for HIV/AIDS; it is the situations they encounter and the behaviours in which they may engage while they are travelling around that lead to and increase vulnerability to HIV/AIDS' (Hope 2001).

Third, poverty structures not only the contours of the pandemic but also the outcome once an individual is sick with complications of HIV infection. A strong feature of HIV infection is that it clusters within families, often resulting in both parents being HIV-positive – and in time falling sick and dying. Poor families have a reduced capacity to deal with the effects of morbidity and mortality than do richer ones, for very obvious reasons. These include the absence of savings and other assets that can cushion the impact of illness and death. The poor are already on the margins of survival, and are unable to deal with the costs associated with HIV/AIDS. These include the cost of drugs – when available – to treat opportunistic infections, the cost of transport to health centres, reduced household productivity through illness and diversion of labour to caring roles, loss of employment through illness and job discrimination, funeral and related costs, and so on. In the longer term such poor households may never recover even their initial level of living, since their capacity is reduced through the loss of productive family members through death and migration, and through the sales of any productive assets they once possessed. As a result, a true process of immiseration is now observable in many parts of the developing world, particularly in southern Africa.

## Feminization of HIV/AIDS

The gendered dimension of deprivation noted earlier becomes particularly significant in considering women's vulnerability to HIV/AIDS. Today, more women than men are dying of HIV/AIDS and the age patterns of infection are significantly different for the two sexes (UNAIDS/WHO 2004). Current trends indicate that existing gendered disparities in access to and control over resources are being exacerbated by AIDS. Resources are defined broadly to include information, decision-making, power, educational opportunities, time, income and other economic resources (such as land, the capacity to inherit, or credit), as well as internal resources (such as self-esteem and confidence). Access is having a resource at hand, while control is the ability to define and make binding decisions about the use of a resource.

There are, however, profound differences in the underlying causes and consequences of HIV/AIDS infections in men and women, reflecting many of the uneven facets of globalization noted earlier. Of particular importance here is the fact that, worldwide, there are increasingly more poor women than poor men, a phenomenon commonly referred to as the 'feminisation of poverty' (Doyal 1995, 2002). As a result, we are seeing differential vulnerability to HIV – with young women showing the highest incidence. This is the direct result of women's lack of autonomy in sexual decision-making and violence against women, both of which intersect with women's poor economic situation which makes negotiation of sexual relations difficult. That society condones such violence, and that women's subordinate position is normative, both attest to women's status as second-class citizens in society.

Imagining for a moment society's response to the full citizen, that is to men, it is hard to envision social acceptance of generalized rape of men; of men having to carry to term a pregnancy that resulted from coerced sex; of men being thrown out of the homes they have created and the relationships they have nurtured simply because they get sick. Yet these are the conditions to which women are subject. As a result, we are seeing differential impacts of HIV, with women more likely to be stigmatized and left without care; more likely to face financial difficulties in accessing treatment or care; more likely to be engaged in a form of income-generation that offers no legal protection and no medical aid. At the community level, women are least likely to be influencing the priorities and budgets of local public institutions, whether local government, health care or schools or local religious institutions or civic groups which shape the 'community' response to HIV/AIDS. Yet, women are most likely to be putting in more time and more strategic thinking on how to create a spiritual, domestic and reproductive environment within which those who are sick and dying, and those who have lost parents, guardians or children have to cope and create futures for themselves. So it is women who are the vast majority of care-givers, both informally and through programmes of care in Africa.

Take Zuki's example in South Africa:

> She works as a security guard at a shopping centre in Johannesburg. Every day she spends two hours getting to work because of the distances apartheid's architects put between city centres and townships that serviced them. Zuki is grateful to have a job. Her two little ones are in KwaZulu-Natal with their grandmother until Zuki can get stable work. She is on a month-to-month

contract with the security company. She watches expensive cars all day, protecting their owner's investments while they work. The company doesn't want to take her on as staff so each month she faces the uncertainty of not having a job the next month. Joining a union is not an option – she's not technically a staff member and anyway, she can't afford to make trouble. Zuki's boyfriend Thabo drives a taxi. Their relationship saves her cash because he drives her to and from work every day – a savings of almost one third of her salary each month. She has another boyfriend at work who often buys her lunch. She has to be careful that Thabo doesn't find out. But last month Zuki discovered that she was HIV-positive. (Poku 2006)

Zuki's story details the vulnerability of millions of women across the developing world who are so economically marginalized that they are reduced to exchanging sex for money, food, shelter and other necessities – with its associated risk of HIV infectivity. In a study of low-income women in long-term relationships in Mumbai, India, the women believed that the economic consequences of leaving a relationship that they perceived as risky were far worse than the risk of contracting HIV/AIDS (Gupta 2000).

## WHERE DO WE GO FROM HERE?

It is clear from the above review that significant changes have been taking place in the world economy that have major social, environmental and public health implications. The globalization of capital is a central feature underpinning these changes. The momentum of globalization is linked to accelerated technological change and consumerism; and to the policies of national governments and global corporations. In its negative aspects, globalization generates strong pressure on nation-states to remove regulations concerned with national protection and the development of local industry. Globalization creates downward pressures on wage rates and tax levels, increases socio-economic inequalities, and can contribute to poor health outcomes and increased mortality. The pursuit of a 'level playing field' for global corporations accentuates other imbalances: between capital and labour, between economy and environment, and between the private power of corporations and the democratic institutions within nation-states. These contradictions make the process of globalization intensely political. Not surprisingly, therefore, responses occur at various levels – global, national and local – and this opens up the possibility of a truly progressive globalization: of human rights, of environmental consciousness, and of a global redress of the causes of health inequalities.

In the face of a pandemic that in a short time has already killed more people than all the wars of the twentieth century combined, we cannot remain silent about the factors that either directly or indirectly contribute to its devastation. To be clear, globalization is not to blame for global AIDS. Blame, if there is any, must reside with humanity's apparent inability to modify sexual behaviour sufficiently to halt the unremitting march of a sexually transmitted disease. But, the underlining societal causes are much broader and familiar and all related to either the process of globalization or the actions of the dominant agents driving the process.

Take the case of poverty: as we have noted, poverty structures not only the contours of the pandemic but also the outcome once an individual is infected with HIV. Thus, until poverty is reduced there will be little progress with either reducing transmission of the virus or creating an enhanced capacity to cope with its socio-economic consequences.

It follows that sustained human development is an essential precondition for any effective response to the HIV/AIDS pandemic. Herein lies the predicament: how to achieve sustainable development in a polarized world, a world underscored by a tectonic struggle between two competing ideological projects: on the one hand, there is the neoliberal project, concerned with first disembedding the market from political influence, and second expanding its reach across social institutions. On the other hand, there is a social-democratic project concerned with the delivery of welfare provisions on a more egalitarian basis rooted in conceptions of social justice. In the context of global marginalization, however, the disconnect between these two ideological projects appears incredibly perverse, even more so, given the fact that both project purports to advance a universal notion of right to basic services.

### References and Further Reading

ADB 2002: *African Development Report 2002.*

Albrow, M. 1996: *The Global Age: States and Society beyond Modernity.* Cambridge: Cambridge University Press.

Allen, J. and Hammett, C. 1998: *A Shrinking World? Global Unevenness and Inequality.* Oxford: Oxford University Press.

Avert 2005: United Kingdom HIV/AIDS statistics summary, at www.avert. org accessed 1 September 2005.

Baylies, C. and Bujra, J. (eds) 2000: *AIDS, Sexuality and Gender in Africa: Collective Strategies and Struggles in Tanzania and Zambia.* London: Routledge.

Berwick, D., Sykes, R. and Achmat, Z. 2002: 'We all have AIDS': Case for reducing the cost of HIV drugs to zero. Commentary: The reality of treating HIV and AIDS in poor countries. Commentary: Most South Africans cannot afford anti-HIV drugs. *British Medical Journal*, 324, 214–18.

Cheru, F. 2000: Debt relief and social investment: linking the HIPC Initiative to the HIV/AIDS epidemic in Africa: the case of Zambia. *Review of African Political Economy*, 86, 519–35.

CHGA 2004: *Impact of HIV/AIDS on Rural Livelihoods and Food Security.* Addis Ababa: UN Economic Commission for Africa.

Chirwa, W. 1998: Aliens and AIDS in southern Africa: the Malawi–South Africa debate. *African Affairs (Lond.)*, 97, 53–79.

Chossudovsky, M. 1996: Global impoverishment and the IMF–World Bank. *Third World Resurgence*, 74.

Cohen, D. 2002: Human capital and the HIV epidemic in sub-Saharan Africa. ILO Programme on HIV/AIDS and the World of Work (June).

Cohen, R. 1997: Diasporas and the nation-state: from victims to challengers. In D. Graham (ed.), *Redefining Security: Population Movements and National Security*, Westport, Conn.: Praeger, 51–66.

Collins, J. and Rau, B. 2000: *AIDS in the Context of Development*. Geneva: UNRISD/UNAIDS.

Decosas, J. and Adrien, A. 1997: Migration and HIV. *AIDS*, 11.

Dicken, P. 1992: *Global Shifts: The Internationalization of Economic Activity*. London: Paul Chapman.

Doyal, L. 1995: *What Makes Women Sick: Gender and the Political Economy of Health*. Basingstoke: Macmillan.

Doyal, L. 2002: Putting gender into health and globalization debates: new perspectives and old challenges. *Third World Quarterly*, 23.

Engh, I. E., Stloukal, L. and Guerny, J. de 2000: *HIV/AIDS in Namibia: The Impact on the Livestock Sector*. Rome: Food and Agriculture Organization of the United Nations.

Falk, R. 1990: Culture, modernism, postmodernism: a challenge to international relations. In J. Chay (ed.), *Culture and International Relations*, New York: Praeger.

Falk, R. 1995: *On Humane Governance*. Cambridge: Polity.

Giddens, A. 1990: *The Consequences of Modernity*. Cambridge: Polity.

Gupta, G. R. 2000: Gender, Sexuality and HIV/AIDS: The what, the why and the how. *Can HIV AIDS Policy Law Rev.*, 5(4), 86–93.

Hope, S. R. K. 2001: Africa's HIV/AIDS crisis in development context. *International Relations*, 15, 15–36.

Hugo, G. 1997: The globalisation of population movements: legal migrants. In D. Graham (ed.), *Redefining Security: Population Movements and National Security*, Westport, Conn.: Praeger.

Lipumba, N., 1994: *Africa Beyond Adjustment*. Washington, D.C.: Overseas Development Council.

Lurie, M., Williams, B., Sturm, A. W., Garnett, G., Mkaya, D. and Karim, S. S. A. 2000: HIV discordance among migrant and non-migrant couples in South Africa. UNAIDS (July).

Morar, N. S., Ramjee, G. and Karim, S. S. A. 1998: Safe sex practices among sex workers at risk of HIV infection. Paper written for UNAIDS.

Mutangadura, G. B. 2000: Household welfare impacts of adult females in Zimbabwe: implications for policy and program development. Paper presented at the AIDS and Economics Symposium IAEN (7–8 July).

National Intelligence Council 2002: The Next Wave of HIV/AIDS: Nigeria, Ethiopia, Russia, India and China, National Intelligence Council (NIC), September.

Orubuloye, I., Caldwell, J. and Caldwell, P. 1993: African women's control over their sexuality in an era of AIDS. *Social Science and Medicine*, 37, 859–72.

Orubuloye, I., Caldwell, J. and Caldwell, P. 1997: Perceived male sexual needs and male sexual behaviour in southwest Nigeria. *Social Science and Medicine*, 44, 1195–1207.

Poku, N. K. 2001a: Africa's AIDS crisis in context: 'how the poor are dying', *Third World Quarterly*, 22 (2), 191–204.

Poku, N. K. 2001b: AIDS in Africa: an overview. *International Relations*, 15, 5–14.

Poku, N. K. 2002a: Global pandemics: AIDS. In D. Held and A. McGrew (eds), *Governing the Global Polity*, Cambridge: Polity.

Poku, N. K. 2002b: Poverty, debt and Africa's HIV/AIDS crisis. *International Affairs*, 78, 531–46.

Poku, N. K. 2006: *AIDS in Africa: How the Poor are Dying*. Cambridge: Polity.

Poku, N. and Graham, D. 2000: *Migration, Globalisation and Human Security*. London: Routledge.

Sachs, J. D. 2001: Macroeconomics and health: investing in health for economic development. Paper presented to Gro Harlem Brundtland, Director-General of the World Health Organization (20 December).

Schoepf, B. 1993: AIDS action-research with women in Kinshasa, Zaire. *Social Science and Medicine*, 37, 1401–13.

Seidel, G. 1993: Women at risk: gender and HIV in Africa. *Disasters*, 17, 133–42.

Smith, S. and Cohen, D. 2000: *Gender, Development and the HIV Epidemic*, UNDP (October).

South Africa Department of Health 2005: *National HIV and Syphilis Antenatal Sero-Prevalence Survey in South Africa 2004*. Pretoria: Directorate, Health Systems Research, Research Coordination and Epidemiology.

Stillwagon, E. 2000: HIV transmission in Latin America: comparison with Africa and policy implications. *South African Journal of Economics*, 5, 985–1011.

UN/DESA 2005: 'World Population Prospects. The 2004 Revision', United Nations Department of Economic and Social Affairs, Population Division, New York.

UNAIDS 2002: HIV/AIDS Fact Sheet: High Income Countries, UNAIDS (October).

UNAIDS/WHO 2004: AIDS epidemic update (December). Geneva: UNAIDS/WHO.

UNCTAD 2000: *Foreign Investment Report*. Geneva: UNCTAD.

UNDP 1999: *Human Development Report 1999*. United Nations Development Programme.

UNDP 2001: *Human Development Report 2001*. United Nations Development Programme.

UNDP 2002: *Human Development Report*. Oxford: Oxford University Press.

UNDP 2004: *Human Development Report*. Oxford: Oxford University Press.

UNFPA 2002: *State of World Population 2002: People, Poverty, and Possibilities*. United Nations Population Fund (November).

UNHCR 1998: *Refugees and Others of Concern to UNHCR: 1998 Statistical Overview*, United Nations High Commisioner for Refugees.

Wallace, L. (ed.) 1999: *Africa: Adjusting to the Challenge of Globalization*. Washington, D.C.: International Monetary Fund Publication Service.

Whitehead, M., Dahlgren, G. and Evans, T. 2001: Equity and health sector reforms: can low-income countries escape the medical poverty trap? *The Lancet*, 358, 833–6.

Whiteside, A. 2002: Poverty and HIV/AIDS in Africa. *Third World Quarterly*, 23 (2) (April), 313–33 (special issue: Global Health and Governance).

Whiteside, A. and Sunter, C. 2000: *AIDS: The Challenge for South Africa*. Cape Town: Human & Rousseau Tafelberg.

WHO/UNAIDS 2003: *Epidemic Spreading Rapidly in New Areas of the World*.

Geneva: World Health Organization and Joint United Nations Programme on HIV/AIDS.

WHO-AFRO 2003: *HIV/AIDS Epidemiological Surveillance Update for the WHO African Region 2002*. World Health Organization Regional Office for Africa: Harare.

Williams, B. G., Gilgen, D., Campbell, C. M., Taljaard, D. and MacPhail, C. 2000: *The Natural History of HIV/AIDS in South Africa: A Biomedical and Social Survey*. Carletonville, South Africa: Center for Scientific and Industrial Research (July).

World Bank 1994: *World Development Report*. Washington, D.C.: World Bank.

World Bank 2000a: *Assessing Globalization*. Washington, D.C.: World Bank.

World Bank 2000b: *Intensifying Action Against HIV/AIDS in Africa: Responding to a Development Crisis*. Washington, D.C.: World Bank.

# 8  Transformations and Constrictions: Globalization and Human Rights in the Third World

*Bonny Ibhawoh*

*Global markets, global technology, global ideas and global solidarity can enrich the lives of people everywhere. The challenge remains how to ensure that the benefits are shared equitably and that global interdependence works for the rights and welfare of all people – not just to profit a few. In this chapter, Bonny Ibhawoh argues that the threats to human rights posed by economic globalization risk outweighing its accidental benefits. The chapter delves beyond economics to recognize and address the ramifications of more subtle, but no less significant, 'bottom-up' dimensions of the phenomenon of globalization. He argues for more efforts to be made to enhance the ability of Third World states and societies to negotiate their own terms within a global economy as it relates to their basic rights.*

None of the developments [of globalization] in itself is necessarily incompatible with the principles of the Covenant on Economic, Social and Cultural Rights . . . Taken together, however, and if not complemented by appropriate additional policies, globalization risks downgrading the central place accorded to human rights by the Charter of the United Nations in general and the International Bill of Human Rights in particular. (UNHCHR 1999)

## INTRODUCTION

The phenomenon of globalization has been subjected to a number of conflicting and sometimes contradictory interpretations. Much of the discussion on globalization since the term gained currency in the middle of the last century has focused on its 'tangible' economic manifestations. Although most scholars acknowledge the multifaceted nature of globalization, there remains a disproportionate concern with its economic dimension – the operations of globalizing economic institutions, international financial institutions (IFIs) and transnational corporations (TNCs); the marked integration of global markets, labour and production; the phenomenal impact of what has been described as 'McWorld' (Friedman 2000) and the obliteration of the 'tyranny of distance' by technological and communication revolutions (Holton 1998: 8). This has created a new orthodoxy about the economic dimensions of globalization that exalts it above all other human values or phenomena. However as several scholars have emphasized, globalization is not just a notion that defines the process of world transformation into one relatively borderless arena of economic life. It is also a notion that defines simultaneous processes of transformation in social, cultural and other subjective matters. Unfortunately, the preoccupation with its economic dimensions has tended to obscure these other important ramifications of globalization.

One possible explanation for this bias in the dominant modes of thinking about globalization is the tendency among scholars, policy makers and other commentators to see globalization from a top-down perspective – as something that comes from above in the form of multinational firms, world markets and international capital flows. Intrinsic in this, is the assumption that the globalizing initiatives originate at the top with the powerful players like multinational corporations affecting the conditions of subaltern actors like Third World workers who have little or no say in the globalizing process (Streeten 1999: 11). This unidirectional view of globalization overlooks important globalizing impulses that come from below such as environmental advocacy movements, women's movements and human rights struggles. This chapter proceeds from the premise that there is need for a more holistic approach to understanding globalization. This must go beyond economics to recognize and address the ramifications of more subtle, but no less significant, 'bottom-up' dimensions of the phenomenon of globalization. There is a need to bring globalization down from the 'rarefied and glorified atmosphere of corporate boardrooms, and home to the daily realities of ordinary human beings' (UN 2000:10). Examining the links between human rights and globalization is one way of bringing down globalization to the level of ordinary people in developing societies.

## ESTABLISHING THE LINK BETWEEN GLOBALIZATION AND HUMAN RIGHTS

One defining feature of globalization has been the emergence of an international moral order in the form of recognized international human rights standards. The universal human rights movement epitomizes an important trend in the globalization of ideas and knowledge. It represents the globalization of thought and consciousness, with people in different parts of the world increasingly concerning themselves with common socio-political issues like human rights, environmental protection and biodiversity in a way that transcends spatial borders. The impact of the phenomenon of globalization on human rights *ideas* and *conditions* around the world has begun to attract the attention of some scholars, policy makers and even the media. A number of studies have addressed the impacts of economic globalization on human rights (McCorquodale 1999; Brysk 2002), the globalization of human rights (Coicaud et al. 2003) and the feminist perspective on globalization and human rights (Orford 1998;

Rowbotham and Linkogl 2001). There is also a growing recognition of the link between globalization and human rights at the level of international policy-making. In 2001 the United Nations Sub-Commission on Human Rights passed a resolution titled 'Globalization and its impact on the full enjoyment of human rights'. The resolution expressed concern about the impact of globalization and the liberalization of trade on agricultural products on the 'promotion and protection of the right to food for members of vulnerable communities'. It reaffirmed the 'importance and relevance of human rights obligations in all areas of governance and development, including international and regional trade, investment and financial policies and practices'. The resolution drew particular attention to the human rights obligations of the World Bank, the IMF, the OECD and the WHO (UNHCHR 2001).

Earlier in 1999 the Public Broadcasting Service (PBS) in the United States released a widely acclaimed documentary entitled 'Globalization and human rights'. Like the UN report, the documentary aimed at exploring the human rights implication of globalization on developing countries in the South. It focused on human rights issues such as the uprisings against IFI and TNC activities in Indonesia and Nigeria, the massive lay-offs of miners in South Africa and worldwide protests against child labour, linking them with the forces of globalization – 'the economic engine that is transforming the world in its own image' (PBS 1999). What both the UN report, the PBS documentary and recent scholarly works call attention to is a growing realization that far from being a purely economic phenomenon, globalization has important ramifications for human rights conditions around the world.

Most writers characterize the link between globalization and human rights, as a 'double-edged sword'. Globalization simultaneously creates opportunities and represents challenges for the international protection of human rights (McCorquodale 1999: 763). Globalization threatens human rights in developing societies but at the same time creates unprecedented opportunities to protect and promote these rights (Brysk and Gonzalez-Cueva 2000). These views are based largely on the evaluations of the human rights implications of economic globalization. They focus mainly on the response of the human rights movement to the adverse economic and social consequences of economic globalization. This presents the globalization/human rights dynamic simply as a dialectic of action and reaction, initiative and consequence. This framework overlooks a third level of the globalization/human rights dynamic – the universal human rights movement as a manifestation of the globalization of consciousness in itself rather than merely as a reaction to economic globalization.

I would argue that rather than being a double-sided affair, the globalization/human rights dynamic in the Third World actually manifests as a 'triple-edged sword'. First, there is the process of 'globalization' (or to use the language of the discourse, 'universalization') of human rights that has occurred quite independently of economic globalization. Since the end of the Second World War and the adoption of the Universal Declaration of Human Rights by the UN, the idea and language of human rights have come to assume unprecedented global appeal and significance, shaping political and social movements across the world. On no other theme is the 'globalization of consciousness' more asserted and contested than on the theme of human rights. Human rights have also become a veritable battlefield where the tensions and contradictions of globalization have been elaborately played out in the debate over universalism and cultural relativism. But while the universalism versus cultural relativism debate rages in academic and policy-making circles, grass-roots social movements in the Third World are increasingly drawing on globalized human rights discourse to articulate and legitimize local political, social and economic demands. This aspect of the link between globalization and human rights has occurred quite independently of economic globalization and may be termed the *transformative potential* of the globalization/human rights dynamic.

The second level of the link between globalization and human rights centres on the effects of economic globalization on the objective conditions of human rights in the Third World. This aspect of the globalization/human rights dynamic has received the most attention. It focuses on the impacts of international trade, investment and finance; IFI-inspired neoliberal economic reforms and free-trade zones like the *Maquiladoras* of Latin America, on economic and social rights conditions in the Third World. Related to this is how globalization impacts popular participation in governance, state-society relations and accountability. On these issues, there appears to be a growing consensus that economic globalization has benefited the global North at the expense of the South. Economic globalization has aggravated poverty and social deprivation in many Third World counties, narrowing or constricting the range of rights and liberties that they enjoy. This may be termed the *constrictive reality* of the globalization/ human rights dynamic.

The third level of the globalization/human rights dynamic borders on how the human rights movement in the Third World has responded specifically to the constrictive effects of economic globalization. As economic globalization threatens human rights, it is also creating new opportunities to respond to these threats and protect human rights. Human rights activists in the Third World are appropriating the 'tools' of globalization such as the Internet, the global media and international NGO networks to counter the adverse effects of economic globalization on their societies. This may be described as the *reactive impulse* of the globalization/human rights dynamic.

Although the reactive and transformative aspects of this dynamic are related, the main difference is that while the former refers to the global spread of human rights ideas and consciousness (which have proceeded quite independently of economic globalization in certain parts of the Third World), the latter refers to trends in the human rights movements that have emerged mainly in response to the economic and social difficulties produced by economic globalization. For example in Latin America and some parts of Asia where international trade and global investment have been pronounced, the main thrust of human rights activism has been reactive – responding to the new challenges posed by globalizing economic institutions and policies like the poor working conditions and labour standards, union rights in the free-trade zones and child labour. However, in much of Africa, where the effects of the global market have been at best peripheral, the link between globalization and human rights are slightly different. The main impact of globalization on human rights in these societies has been the increased ability of local activists to draw on the universal human rights discourse and international networks of activists to promote their agendas. In many parts of Africa, where the vast majority of the populace is based in the rural areas eking out subsistence existence, the main human rights issues are not working conditions in 'sweatshops' because there are no sweatshops. Sub-Saharan Africa remains largely unpenetrated by global capital. The position of Africa in the economic globalization process evokes the old aphorism that the only thing worse than being exploited is not being exploited. A French diplomat is reported to have stated that economically speaking, if the whole of black Africa, with the exception of South Africa, were to suddenly disappear it would have little or no effect on global markets and financial systems (quoted in Chege 1992: 148). Such is the marginal role of African economies in the world even in an era of unprecedented global economic integration. This further underscores the limitations of seeing the phenomenon of globalization solely or even essentially as an economic phenomenon. In some parts of the Third World globalization has manifested more in the transformation of consciousness than of economies. Apart from a few exceptions, local human rights activists in Africa have been concerned more with state violations and cultural limitations on individual liberties rather than on the activities of TNCs and IFIs. The global human rights discourse has provided local activities with an effective means of addressing issues like female genital mutilation (FGM), ethnic minority rights, press censorship and arbitrary arrests and detentions. Under these circumstances, the globalization/human rights dynamic resonates more in its potential to transform local socio-cultural and political conditions than as a reaction to the adverse effects of the global trade and investment.

The paradox of globalization at all these levels, however, is that while the 'globalization of consciousness' in the form of the universal human rights movement has empowered subaltern groups in the Third World like workers, women and ethnic minorities, the 'globalization of labour and markets' has had exactly the opposite effect. Economic globalization has, for the most part, furthered the alienation and marginalization of these groups. The questions that arise are: how do we explain this paradox of globalization? How can people and societies in the Third World take advantage of the transformative potential of the globalization of consciousness in the human rights movement while redressing the devastating impact of economic globalization on their rights?

## TRANSFORMATIVE POTENTIALS: GLOBALIZATION AND 'UNIVERSAL' HUMAN RIGHTS

Long before the phenomenon of globalization gained currency, the human rights movement had laid claim to a universalizing/globalizing mission. This is evident in the assertion that the regime of rights and freedoms established through the Universal Declaration of Human Rights (UDHR) in 1948 – and related UN human rights conventions – extended beyond national or regional concerns to set a global agenda for human rights protection (UN 2000: 6). Indeed, the inauguration of the UDHR marked the first time in world history that certain fundamental rights and freedoms were set forth, at an international forum, as inalienable values to which *all* individuals were entitled simply by virtue of their humanity. This ideal marked a shift from earlier notions and instruments of rights because, at least in theory, it was applicable to every human being irrespective of nationality, race, gender and social status. The UDHR affirmed human rights as a global project stating that the 'inherent dignity of all members of the human family is the foundation of freedom, justice and peace in the world'. Global freedom and peace, it declared, is 'linked to the recognition of fundamental rights, towards which, every human being aspires''. This principle has become widely acknowledged as the cornerstone of the contemporary human rights movement.

At its adoption in 1948, the UDHR was heralded as 'a world milestone in the long struggle for human rights' and 'a magna carta for all humanity' (UN 1997). However, the UDHR's claim to universality and global legitimacy was significantly undermined by the fact that even as it affirmed the rights of all humanity in 1948, half of the world's peoples still lived under colonial domination. Added to this was the fact that most colonized peoples were, at the time, not represented at the United Nations and had no opportunity of making any input into the preparation of the UDHR. The exclusion of the voices of these mostly Third World peoples in the process of drawing up the UDHR remains one of the strongest challenges to its claim to universality. It has become a powerful tool in the hands of those who argue that the UDHR represents mainly Western values and bears little relevance to non-Western, Third World societies (Cobbah 1987; De Bary 1998).

In spite of these challenges to the globalizing claim of the UDHR, the human rights movement can today lay claim to some level of global legitimacy if not acceptance. At the 1993 United Nations World Conference on Human Rights held in Vienna, 171 countries, including many Third World states, reaffirmed their commitment to the Universal Declaration of Human Rights and reiterated the 'universality, indivisibility and interdependence of human rights'. Moreover, beyond the level of states and international politics, the human rights movement has also been embraced by grass-roots movements around the world and particularly in the Third World. In the past five decades there has been an increasing and unprecedented globalization of the idea and ideals of human rights. These ideals have the potential of transforming political and social conditions in the Third World.

The advent of information globalization through avenues like CNN and the Internet has strengthened the human rights movements in many developing societies by transforming the nature of individual participation in discourses on foreign and domestic politics. These changes have boosted the capacity for individual autonomy, and, in consequence, fuelled the demand for more personal rights and liberties (Franck 2001).

Information globalization has brought down many of the walls that limited the movement and reach of people in the Third World and given more power to individuals and grass-roots movements. In this respect, globalization has created not just superpower states, IFIs and TNCs but also 'super-empowered' individuals and NGOs (Friedman 1999). Working within human rights and pro-democracy movements across the Third World, these super-empowered individuals and NGOs have been able to act directly on a world stage to challenge governments, corporations and social traditions.

Across Africa, NGOs are increasingly drawing on globalized human rights discourses in their advocacy for political participation and social welfare issues. Globalization has provided new discursive frameworks and spaces for these groups to address local issues from worldwide perspectives. For instance, NGOs working for women's rights across Africa – whether in the form of church councils as in Swaziland, Kenya and Namibia or as groups of women lawyers in Ghana, Uganda and Nigeria – are using the global discourse on women's rights to address local issues like FGM and property laws that discriminate against women. In Ghana, the local branch of the International Federation of Women Lawyers has been working to ensure that local laws and cultural practices are reformed to conform to global standards on women's rights. One of the organization's declared objectives is to make 'non-literate women literate in modern international laws that protect women's rights' (FIDA, 2002). Similarly, in Swaziland, one of the dominant NGOs working to promote women's welfare, the Council of Swaziland Churches (CSC) uses the global human rights debate to criticize cultural practices that discriminate against women (Jensen and Poulsen 1993: 16–17).

Globalization has made it easier for these groups to use universal human rights discourse to address domestic concerns in a way that would not have been possible five decades ago. The increased information flows and advances in communication technology that have come with globalization have facilitated the building of networks, alliances and coalitions among human rights movements in the Third World. New institutions, information and organizations have contributed to new levels of collective mobilization. As a result of information globalization and new links between local and international activists, issues like FGM which affect Third World women, many of whom are voiceless within their own patriarchal societies, now command international attention and have become central to the global feminist and women's rights agenda. In other areas of human rights advocacy and the environmental protection, international NGOs such as Amnesty International, Greenpeace and the World Wildlife Fund are increasingly able to work with local groups to mobilize people directly for political ends. Once fragmented, social movements in the Third World are becoming part of an emerging global civil society that exists independently from traditional patterns of interstate relations.

In Latin America, local human rights activists have collaborated across national borders to form new web-based human rights organizations like Derechos Human Rights which have been hugely successful in their action campaigns and as documentation resource for human rights groups across the subcontinent.[2] Another example of such international coalitions in Latin America is the Argentina-based Federation of Families of the Disappeared (FEDEFAM), founded in the 1980s to unite national and international NGOs working to promote political rights and to draw attention to the fate of the 'disappeared'. Although there are concerns that these trends in globalization have established the dominance of a Western oriented, neoliberal view of human rights (Evans 2001: 415), many agree that these NGO coalitions have transformed the mobilizing power of human rights movements in Third World. In this regard, the link between globalization and human rights in the Third World is most apparent in its potential to transform social and political conditions by empowering non-governmental sectors. However, the globalization of knowledge and consciousness, whether in the human rights or environmental arena, represents only one dimension of the globalization/human rights dynamic. The other dimension has to do with the globalization of capital and markets where human rights are more directly linked to the activities of globalizing economic institutions in the Third World.

## CONSTRICTIVE REALITIES: THE HUMAN RIGHTS COSTS OF ECONOMIC GLOBALIZATION

Much of the discussion on the effects of globalization on human rights has focused on the point that economic globalization has resulted in the deterioration of living conditions in many Third World countries and widened domestic and global inequalities. Indeed the integration of global production has been accompanied by the growing integration of the global elite and the further marginalization of the masses. Globalization worsens economic inequality when the economic interests that are protected by the institutions of globalization are those of the rich and economically powerful – usually elite urban males (McCorquodale 1999: 748) Even in the poorest of countries, local elites are becoming increasingly interconnected with the global elite through satellite dishes and the Internet while the poverty-stricken majority are more disconnected and fragmented. At the global level, the benefits and costs of economic globalization have divided the world more starkly into two halves – a prosperous 'core' (mainly in the West), which enjoys much of the benefits of global trade and investments, and an increasingly impoverished Third World 'periphery', which bears much the cost of economic globalization. Even advocates of globalization like the Nobel Prize-winning economist and former Vice-President of the World Bank, Joseph Stiglitz, concede that the process of globalization is clearly 'not working for the interests of the world's poor' (CCEIA 2002: 1).[3]

This view is not merely a matter of speculation. Available statistical data bear out this fact. In spite of the enormous benefits accruing to TNCs and some industrialized countries from global trade and investment, poverty, illiteracy and disease are on the rise in much of the Third World. In its Human Development Report for 1999, *Globalization with a Human Face*, the UNDP called attention to the stark disparities between the rich and poor in global opportunity. According to the UNDP, the decade of the 1990s witnessed the 'increasing concentration of income, resources and wealth among people, corporations and countries'. In 1997, the richest 20 per cent of the world's population living in Western countries accounted for 86 per cent of the worlds GDP while the poorest 20 per cent living in the Third World accounted for only 1 per cent (UNDP 1999: 2). These grim statistics underscore the connections between globalizing forces of inequality and human rights conditions in the Third World. More progress has been made in norms, standards, policies and institutions for open global markets than for people and their rights. Deteriorating living conditions in Third World countries have meant that a vast majority of the people are denied such basic rights as the right to food, shelter and fair working conditions which are stipulated in the UDHR and other international human rights covenants.

However, not everyone agrees that economic globalization has negative impacts on human rights conditions. Some policy makers and business leaders contend that globalization actually aids the cause of human rights. James Robinson, a former head of an American TNC, argues that by giving jobs to people in developing countries at salary levels that they never would have had access to before, globalization actually improves their human rights conditions (PBS 1999: 4). Moreover, the greater integration of Third World economies into the international community enlarges the role of the private sector in developing societies. This promotes a stable legal environment and restructures the state's relations with its citizens. In this sense, it is argued, globalization and international economic cooperation widens political participation and promotes political rights (Monshipouri 1995). Related to this is the argument that globalized economic institutions such as the World Bank and IMF tend to demand that certain conditions of 'democratic governance' must exist in a state before they invest. These investment conditions, which sometimes include the acceptance of the rule of law, accountability and transparency in government, ultimately lead to the protection of human rights. The most frequently cited example of this is Malawi, where in 1992 all the major donor states threatened to stop investment in the country until President Kamuzu Banda dealt with gross breaches of human rights in that country (McCorquodale 1999: 754).

True, World Bank and IMF 'good governance' conditionalities introduced in the 1980s and 1990s have succeeded in twisting the arms of some authoritarian regimes in the Third World to carry out marginal political reforms, but can this alone be a valid basis for concluding that globalization promotes human rights? Would this be an accurate 'balance sheet' of the impact of globalization on human rights in the Third World? I would think not. For one thing, examples like Malawi have been the exceptions rather than the norm. The IMF and the World Bank have not pushed their 'good governance' conditionalities quite as forcefully as they have pushed their economic structural adjustment programmes. Moreover, the argument that these good governance conditionalities actually translate into an improvement in the objective human rights conditions of local people is at best conjectural. Focusing on the persuasive influence of World Bank conditionalities seems a narrow approach to the evaluation of the impact of economic globalization on human rights. A much broader approach would be to examine not just IFI conditionalities, but also the full ramifications of the activities of globalizing economic institutions – IFIs, TNCs and the WTO – on economic and social conditions in the Third World societies.

## THE IMPACT OF GLOBALIZATION ON SOCIAL AND ECONOMIC RIGHTS

The IMF, World Bank, the OECD and the WTO have been described as the 'practical manifestations of globalization in its trade and commercial aspects' (UNHCHR 2001). Their globalizing economic activities generally produce winners and losers. In some countries, World Bank-inspired economic reforms and WTO regulation have led to economic growth and raised national GDPs. In most countries however, these reforms and regulations have resulted in economic crisis and a precipitous decline in living standards. In many parts of the Third World, WTO regulations in particular have produced more losers than winners, spelling significant implications for human rights. As one UN report clearly outlined, the activities of the WTO do not simply end with trade and commerce – they also have 'serious human rights implications' (UN 2000: 6)

The main threats to human rights and security posed by global trade and financial regulation in developing societies include job and income insecurity, health insecurity, political insecurity and environmental insecurity (UNDP 1999: 4). These are often the direct result of strict funding conditions and structural adjustment programmes imposed on developing nations by international financial institutions. Such IMF and World Bank-inspired structural adjustment programmes (SAPs) and lending conditionalities typically include the devaluation of national currencies, which results in high inflation; market liberalization; cuts in public wages and social sector programmes; and the elimination of subsidies and price controls. These 'reforms' and conditionalities adversely affect the living conditions of the poor and vulnerable sections of the population.

In Africa the liberalization of labour markets has left millions of breadwinners unemployed, while the introduction of fees in the delivery of formerly free social services like health and education have raised the cost of living. In circumstances where there are no reliable social welfare systems – as in most African countries – millions of dependants have become destitute or 'economic refugees' in the already overcrowded urban centres. Mass retrenchments in the public sector swell the ranks of the unemployed, creating social tension and a discontented and restive population. For instance, the drastic fall in the price of South African gold in 1997 – a result of international financial speculation – led to a crisis in the gold-mining industry. Thousands of South African gold miners found themselves out of work and those that remained faced an uncertain future in the weakened gold-mining industry. In Tanzania, the devaluation of the shilling by 26 per cent in 1984, the de-subsidization of the staple maize meal, and the relaxation of import regulations in line with IMF conditionalities had a disastrous impact on the living conditions of the vast population of rural and urban poor (ARB 1984: 275).

In Asia, the devastating impact of economic globalization became particularly evident in the economic crisis that engulfed the continent of the late 1990s. Two of the hardest hit countries were Indonesia and Thailand, which a few years earlier had been hailed as a miracle of globalization. The Asian crisis proved that the miracle had been a myth. In Indonesia, the local currency lost 26 per cent of its value in one day. Local people saw their savings wiped out and their standard of living drop precipitously as workers could no longer afford basic necessities for their subsistence. Many saw the widespread rioting that subsequently broke out as a protest against globalization.

Increasingly, economic decision-making is being taken away from Third World governments and put in the hands of foreign financial 'experts' in globalized economic institutions. This often means that people and their elected representatives in developing countries become less involved in making important economic decisions affecting their lives (McCorquodale 1999: 746). Thus, the globalizing activities of IFIs in the Third World raise questions not only about economic and social rights but also about the right to political participation and self-determination.

With TNCs, the major human rights issues that arise in connection with their globalizing activities in the Third World are labour and environmental conditions in the export processing zones (EPZs) or special economic zones (SEZs) where they operate. Since the 1980s, the EPZs have been created in Third World countries by governments eager to attract foreign investments. These EPZs mainly comprise labour-intensive industries in search of cheap Third World labour. Although TNCs working in the Third World EPZs have quantitatively increased work opportunities, these have come at the expense of poor, and sometimes inhuman, working conditions. The shrinking role of the state in national economies along with the deregulation of the labour market, de-unionization of workers, and decentralization of wage bargaining, have contributed to a progressive decline in working conditions in these industries. Women, who dominate the workforce of the EPZs, have been particularly vulnerable to these difficulties. In Latin America, the semi-skilled, poorly paid women who make up 80 per cent of the workers employed under deplorable conditions in the *maquiladoras* (export assembly plants) bear many of the problems of globalization. UN Secretary-General Kofi Annan has described this trend as the global 'feminisation of poverty' (UN 1999; 19).

Two issues that particularly underscore the link between global trade and human rights are environmental pollution and the use of child labour. In many parts of Asia like India, Bangladesh and Thailand, the use of child labour either directly by TNCs or their local contractors have come to symbolize the dark side of globalization. Anti-globalizers often draw attention to the use of child labour and the 'sweatshop' phenomenon as examples of burdens of economic globalization on Third World societies. In Nigeria, the campaign by the Movement for the Survival of the Ogoni People (MOSOP) and other minority ethnic groups of the Niger Delta against the environmental pollution caused by TNCs prospecting for oil in their land, also symbolizes the link between the forces of globalization and human rights.

That the globalizing activities of TNCs and IFIs sometimes have negative fallout on living conditions in Third World countries is hardly a matter of contention. However, questions have been raised as to whether these are human rights issues. Can we really link the socio-economic and political fallout of globalization with the violation of specific human rights guarantees under international and domestic laws? This question arises out of a tendency to see the negative consequences of economic globalization merely as the inevitable 'social costs' of economic growth, which can be overcome with time, rather than as human rights issues. It is also informed by the tendency to draw a distinction between civil and political rights on the one hand and social and economic rights on the other. The assumption is that civil and political rights are more important than economic and social rights, and since globalization has a more direct impact on economic and social life, it has little to do with 'real' human rights issues. This assumption is erroneous. The UN Vienna Declaration and Programme for Action on Human Rights (1993) emphasizes that human rights are 'indivisible, interdependent and interrelated'. Economic and social rights are integral parts of the international human rights corpus. In addition to its explicit civil and political rights provisions, the Universal Declaration of Human Rights affirms such economic and social rights as the right to an adequate standard of living, the right to work and just and favourable conditions of work, and the right to education. The UDHR also recognizes the right of everyone to a social and international order in which the rights and freedoms set forth in it can be fully realized (UN 1948, article 28). The International Covenant on Economic, Social and Cultural Rights (ICESCR) elaborates on these economic and social rights.

A related question that arises is whether non-state actors like global economic institutions have any obligation under international law to promote human rights. Underlying this question is the assumption that human rights are the obligations of state rather than non-state actors. This, too, is erroneous. Although states are the primary concern of international human rights law, the obligation to protect and promote universal human rights is not limited to them. The UDHR calls on every individual and *organ of society* (including IFIs and TNCs) to take action to secure the universal and effective recognition of human rights.[4] Similarly, the UN's 'Guidelines on evaluating violations of economic, social and cultural rights' adopted in Maastricht in 1997 recognizes that violation of economic and social rights can result though omission or commission of both state and non-state actors. Human rights violations can result either from the direct transgressions of states and TNCs, or from the failure of states to exercise control over the operations of TNCs. The guidelines also state that given the far-reaching impact of their activities on the lives of a great number of people around the world, TNCs and IFIs cannot absolve themselves from the obligation to uphold international human rights standards.

## GLOBALIZATION AND POLITICAL RIGHTS

Apart from the direct impacts of IFI and TNC activities on economic and social rights in Third World countries, there are also important ramifications for the right to self-determination and the enjoyment of civil and political rights. Several studies have linked IMF and World Bank inspired SAPs and lending conditionalities to political repression and authoritarianism in the Third World (Bangura 1986; Hutchful 1987). Because IMF and World Bank adjustment programmes and lending conditionalities create economic difficulties for local peoples and are thus unpopular, they predispose governments in Third World countries, many of which already have problems of legitimacy, to resort to the excessive use of repression and coercion to enforce them (Rusk 1986). Claude Ake argues that there is no way that Third World regimes can implement structural adjustment programmes recommended by global financial institutions without resorting to some level of political repression (Ake 1989: 62).

The structures of globalization and the pressures they place on vulnerable Third World states sometimes make repression and the circumscription of political rights and freedoms inevitable. For instance, following the devastating impact of the Asian financial crisis on Indonesia in the late 1990s the International Financial Community promised the government a $40 billion bailout on the condition that Indonesia restructured its economy and drastically cut subsidies on social programmes. Under this pressure the government increased fuel prices by 70 per cent and started a programme of massive lay-off of civil servants. The result was an outbreak of popular public protest which the Suharto government tried to suppress with armed force, arbitrary arrests and detentions and press censorship until it was overthrown in 1998.

In this regard, globalization represents a surge in the power of capital over social classes which ultimately results in the narrowing of the scope of democracy and popular participation in national politics. It represents a world-view through which the transnational elite attempts to reduce the scope of national and regional decision-making, blocking any alternatives to the patterns of social organization it projects. Economic globalization espouses the triumph of the neoliberal political paradigm and, as some scholars argue, the 'end of ideology'. The governing institutions of economic globalization such as the IFIs reward governments and countries that play by the rules of neoliberalism with investment and credit. Those that dare to differ and explore alternative paths are punished with divestments and exclusion. Thus globalization, which has created barrier-free global space for market networks, has also created a rigid ideological boundary which ultimately imposes limits on the scope of local participation in the decision-making process and people's right to self-determination (Mengisteab 1999; Latham 1997: 56)

Because global investment and marketing decisions are being made by IFIs and TNCs beyond the control of states, many Third World governments are unable to control macroeconomic monetary policies. This ultimately affects the ability of people to influence their governments since their governments have no control in the first place.

For instance, facing hyperinflation and economic collapse in 2000, the government of Ecuador was forced to go against the grain of public opinion and adopt the US dollar as the national currency in 2000. This raises important questions about the right to self-determination. The UN Covenant on Civil and Political Rights recognizes the right of self-determination of peoples as being fundamental to the enjoyment of other rights. An important aspect of this is the right of peoples to exercise sovereignty over their natural wealth and resources. Economic globalization increasingly denies this right to vulnerable states and societies in the Third World.

Related to this is the right to development. As globalization increases the gap within and among nations it limits the capacity of Third World states to break out of the circle of poverty and achieve sustainable economic development. The United Nations 1986 Declaration on the Right to Development (UNDRD) recognizes that individuals and societies have a right to development and that this right cannot be assessed solely on the basis of economic and GDP indices. Rather, UNDRD affirms, the central focus of the process of development must be the human person – the socio-economic well-being of the individual. The right to development means that 'every human person and all peoples are entitled to participate in, contribute to, and enjoy economic, social, cultural and political development, in which all human rights and fundamental freedoms can be fully realized' (UN 1986). In many parts of the Third World, economic globalization threatens both the political right to self-determination and the right to development as spelled out in the UNDRD. This is recognized even by institutions of economic globalization like the World Bank, which has acknowledged that, 'globalization is a threat to weak or capriciously governed states' and has made efforts to address some of the concerns about the impact of its activities on human rights in the Third World (World Bank 1997: 1).

After years of insisting that its mandate was purely economic rather than political, the World Bank issued a set of guidelines in 1998 linking its activities to what it perceived as its human rights obligations (World Bank: 1998).[5] The Bank acknowledges that it policies can no longer be restricted to economic considerations alone but must also involve considerations like the social costs of economic reforms, good governance, public sector accountability and the objective living conditions of affected people. The IMF issued similar guidelines on 'Good governance' in 1997 (IMF 1997). The shift by IFIs towards incorporating non-economic indices like human rights guidelines into their operations clearly represents the growing awareness among the governing institutions of globalization that they can no longer ignore the adverse effects of economic globalization on the enjoyment of human rights in the Third World.

However, these policy statements tend to focus on civil and political rights rather than economic and social rights, which are the more direct outcomes of economic globalization. The economic and social rights issues arising from the globalizing activities of IFIs, TNCs and the WTO in the Third World have not been adequately addressed. Recognizing this, the UN Committee on Economic and Social Rights has called on institutions of economic globalization, particularly the IMF and the World Bank, to pay enhanced attention to economic, social and cultural rights in their activities by broadening their lending policies and by 'encouraging explicit recognition of these rights' (UNHCHR 2001). Thus, although there is a growing awareness of the adverse impacts of economic globalization on human rights, the institutional mechanisms of globalization have yet to address them seriously and fundamentally.

## REACTIVE IMPULSES: CHALLENGING THE MARKETS

Economic globalization has had some negative impacts on human rights conditions in the Third World. Yet, it has created new fronts and strategies with which Third World people have tackled the difficulties arising from economic globalization. This is particularly true of Latin America which has been most affected by economic globalization. In many Latin American countries, global relations have become a vehicle for challenging the excesses of economic globalization and developing more humane political, social and economic relations. Unlike in most parts of Africa, the human rights movements in Latin America have responded more directly to the globalization of labour and markets. Human rights activists in Latin America have been more involved in using human rights to challenge the activities of globalized economic institutions than has been the case in Africa. Many human rights activists are shifting from their traditional focus on abuses by governments and are now confronting the multiple impacts of economic globalization on the working and living conditions of people within their countries.

In Colombia, land rights conflicts between peasants and transnational corporations involved in the lucrative oil and coffee export trades have contributed to rural violence and widespread human rights abuses. But at the same time, these conflicts have led to an unprecedented awareness of universal human rights and have strengthened the human rights movement in the country. Both local and international human rights organizations have become more involved not only in the conflict between local peasants and transnational corporations but also in other human rights abuses arising from the Colombian military's campaign against leftist guerrillas. The renewed attention accorded to human rights in Colombia has led to the emergence of several new non-governmental institutions dedicated to the promotion of these rights. For instance, the UN set up a special division of its Human Rights Office in Colombia and helped found and fund human rights-oriented organizations like the Children's Peace Movement, which has led nationwide demonstrations against human rights abuses resulting from the activities of TNCs and the Colombian government. Other international NGOs in Latin America like the International Peace Brigade have worked with local activists on issues of human rights, democracy and accountability in activities of TNCs in the country (Brysk and Gonzalez-Cueva 2000).

Seeking ways to respond to the negative impact on TNC activities, local human rights activists in the Third World have achieved greater success by building on global cooperation and networks with advocacy groups in the North and the South. Transnational information campaigns have been effective in bringing to international focus the human rights implications of TNC activities. Working with groups like Amnesty International and Human Rights Watch, local activists have adopted an effective strategy of 'naming and shaming' corporations implicated in human rights abuses. In Mexico, local activists collaborated with Human Rights Watch in the 1990s to publicize and lead an international campaign against the practice of compulsory pregnancy testing of Mexican workers by some US border assembly plants. As a result of this campaign, several TNCs were forced to discontinue the practice. Similarly, the Coalition For Justice in the *Maquiladoras*, which focuses on monitoring and improving labour conditions in the export plants concentrated along the US-Mexico border, has been successful in using the global media in its advocacy work. In Asia, the South Asia Coalition on Child Servitude had built a global coalition of NGOs and other interest groups working to address the problem of child labour in India, Bangladesh and Thailand. Thus, the same 'instruments' that further economic globalization, such as the Internet, global banking and the media, have become effective means of challenging it.

It is evident, however, that challenges from activist and the non-government organizations alone cannot redress the adverse impacts of economic globalization on human rights conditions in the Third World. Meaningful and sustainable changes can only come when the activities of NGOs working from below are complemented by a fundamental reform of the rules and institutions of economic globalization from above.

## CONCLUSION: REINVENTING GLOBALIZATION

The links between globalization and human rights in the Third World is multi faceted. Globalization has the potential of both transforming and constricting human rights. On one level the globalization of knowledge and information have strengthened human rights movements in the Third World. Local activists are increasingly able and successful in using the universal human rights discourse to address local issues. On another level, economic globalization has limited the enjoyment of human rights in many Third World Societies by creating economic and political conditions that have worsened individual living conditions and made it difficult for states to meet their social welfare obligations to citizens. On a third level global human rights networks and coalitions have become effective means of challenging the excesses of economic globalization and moderating their effects on Third World societies.

Finally, the question that arises is: what more can be done to ensure that the forces of globalization increasingly benefit rather than threaten human rights in the Third World? The emerging consensus is that the threats to human rights posed by economic globalization risks outweighing its accidental benefits (McCorquodale 1999: 764). In its 1999 Human Development Report, 'Globalization with a human face', the

UNDP called for a reorientation of global governance that ensures equity in international trade negotiations and that has, as its central focus, human development and human rights (UNDP 1999). Indeed the formulation of the rules of global trade and investments are presently unacceptable and needs to shift. As presently constituted, the rules of global trade and investments, as set by the powerful state, IFI and TNC players seem to be guided by one question alone: how can global trade and investments be protected and sustained? This questions needs to be mediated by a more important question: how can global trade and investments be conducted in a way that conform to international human rights standards?

The integration of human rights principles more fully into the rule-making processes of global trade and investment should be the first step in the reform process. The rules of globalization have to be reinvented with human rights and human development at their core. Such reform must deal not only with markets, investments and profits, but also with issues concerning participation and involvement of local people in decision-making processes, the transparency of such processes, negotiations, leadership, inclusiveness and dispute-settling. More importantly, international human rights law has to provide more effective mechanisms though which non-state actors like IFIs and TNCs can be held accountable for human rights violation resulting directly or indirectly from their activities. Presently, international human rights law places much of the obligation on human rights protection and promotion on states. While this may have been adequate in a post-Westphalian age of absolute state sovereignty, this is no longer tenable today. In an era where the power of states over their citizens is increasingly replaced by the influence of global economic institutions, these institutions must bear as much responsibility as states in upholding human rights.

Fortunately, some steps have already been taken in this direction. The UN Sub-Commission on Economic and Social Rights has formulated a draft code of conduct for TNCs which stresses the responsibility and obligations of corporations to promote the core human rights values of respect for life, liberty, justice, equality, tolerance, mutual respect and integrity that underlie the Charter of the United Nations and the Universal Declaration of Human Rights. The hope is that this code of conduct will constitute the basis of a regime of enforceable international law that spells out the human rights obligations of non-state actors within the context of globalization (UN 2000: 21). However, to be relevant and effective, such efforts at integrating human rights standards into the rules of global trade and investment must have the direct input of Third World states and peoples who bear much of the social and economic cost of globalization. There should be an effort to enhance the ability of Third World states and societies to negotiate their own terms within a global economy as it relates to their basic rights – the right to political and economic self-determination, the right to development, the rights to fair labour conditions for workers and their right to organize, negotiate and bargain collectively. Global markets, global technology, global ideas and global solidarity can enrich the lives of people everywhere. The challenge remains how to ensure that the benefits are shared equitably and that global interdependence works for the rights and welfare of all people – not just to profit a few.

## Notes

1 See the preamble of the Universal Declaration of Human Rights.
2 More information about the activities of Derechos Human Rights can be found at www.derechos.org/.
3 Also see Stiglitz (2002).
4 See preamble of the UDHR.
5 For a more incisive discourse on the human rights obligations of the World Bank and the IMF see Skogly (2001).

## References and Further Reading

Adams, F. et al. 1999: *Globalization and the Dilemmas of the State in the South*. New York: Macmillan and St Martin's Press.

Ake, C. 1989: *The Political Economy of Crisis and Underdevelopment in Africa: Selected Works of Claude Ake*, ed. J. Ihonvbere. Lagos.

ARB 1984: *Africa Research Bulletin*, 2, 4.

Bangura, Y. 1986: Structural adjustment and the political question. *Review of African Political Economy*, 37.

Brysk, A. and Gonzalez-Cueva, E. 2000: *NACLA Report on the Americas*, 34 (1).

Brysk, A. (ed.) 2002: *Globalization and Human Rights*. Berkeley: University of California Press.

CCEIA (Carnegie Council for Ethics and International Affairs) 2002: Edited transcripts of remarks by Joseph Stiglitz at the *Books for Breakfast* 05/15/02 at www.carnegiecouncil.org/about/transcript_stiglitz.html (accessed 13 October 2002).

Chege, M. 1992: Remembering Africa. *Foreign Affairs*, 71.

Cobbah, J. 1987: African values and the human rights debate: an African perspective. *Human Rights Quarterly*, 9, 3.

Coicaud, J.-M. et al. (eds) 2003: *The Globalization of Human Rights*. Washington, D.C.: The Brookings Institution.

De Bary, W. T. 1998: *Asian Values and Human Rights: A Confucian Communitarian Perspective*. Cambridge, Mass.: Cambridge University Press.

Evans, T. 2001: Globalization, human rights and international citizenship. *Alternatives*, 26 (1).

FIDA 2002: International Federation of Women Lawyers, Ghana, 'FIDA objectives', at http://iisd1.iisd.ca/50comm/commdb/list/c29.htm (accessed 13 November 2002).

Franck, T. M. 2001: Are human rights universal? *Foreign Affairs* (January–February).

Friedman, T. 1999: DOScapital. *Foreign Policy* (Fall).

Friedman, T. 2000: *The Lexus and the Olive Tree: Understanding Globalization*. New York: Anchor Books.

Holton, R. 1998: *Globalization and the Nation State*. London: Macmillan Press.

Hutchful, E. 1987: The crisis of the international division of labor: authoritarianism and the transition to free market economies in Africa. *Africa Development*, 12, 2.

IMF 1997: Good governance: the role of the IMF at www.imf.org (accessed 13 October 2002).

Jensen, M. and Poulsen, K. 1993: *Human Rights and Cultural Change: Women in Africa*, 6.

Latham, R. 1997: Globalization and democratic provisionism: reading Polanyi. *New Political Economy*, 2, 1.

McCorquodale, R. with Fairbrother, R. 1999: Globalization and human rights. *Human Rights Quarterly*, 21, 3.

Mengisteab, K. 1999: Globalization and the struggles for democratization in Africa. Unpublished seminar paper. Old Dominion University.

Monshipouri, M. 1995: *Democratisation, Liberalization and Human Rights in the Third World*. New York: Lynne Rienner.

Orford, A. 1998: Contesting globalization: a feminist perspective on the future of human rights. *Transnational Law and Contemporary Problems*, 8, 2.

PBS 1999: The view from the top. Transcripts of PBS documentary *Globalization and Human Rights* at www.pbs.org/globalization/home.html (accessed 16 November 2002).

Rowbotham, S. and Linkogle, S. (eds) 2001: *Women Resist Globalization: Mobilizing for Livelihood and Rights*. London and New York: Zed Books.

Rusk, J. 1986: Structures of neocolonialism: the African context of human rights. *Africa Today*, 33, 4.

Skogly, S. 2001: *The Human Rights Obligations of the World Bank and the International Monetary Fund*. London: Cavendish.

Stiglitz, J. 2002: *Globalization and its Discontents*. New York: W. W. Norton.

Streeten, P. 1999: Globalization and its impact on development cooperation. *Development*, 42, 3.

UN 1948: *Universal Declaration of Human Rights*. New York: UN.

UN 1986: *Declaration on the Right to Development*, General Assembly Resolution 41.128 of 4 December 1986.

UN Department of Public Information 1997: *The Universal Declaration of Human Rights: A Magna Carta for all Humanity*. Vienna: UN.

UN 1999: The role of employment and work in poverty eradication: the empowerment and advancement of women. Report of the Secretary-General (E/1999/53).

UN 2000: Globalization and its full impact on the enjoyment of human rights (June) (E/CN.4/Sub.2/2000/13).

UNDP 1999: *Human Development Report 1999*. London: Oxford University Press.

UNHCHR 1999: Globalization and its impact on the enjoyment of economic, social and cultural rights. Decisions adopted by the Committee at its eighteenth session, 15/05/98 (E/1999/22).

UNHCHR 2001: Globalization and its impact on the full enjoyment of all human rights. Sub-commission on Human Rights resolution 2001/5, 2001 at www.unhchr.ch (accessed 27 October 2002).

World Bank 1997: *World Development Report 1997*. Washington, D.C.

World Bank 1998: *Development and Human Rights: The Role of the World Bank*. Washington, D.C.:

# 9  The Political Economy of Globalization and Grass-Roots Movements

*Dong-Sook S. Gills*

*Rejecting economic determinism, in this chapter Dong-Sook S. Gills sets out to establish the centrality of the 'political' in our understanding of globalization. She engages in a critical rethinking of what practices now constitute viable political strategies in the world economy, focusing on popular responses to neoliberal globalization. She argues that a key political and social tension in the coming years will be between the forces of neoliberal economic globalization, seeking to expand the freedom of private capital and the market, and the forces of social resistance, seeking to preserve and redefine communities and solidarity.*

## INTRODUCTION

This chapter is an attempt to outline the essential features of the political economy of globalization, unpacking the politics of the social relations too often obscured by the rhetoric of neoliberal economics. I will seek to investigate the common characteristics of the seemingly disjointed and diverse grass-roots movements that have been gathering force over the last few years in response to neoliberal globalization. By doing so, I intend to arrive at a more holistic analysis of the political economy of globalization and its relation to the new grass-roots movements of resistance and social transformation.

## THE POLITICAL ECONOMY OF NEOLIBERAL GLOBALIZATION

The current processes of globalization are largely driven by the forces of the market economy supported by neoliberal ideology. The first and most important point about the underlying economic structure of globalization is the move from the 'national economy' to the 'global economy'. National economies are being restructured through the process of the transnationalization of capital, and economic space has been expanding beyond the national boundaries. The national economy is under increasing pressure from external economic and political forces which endanger its autonomy or even its sovereignty. The range of manoeuvre for managers of the national economy is being undermined by the growing power of globalized capital, also known as 'global finance' or 'transnational capital'. This by definition is money that is highly mobile across state boundaries.

The shift from a national economy to a global economy has been taking place through the shift from national production structures to global production systems. With technological advancements in information, communication and transportation, industrial production is increasingly organized into segregated segments which are processed in different locations around the world. This globalization of production is facilitated by the increase of free trade and the decline of national protectionism, and the rise of global finance as opposed to closed or restricted national financial systems. The free flow of global capital, made possible through increasing financial liberalization, and globalized production, now supersede the old idea of international comparative advantage, in practice if not yet in theory.

A large proportion of commodities in the global market today can no longer be identified as the product of a single or particular country, except perhaps for certain primary commodities. Metaphorically speaking, in today's world, 'British' woollen cloth and 'Portuguese' wine, the classic examples used by Ricardo in his explanation of the case for comparative advantage, are no longer necessarily produced in Britain and Portugal. The British wool may be woven by subcontracting companies in Bangladesh and dyed in Sri Lanka, at factories owned by Korean capital. A Portuguese wine-producing company might well be in operation in the Napa Valley in California, using local grapes and migrant Mexican labour. So under the conditions of global production and global finance, old assumptions about national production break down.

Theoretically it could be the case, as neoliberal advocates claim, that the best and the cheapest commodities are those produced through such global organization. However, the benefits of international comparative advantage, that were once thought to accrue to national economies are now transferred to transnational capital. The national economy is no longer a coherent single unit within which the economic cycle of investment, production, consumption, distribution and accumulation is completed. In other words, accumulation of capital at the world scale – 'global accumulation' – now increasingly supersedes 'national accumulation' or 'the wealth of nations' as understood by either Adam Smith or Karl Marx. Thus, both traditional liberal economic thinking and Marxist thinking are inadequate in terms of understanding the dynamic of 'national economic development' under the conditions of globalization.

The second point about the political economy of globalization is that this new global economic structure brings with it a new global power structure, which is both economic and political. In the new mode of control, global capital, rather than national capital, is paramount. National economic policy is held hostage to the demands or dictates of global economic interests, led by globalized firms and banks. In this new global power structure, the space for the struggle for popular rights within the national political context becomes more constricted than before. This narrowing of the social space for the struggle for popular rights is related to the increasing power of market forces.

The market ideology that accompanies neoliberal globalization promotes a value system based fundamentally on extreme individualism. This doctrine preaches that individual freedom is the supreme human value above all others. In neoliberal or 'market' ideology the primary emphasis is given to individual freedom, and specifically to the freedom to compete and consume. Moreover, such 'rights' are regarded as best guaranteed in a free market. Theoretically, in a truly free market society, everyone is equal and equally free to make their choices. Only the individual's own efforts and abilities account for the existence of 'winners' and 'losers'. Thus, the free market is assumed to be politically neutral; it does not have any prejudice against or bias towards anyone. Every person's individual freedom is protected and no one's freedom is curtailed by any conscious political intervention. According to this view, the virtue of a market society is that it gives everyone, including the poor, true freedom (Hayek 1944). The counter-argument to this view is that such freedom is contingent on access to money, and that nothing so constrains the freedom of the individual in such an economic system as a total absence of money (Galbraith 2000). That is, the poor do not experience real freedom. Poverty, and especially extreme poverty, constrains 'choice' in the market, and therefore constricts 'freedom'. Therefore it can be argued, contra Hayek and the neoliberals, that poverty and freedom are mutually exclusive in a market economy.

While neoliberal economic theory assumes that the market is a neutral institution and that there is thus no need for a critical theory of the market in regard to the question of power, a critical view of the market begins by rejecting the social neutrality of the market. Historically, markets are institutions that tend to reflect the pre-existing inequalities in the social structure, whereby those who are already advantaged, e.g. through ownership of property or control of capital and technology, tend to have more power in the market. Those who are already disadvantaged, e.g. by the absence of property, capital or technology, tend to become powerless. Through interviews with thousands of poor people in the world carried out as part of the 'Voices of the Poor' initiative, it is reconfirmed that the poor feel they have no voice and are powerless against forces beyond their control (World Bank 2000). This applies not only among individuals and families in a domestic economic context, but also in the relations between countries in the international economic system. The result of such market-mediated social relationships is that power and wealth tend to become more concentrated in a few hands, therefore perpetuating inequality and even widening the gap between the rich and the poor, the powerful and the powerless. The market alone therefore is not a mechanism for making society more equal, nor is it capable on its own of creating a just distribution of goods and meeting all human needs. As neoliberal economic globalization proceeds on the basis of strengthening the market mechanism it also strengthens the tendency towards increasing inequality in wealth and power on a global scale.

It is important to keep in mind that neoliberal ideals of individual freedom address only a limited sense of rights. The classic typology of rights developed by T. H. Marshall (1950) is useful to help us recognize the limitations of the ideology of individualism. Marshall distinguishes three different types of rights: civil rights, political rights and social rights.

1   Civil rights are those legal rights that entitle citizens to basic freedom and security under the law, for example, freedom of the press, freedom of speech, freedom of religion and habeas corpus (i.e. freedom from arbitrary arrest and detention).
2   Political rights refer to those rights that allow participation in a democratic political process, which includes the right to vote, the right to assembly and the right to political association. These first two types of rights are emphasized in neoliberal thought, but often at the expense of the third category, i.e. social rights. However, as Marshall argued, citizenship in a democratic society is only completed when fundamental social rights are included and guaranteed.
3   Social rights include the right to education, welfare, health, social care and social security. In other words, social rights represent the right to fulfilment of basic human needs, not necessarily provided by the market.

Since the market alone cannot meet all human needs or satisfy fundamental social rights, a political process is thus necessary to ensure basic guarantees of social rights. For example, in developed countries, a state pension for old age is regarded as an entitlement of citizenship. After the Great Depression, which was a global crisis of capitalism, a new social compromise was reached between labour, capital and the state which resulted in the expansion of welfare states and social democracy, with guarantees of social rights for all citizens. This recognition of social rights included the expansion of the idea of human rights to include many fundamental social rights, as formally embodied in the Universal Declaration of Human Rights.

However, neoliberal economic globalization undermines these social rights, exerting the pressure of competition in the world market place, thus limiting the ability of national states to provide the necessary level of welfare for all citizens. In other words, the argument is made by neoliberals that social rights are too expensive to be economical and therefore undermine competitiveness in the market. This process of undermining social rights should be recognized for what it is: a historical retrogression in the history of capitalism and democracy. It is retrogressive in relation to the social progress, especially in the West and also in many other developing countries, achieved over the past century. In particular, during the period of post-Second World War Fordism, social rights were expanded under a more humane and democratic political order than had previously characterized capitalism. Globalization should not come at the expense of the social gains of the past century. Although the UN Special Session in Geneva in 2000 failed to reach agreement on Global Principles for Social Policy, it has been increasingly recognized in recent debates that 'social policy is inextricably linked to economic policy' (Pearson and Seyfang 2001: 72).

In neoliberal thought, as discussed above, the parallel of individual political freedom is the economic freedom to choose and to compete with others in the market. This economic freedom is actually just a freedom to choose among commodities, on the (false) assumption that everyone already has the power to purchase all the commodities they need. This ideology, sometimes called consumerism, encourages the trend to commodify everything. That is, the logic of consumerism is that you can buy everything and anything in the market and therefore every human need can be met and satisfied via commercial exchange. This helps explain the recent global trend to privatization under neoliberal economic globalization. It encourages the idea that to privatize is the best way to compete in the market. Over the last two decades the process of privatization has extended even to include basic human needs such as water, health care, education, and pensions. This deepening of commodification via privatization leads to the weakening of social rights. In fact, privatization of basic human needs is a direct attack on the idea of social rights as human rights and a fundamental entitlement of citizenship.

On the surface, neoliberal economic globalization appears to promote democracy. Indeed, the promotion of democracy based on the paradigm of liberal constitutionalism is compatible with the promotion of individualism and its economic manifestation through marketization and privatization. The parameters of democracy in this context are based on an economy organized by the free market. Thus, (neo)liberal democracy is confined to a minimalist state which is to be socially legitimized via a formal electoral system. This structure however, has the effect of granting autonomy to capital and the market, with a minimum of state interference.

There is a necessary and useful distinction to be made between two forms of democracy: formal democracy and substantive democracy. In formal democracy, which is encouraged by neoliberalism, the status quo remains untouched despite periodic competitive elections. In this form of democracy, known as 'low intensity democracy'(Gills et al. 1993), the formal exercise of legal and political rights as discussed above actually serves to preserve the status quo, to legitimize it, and above all to prevent any radical change or meaningful redistributional reform from happening. Moreover, it is a form of democracy that actually facilitates the imposition of neoliberal economic policies, including liberalization, marketization and privatization, the three pillars of the 'Washington Consensus' that dominated the 1980s and 1990s. A very similar concept is 'polyarchy', which refers to 'a system in which a small group actually rules, on behalf of capital, and participation in decision-making by the majority is confined to choosing among competing elites in tightly controlled electoral processes' (Robinson 1996: 20–1).

In substantive democracy, in contrast, there is a change in the status quo, in terms of the distribution of assets, income, and power. Thus, in substantive democracy there are definite redistributional outcomes. The status quo is not accepted, but rather challenged and transformed. Therefore democracy is a means for bringing about social change, which can be quite radical change. At its most radical, substantive democracy aims at achieving distributional equality in terms of wealth and political power, i.e. a society of equals in which all participate with equal rights and dignity.

The prevailing neoliberal formula is very simple: free markets equal democracy. However, as argued above, the emphasis in neoliberal democracy is squarely on individual freedom and formal political rights. In reality, this de-emphasizes social rights, marginalizing their significance and questioning their necessity or validity. Neoliberal globalization promotes only low-intensity democracy. Contrary to its claims, the real effect of neoliberal economic globalization is not to strengthen democracy but rather to weaken it by actually undermining social rights. Thus formal democracy is promoted at the expense of substantive democracy, where social rights and welfare rights are higher priorities than mere voting.

## GLOBALIZATION AND GRASS-ROOTS SOCIAL MOVEMENTS

A key problem in the political economy of globalization is that while the economy is more and more managed and operated on a global scale, democracy is still based on national politics, not global politics. This represents a serious contradiction between the economics of globalization and the politics of globalization. On the one hand, the sovereignty of the nation-state is a very important conceptual element in liberal democracy. The terrain of democracy in liberal theory is limited to the nation-state. Therefore, in conventional thinking, the democratization process, in particular formal democracy, which includes the elimination of military dictatorships and authoritarian regimes, and the establishment of multi-party systems, applies only to sovereign nation-states.

On the other hand, an increasingly large part of our global economy is organized and managed by transnational capital. The revenues of the top five global companies in 2005 together reached $1306 billion, which is far greater than the GNP of all low-income countries in the world put together. The revenues of Wal-Mart, the largest global corporation, were listed in 2005 as close to $288 billion (Fortune 2005), and this is larger than the GNP of Norway – the most 'livable' country in the world (UNDP 2005). Two-thirds of the world's fixed assets are owned by a few hundred global companies which together control over 70 per cent of world trade.

Given that transnational capital is by nature highly mobile in relation to national borders, its operations are not always bounded by national political rules. Economic globalization is loosening 'non-market structures that in the past placed limits on the accumulation of capital' (Robinson 1996: 15). Neoliberal economic globalization is undermining the economic sovereignty of the nation-state and at the same time it is narrowing the space for democracy even within the confines of existing national boundaries. In other words, the national boundary of the economy is becoming more obscured, and yet, the political boundary in which the economy is disciplined and controlled, especially for redistribution, has not been altered. This discrepancy of the boundaries between economic accumulation and distribution further obstruct the opportunity for substantive democratization.

In the past, the national struggle for social rights was fought between a set of recognizable national forces. Class struggle, for example took place in a clear national context between the elite social class and the 'masses'. The national state was a crucial political terrain where the class struggle had to be fought out and mediated and the state implemented decisions that expressed the outcome of these struggles. The transnationalization of the national economy has rendered these old relationships tenuous at best. Capital is not really very tangible on the 'national' level, when so much of it is not national, but rather 'foreign', transnational, or global. How does a national social movement fight the transnational banks and corporations or the IMF? Where does their national government come into this struggle? To what extent does the nation-state have any mediating power between transnational capital and national labour?

The political economy of neoliberal globalization generates a situation in which electoral competition between parties becomes increasingly meaningless. This is because, unlike in the past, present-day political parties are much more constrained by economic globalization when they come into power. In some cases, the party opts for neoliberal globalization by choice, e.g. the New Labour Party in the UK as led by Tony Blair and guided by the so-called 'Third Way' ideology. In other cases, a party and a leadership that might have pursued more progressive policies, such as Kim Dae-jung and his Millennium Democratic Party in South Korea, were heavily constrained by IMF policies and the existence of a huge foreign debt. Still others, such as the Workers' Party of Brazil, maintain a radical programme and strong links to vibrant autonomous social movements based on popular struggles for justice, but even they must tread a very cautious path in order to avoid punitive actions by the international financial institutions.

In the current globalization, national politics are not fully free to fulfil their intended radical political goals. They are constrained in how much they can do by the power structure of the global economic system. As a consequence – and this is a common symptom of neoliberal globalization – rival political parties do not always offer a very strong contrast between their policy positions, but rather tend to look alike. This alienates many voters, who decide that the outcome of elections will alter nothing, and therefore many choose not to participate. It is an environment in which politicians and political parties compete on the basis of who can present themselves as better managers, over a system that will be essentially unchanged whoever wins the election.

Given that the national political space in which parties operate is constricted by globalization, this obviously affects the activity and focus of social movements. That being said, this constraint clashes with the very nature of popular movements, which embody the struggle for social change through social rights and substantive democracy. Historically, grass-roots movements have challenged political party politics and state-centric politics. Their politics is people-centric, more interested in making concrete and specific social change than in gaining state power.

Grass-roots social movements are thus frequently autonomous from any political party or organization and can therefore more freely criticize the practices of both political parties and governments (Routledge 2002). They are less prone to compromise and more capable of direct action and self-help. Grass-roots organizations are freer to broaden their movement and strengthen it through their inclusiveness, addressing a wide range of economic, political, cultural, environmental and social issues. Alliances with political parties are always possible, as in the case of the Workers' Party in Brazil, but the autonomy of the social movements should remain a first concern, to maintain their mobilization and integrity as movements (Frank and Fuentes 1992).

In the recent 'new' social movements, the strengthening of many types of grass-roots approaches to decision-making and self-determination represent an indispensable form of opposition to corporate globalization (Klein 2001). Maude Barlow and Tony Clark conclude that not only has the assault on democracy by neoliberal globalization produced new grass-roots movements of resistance, but that developing 'new democracy' through grass-roots movements 'at local, national and international levels is the only possible antidote to corporate globalization' (Barlow and Clark 2002: 208).

The intensification of cross-border economic activities and global financial transactions requires a corresponding transnational social and political response. As Barry Gills argues, 'to the extent that there is now . . . already a truly global economic system based on the free movement of capital, then there is also an objective and logical need for new forms of global political order to accompany this global economic system' (Gills 2002: 160). The main question is therefore, how will such a new global political order be built, and whose interests will it represent – the global elite or the global majority? In relation to either governments or political parties, social movements seem to have more manoeuvrability and potential to bridge the gap between national and global political spaces. It is the grass-roots social movements, organizing on a transnational basis, that have the potential to embody the new values and ethics of global democracy and global justice. 'The increasingly globalized world economy calls for a similarly globalized approach to basic ethics and political and social procedures' (Sen 2000).

In fact, many of the grass-roots movements today are concerned not only with local and national justice, but also increasingly with global justice. Through practice they have recognized that justice at all these levels is linked or integrated. Very often they are contingent on each other. For example, local and national justice today is increasingly contingent on decisions and power located at the global level. This means that it is not enough simply to be concerned about the local or national level of political action. It is necessary to understand the local and national problems within a global context and to address the global situation as well as the local and national.

Although the economic or material structure of neoliberal globalization is constraining the political space for substantive democracy and social rights, nevertheless neoliberal globalization is also activating grass-roots movements in response to its effects on the lives of ordinary people around the globe. It is not contradictory that neoliberal economic globalization depoliticizes or desocializes the social forces while simultaneously provoking further resistance. The dynamics in the politics of globalization are the dialectic nature of trend, that is to say, neoliberal economic globalization and counter-trend – political and social action by grass-roots movements. So widespread, deep and disruptive are the effects of neoliberal globalization that it works to stimulate people from many sectors and occupations into action in defence of their own interests. This diversity requires the creation of broader coalitions, alliances and solidarity among movements from many countries. Economic globalization encourages a great diversity of movements and creates the need for these diverse movements to unify at the global level. Therefore, the political economy of globalization leads to globalization of political activism.

## THE GLOBAL POLITICS OF RESISTANCE

Precisely because neoliberal states no longer truly serve the interests of the majority, popular social forces have a much greater need to mobilize and organize in order to serve their own needs. They cannot rely on the state, or on political parties, as they may have felt they could do in the past. Elites that have been co-opted into neoliberal globalization no longer put the interests of their own people first, but rather attempt to discipline their people into acceptance of neoliberalism. This situation changes the nature of national politics, because the focus on the state to provide popular welfare no longer necessarily works. So people and movements have to create a new space for their struggle for popular rights, social rights and substantive democracy.

The new global grass-roots movements of resistance are mainly organized and led from the South. This reflects the fact that many of the gains of neoliberal economic globalization have been at the expense of the South. That is, the negative impact of neoliberalism has been more deeply felt among the ordinary people of developing countries. It is now a well-established fact that over the past two decades of globalization the gap between the rich North and the poor South has widened and the scale of global inequality has been enlarged (UNDP 2002). In addition to the centrality of movements from the South in the new global resistance to neoliberal globalization, their very composition and diversity reflects the many effects of neoliberalism around the world, such as on environment, women, labour, farmers, indigenous peoples, children, migrants and many others.

Networking among these diverse movements has now become one of the distinctive characteristics of the global movement against neoliberalism. The advent of electronic communications media and easier global transportation has facilitated new types of transnational organizing, having sped up and simplified personal and organizational contacts between activists throughout the world (Keck and Sikkink 1998). We might call this 'globalizing anti-globalization'. These new transnational social movements pursue forms of social action that are becoming more participatory as well as direct compared to the past (Cohen and Rai 2000). The inclusiveness of the movement is deliberate, in order to mobilize the maximum support in opposition to neoliberal economic globalization, and, post-11 September 2001, also in opposition to war.

There are two overarching grounds that unify such a wide range of movements. First, opposition to neoliberal corporate globalization is the primary unifying theme of the new global grass-roots movement of resistance. In the words of the World Social Forum-India secretariat, inviting participation in the first Asian Social Forum, in Hyderabad (2–7 January 2003), 'The forum is a major event of protest against Globalization, organized in concert by a wide variety of organizations and associations spread across the length and breadth of Asia, committed to the idea that another world, a world different from that promoted by multinational capital and the Bretton Woods institutions, is possible' (Asian Social Forum 2003). Robin Broad also shares this view, that the 'overarching umbrella uniting the backlash' of globalization is 'opposition to corporate control of the global economy' (Broad 2002: 3).

Second, democratic participation and democratic global governance are the common goals of the movements. The social movements are ultimately about redefining and reinvigorating participatory democracy that extends beyond the national politics. They are organized on the principle based on decentralization and autonomy with minimal central structures (PGA 2001: appendix 4). Both of these bases of unity are founded in a common set of values that animates and defines the character of the new global grass-roots movements of resistance.

The core values of the global grass-roots movement of resistance to neoliberal globalization are:

■ non-violent struggle;

■ democratic practice at all levels;

■ social justice for all;

■ inclusiveness and non-discrimination on the basis of colour, sex, class, creed, etc.;

■ secularism, as opposed to religious fundamentalism;

■ membership in one human community as opposed to parochialism.

There are in fact, however, also certain 'exclusions' in this movement. The new global social movement excludes movements based on a different set of values, including the following:

■ violent action;

■ communal or ethnic hatred;

■ nationalist militarism and aggression;

■ religious fundamentalism;

■ patriarchal domination;

Taken together these give us an idea of the new political ideology of the global grass-roots movements. The new social movements do not resemble the traditional armed guerrilla movements, with their goal of taking state power by force. Neither do they resemble the old socialist or left-wing political parties of the past, with their emphasis on hierarchical discipline and a single ideology. Tolerance and secularism have arisen as central concerns given the circumstances of the present and the great importance of these issues to many communities in both the North and the South. The increasing participation of women in all these movements has been a reflection of their core values of democratic practice, inclusiveness and non-discrimination.

However, the nature of the grass-roots movements is largely ad hoc and spontaneous, and therefore in the initial stages they appear to be somewhat erratic and disorganized. The movements themselves recognize this situation and they are not yet prepared to attempt to truly unify all the movements under a single ideology, organization or even a federation. Rather, they are primarily concerned to create a political space at regional and global level, where the many movements can meet together to 'share each other's experience and learn from each other . . . open up channels of communication between the ideologically diverse protest movements', and 'bring together at one place the vast masses of people whom globalization has marginalized, and whom each of these movements is separately organizing'. They hope that this will eventually 'lead over a period to a more substantial unity' (Asian Social Forum 2003).

The International Council of the World Social Forum, at its meeting in Porto Alegre on 21–22 January 2003, adopted a set of resolutions which emphasize their desire to continue promoting a process that is 'open and plural' and that 'works with the diversity of resistances, organizations and proposals' (WSF 2003). The statement entitled 'Call of the World Social Movements' issued at Porto Alegre in 2003, reflects the extremely broad agenda of the new global social movements of resistance.

> We are social movements that are fighting all around the world against neoliberal globalization, war, racism, castism, poverty, patriarchy, and all the forms of economical, ethnical, social, political, cultural, sexual and gender discriminations and exclusions. We are fighting for social justice, citizenship, participatory democracy, universal rights and for the right of peoples to decide their own future. (WSF 2003)

We can identify three main activities of the emerging global grass-roots movements against neoliberal globalization:

- protest;

- teach-ins;

- networking.

Beginning with Seattle in November 1999, there have been a series of large-scale global protests including those in Washington D.C. (April 2000); Prague (September 2000); Davos (January 2001); Porto Alegre (January 2001); Quebec City (April 2001); Genoa (August 2001); Florence

(2002); Mumbai (2004); and Gleneagles (2005). The growth of such global protests at or in relation to meetings of the major international bodies supervising neoliberal economic globalization such as the IMF and World Bank, the WTO, and the G8 summits has been a key feature of the movement to date. These global protests have been very successful in raising awareness about the issues of global trade and development in relation to neoliberalism. In terms of their political impact, the protests have made these formerly secretive elite meetings more subject to public scrutiny and accountability. The making visible of what was invisible, i.e. the important social-political relations underlying the technical economic decision-making of these organizations, was a crucial achievement of the protests. This put the deliberations of these bodies firmly on the political agenda of world public opinion.

In terms of the scale of these protest mobilizations, the actions have been impressive, involving a very large number of people from many different parts of the world. The numbers have ranged from tens of thousands to hundreds of thousands. The social forum meetings started as a protest against the elite meetings, and have featured large marches as an aspect of the forum activities. For example, the World Social Forum (WSF) 2003, the third such forum held in Porto Alegre, Brazil, in parallel with the World Economic Forum held in Davos, Switzerland, brought together 100,000 activists drawn from all continents. The meetings commenced with a march of the movements against neoliberal globalization, under the slogan of 'Another World is Possible', by some 70,000 people and concluded with a march against war in Iraq. The European Social Forum held in late 2002 in Florence had 50,000 participants and culminated in a gigantic anti-war march of a million people. Over 20,000 participants, including a number of South Asian grass-roots organizations, attended the first Asian Social Forum in 2003 in Hyderabad.

A second main purpose of the movements has been the organization of international meetings among grass-roots movements and activists in order to conduct teach-ins. The largest of these to date was the third World Social Forum in Porto Alegre in January 2003. The WSF International Council identified five thematic areas to guide the discussions and exchange of information. These five thematic areas were:

- democratic sustainable development;

- principles and values, human rights, diversity and equality;

- media, culture and counter-hegemony;

- political power, civil society and democracy;

- democratic world order, fight against militarism and promoting peace.

Conferences were organized around these themes, aiming 'to socialize views and analyses to the broader public at the Forum' and to 'contribute to strengthening a broad movement of public opinion' on the need for alternatives to neoliberal economic and financial globalization (WSF 2003: Programme). In addition, there were some 1,710 workshops and seminars, most with simultaneous translation in English, French, Portuguese and Spanish. These were mostly on a self-organizing basis, and represented an enormous range of topics and organizations.

These represent what Roberto Savio calls 'horizontal participation', which is not the mere gathering of persons together but rather 'the multiplication of knowledge, such as in the thematic and regional forums, which allow the experiences of this process to be shared with the whole world' (Terra Viva 2003: 6). This process is being repeated and expanded in regional and national social forums throughout the world, with the encouragement of the WSF secretariat. The focus of teach-in workshops, seminars and conferences is the sharing of information, ideas and experiences among diverse groups that might not otherwise have been in communication with one another.

Most grass-roots groups are concerned with networking, vigorously utilizing web-based contacts as well as physical meetings in international gatherings. Their international links and networking are now stronger than ever, including among the 'old' social movements (e.g. trade unions) and 'new' social movements. Networking takes place naturally in a casual way, but it is also a conscious concern of social movement organizers. For example, a proposal for a new 'network of social movements' emerged from the Porto Alegre process in 2003 with the hope to establish a coordinating mechanism for common actions. A similar initiative for Asian social movements emerged from the Hyderabad meetings in 2003. They recognize a need for a wide debate to formulate proposals for a more permanent and representative structure. This indicates a gradual shift in emphasis from the ad hoc spontaneous networking of the first phase of the movements towards a formal organizational structure and institutionalization.

A successful example of effective global networking between different social movements and grass-roots resistance groups is the People's Global Action (PGA). The Zapatistas in Mexico organized a global meeting of resistance to neoliberal globalization in Chiapas in 1996 and in Spain in 1997. Out of these meetings there emerged a network between ten social movements including Movimento Sem Terra (the landless peasants' movement) of Brazil, the Ogoni People of Nigeria, the Peasant Movement in the Philippines, the Karnataka State Farmers' Union of India, the Indigenous Women's Network and the Central Sandinista of Trabajadores (Workers) of Nicaragua. At their founding meeting in Geneva in February 1998, there were over 300 representatives from 71 countries. In their statement they said that 'Despite great material differences the fights are increasingly similar in every part of the global empire, setting the stage for a new and stronger sort of solidarity' (PGA 2001).

The PGA's example has inspired emulation by a number of other networks, including in North America by Direct Action Network (DAN) and the Montreal Anti-Capitalist Convergence (CLAC), in Europe by Ya Basta (Italy) and Reclaim the Streets (UK) and other associated groups around the globe. The PGA's call for 'global days of action' in support of local protests against institutions of global capitalist governance was an aspect of the initiation of the Seattle protests in 1999 and in September 2000 was met with demonstrations in 100 cities around the world. The objectives of the PGA include 'offering an instrument for coordination and mutual support at the global level for those resisting corporate rule and the capitalistic development paradigm' (Routledge 2002: 323). They emphasize that the PGA is not a centralized organization, but rather describe themselves as a process and an 'evolving coordination' of grass-roots groups (Rupert 2002: 5–6).

Critics of the grass-roots movements charge that there is a lack of clear specific goals and a coherent alternative agenda and that the tactics and the strategy are not clear. What do they collectively want to achieve? How do they intend to achieve their goals? What is their political effectiveness? The weaknesses of the grass-roots movements can be summarized as:

- the lack of a coherent ideology;

- the lack of formal global organizational structure;

- the lack of a common political programme.

This lack of any overarching ideology is a consequence of the inclusiveness of the movement as a whole and the desire to inspire and mobilize the greatest number of people to act against neoliberal corporate globalization. The only ideology recognized is a very broad one, in which the lowest common denominator is opposition to neoliberal economic globalization.

Again, it is this same inclusiveness and mobilizational motive that creates the conflict between the need to maintain the essence of grass-roots movements, with their preference for spontaneity and decentralization, and the need for more formally coordinated organization. The great diversity of the movements itself explains not only the impossibility of a single ideology but also the great caution exercised within the movement not to prematurely impose a unified organizational structure. However, the WSF, for example, is pursuing an enlargement of its International Council to integrate 'all the international and regional networks, movements and organizations' that can accept its Charter of Principles (WSF Resolutions 2003)

The question is whether they can overcome the political weakness inherent in such a broad inclusiveness and work towards achieving more coherence in organization, programme and action. Can they move beyond the initial phase of mobilization, education and networking, beyond large protests and teach-ins to a more developed and structured organizational form? The challenge is to maintain the impetus to action and to achieve more concrete and tangible results, without losing the sense of global solidarity that has emerged in recent years.

## CONCLUSIONS

Economic globalization is separating the economic domains of accumulation and the political domains of redistribution. Economic activities are increasingly shifting from the national economy to the global economy. Transnational companies, which dominate global finance, global production and world trade operate on the basis of global economic rationality. The national identity of banks and firms is less clear, as expressed in HSBC's slogan 'The World's Local Bank'. Yet, the recognized political boundary within which the regulation of capital and the redistribution of wealth can be carried out is still the nation-state. National policy is more and more subjected to the interests of global capital, and by this process social rights are being increasingly undermined. All of this amounts to nothing less than a global crisis of democracy.

The grass-roots movements against neoliberal globalization need to be understood in this context of the political economy of neoliberal globalization. These movements of resistance are fighting for substantive democracy which will ensure the basic social rights of all, including the weak, the powerless and the poor. Democracy without social rights is an empty vessel, now more than ever since global capital is threatening to commodify and marketize even the most basic social rights. The weakening of the political ability of the nation-state to reign in capital and redirect resources to meet social needs necessitates the entry into the political arena of other social forces from the 'bottom' to counteract this tendency. Neoliberals did not expect this as an outcome of their policies, but their actions invoke this response, not only nationally, but increasingly on a global scale.

The new configuration of the social forces of resistance focuses on global capitalism itself, in all its manifold expressions. These movements resist neoliberalism from an extremely wide range of viewpoints and positions. This represents a shift away from the traditional idea of national revolution, with its emphasis on the capture of state power. We now see a coalition of many different forms of struggle, with many different objectives and styles of action. Some movements see themselves as anti-capitalist, but others are more concerned with the strengthening of civil society and the rights of citizenship, whatever the specific issue area they address.

This is about a newly conceptualized global struggle – a struggle against capitalism in its neoliberal mode and against the global elites and global institutions that promote this form of capitalism. It is about resistance and reform on a global scale, but also about direct action taken by local and national popular movements. There is a tremendous diversity in these movements, reflecting many different ideologies and organizational forms. It is this great diversity of the new movements that gives them so much energy and momentum. Yet, this is also at the root of a central political problem of representation and action in the new global politics.

There is indeed a great need for the emergent global civil society represented by these movements to be able to advance concrete proposals for change. A growing concern is that the movement focus on creating a space for strategic debates in order to elaborate a concrete political programme. However, since the grass-roots movements articulate such a wide range of proposals for alternatives to neoliberal globalization, it seems impossible to find a single unified programme. In addition, in order to advance a common political programme a common unifying organizational structure is required. Thus, a new challenge that global resistance must confront is to find the right balance between the need for institutionalization of the movements and the need to maintain the autonomy of grass-roots movements, which is one of their essential features. The future success of the movements will depend on finding the ways of coordinating diverse grass-roots movements under a more structured organization without compromising the strength of decentralized movements.

### References and Further Reading

Asian Social Forum 2003: Make the Asian Social Forum Programme a success. (January 2–7).

Barlow, M. and Clark, 2002: *Global Showdown*. Toronto: Stoddart Publishing.

Broad, R. (ed.) 2002: *Global Backlash*. Oxford: Rowman and Littlefield.

Cohen, R. and Rai, S. (eds) 2000: *Global Social Movements*. London: Athlone Press.

Fortune 2005: The 2005 Global 500. Fortune's annual ranking of the world's largest corporations. Available at www.fortune.com/ fortune/global500/fulllist (accessed 5 September 2005).

Frank, A. G. and Fuentes, M. 1992: Ten theses on social movements. *Third World Quarterly*, 13 (2).

Galbraith, J. 2000: Forward: the social left and the market system. In B. K. Gills (ed.), *Globalization and the Politics of Resistance*, London: Macmillan.

Gills, B. K. 2002: Democratizing globalization and globalizing democracy. *The Annals of American Political Science*, 581, 158–71.

Gills, B., Rocamora, J. and Wilson, R. (eds) 1993: *Low Intensity Democracy: Political Power In New World Order*. London: Pluto.

Hayek, F. A. 1944: *The Road to Serfdom*. London: George Routledge and Sons.

Keck, M. E. and Sikkink, K. 1998: *Activists beyond Borders*. Ithaca, N.Y.: Cornell University Press.

Klein, N. 2001: The vision thing. In E. Yuen, G. Katsiaficas and D. Burton-Rose (eds), *The Battle of Seattle*. New York: Soft Skull Press.

Marshall, T. H. 1950: *Citizenship and Social Class, and Other Essays*. Cambridge: Cambridge University Press.

Pearson, R. and Seyfang, G. 2001: New hope or false dawn? Voluntary codes of conduct, labour regulation and social policy in a globalising world. *Global Social Policy*, 1 (1), 49–78.

Peoples' Global Action, 2001: Organizational principles of the Peoples' Global Action, Cochabamba, Bolivia, at www.nadir.org/nadir/ initiativ/agp/cocha/cocha.htm.

Robinson, W. 1996: Globalization: nine theses on our epoch. *Race and Class*, 38 (2), 13–31.

Routledge, P. 2002: Resisting and reshaping destructive development: social movements and globalizing network. In R. J. Johnston, P. J. Taylor and M. Watts (eds), *Geographies of Global Change: Remapping the World*. Oxford: Blackwell, 310–27.

Rupert, M. 2002: Anti-capitalist convergence? Conference paper prepared for the conference on 'Ideological Dimensions of Globalization', Globalization Research Center, Honolulu, Hawaii (Dec. 9–12).

Sen, A. 2000: Work and rights. *International Labour Review*, 139 (2), 119–28.

Terra Viva 2003: Interview with Roberto Savio, President of IPS and WSF IC member (24 January), 6.

United Nations Development Programme 2002: *Human Development Report*. New York: UNDP.

United Nations Development Programme 2005: *Human Development Report*. New York: UNDP.

World Bank 2000: *World Development Report*. New York: Oxford University Press.

World Bank 2002: *World Development Indicators*. Washington, D.C.: World Bank.

World Social Forum 2003: Call of the world social movements. Porto Alegre, Brazil (27 January) at www.focusweb.org.

# 10 Gender, Power and Governance in a Globalizing World

*Jane Parpart*

*As Sen has argued, one of the most critical aspects of development and human security concerns gender. This final chapter considers the gendered nature of the good governance agenda and its significant consequences for the empowerment of women in developing societies. It reflects critically upon the limits and contradictions of 'good governance' with particular reference to the concrete ways in which it impacts upon women's lives and prospects in the poorest regions of the globe. In doing so, it argues that the global development complex must take into account the gender implications of its good governance agenda if real development, in Sen's terms, is to be realized. In short, analyses of the relation between globalization, governance and human security which neglect the gender dimension are, at best, significantly flawed.*

'Governance' has become one of the watchwords of current development discourse. It has developed out of the growing concern for the corruption, venality and incompetence of many Third World (and Northern) governments. The failure of development efforts to stimulate effective, efficient governance in the South has become a concern both for the voters who pay for Northern development efforts and for those in the North who administer these efforts. Consequently, earlier reluctance to interfere in sovereign states was replaced by deliberate efforts to improve governance. Indeed, in the mid-1980s, 'good governance' became one of the conditionalities for those seeking development assistance (Stiglitz 2002).

Yet this concern with governance has largely ignored both gender and power. For the most part, governance has been seen as a gender-free concept, associated with those who run political parties, bureaucracies and the military. Some scholars and policy makers acknowledge the important role played by NGOs, particularly as pressure groups demanding good governance from autocratic bureaucracies and government officials. Yet all too often, even the inclusion of NGOs fails to interrogate the gendered, complex and fluid nature of governance. The analysis is still about people (i.e. men), running the ship of state (Prakash and Hart 1999). This chapter argues for a different approach, one that takes account of both the gendered nature of governance and the need for new thinking about gender, power and empowerment before effective, more gender-equitable governance can be achieved.

For this task, feminist theorizing has much to offer. However, an eclectic approach to theory is required, one that draws on both materialist and discursive analyses. Governance is shot through with power. It is also highly gendered. Creating policies and practices that will ensure more gender-equitable governance is a difficult business, taking place within institutional and discursive contexts that both enable and constrain efforts to transform society. Thus, encouraging good governance requires more than just evaluating the practices and language of government officials. It requires close attention to the broad political and economic structures, cultural assumptions and discourses, notions of human rights, laws and practices in which women (and men) seek to ensure or at least struggle for (or against) more gender-equitable, accountable governance at all levels of society. Moreover, this takes place in many different ways, from the personal encounters of daily life to involvement in formal and informal organizations.

## WHY GENDER AND GOOD GOVERNANCE?

The business of government has been seen largely as a male affair, and indeed, statistics bear this out. Around the world, men dominate executives, parliaments and cabinets. They run the civil service, create most policies and carry them out as well. Women are often there, but largely in a subordinate role (Enloe 1990, 1993). Thus, if one takes a neoliberal, or even Marxist approach to the issue of government and state power, it is clear that we live in a very gendered world (Parpart and Staudt 1989; Peterson and Runyan 1993).

The gendered (male) nature of state power has led to a preoccupation with women's representation and participation in government structures, and the consequences of their minimal participation for governance practices. This is important work that has inspired women (and some men) around the world to lobby for more women in politics, parliaments and bureaucracies, particularly in command positions, and it has been frustratingly slow although some improvements have taken place. While this is a crucial struggle one cannot assume that women in politics are inevitably committed to improving women's lot – witness the policies of Margaret Thatcher. Nevertheless, many women in representative governments do carry some of their personal concern for women's rights into the political arena (Rai 2002). Moreover, improving the gender balance in government is an issue of women's rights and human equality as well.

At the same time, governance does not operate only at the highest levels of state power. Relations of power and dominance occur in many sites. All relationships are shot through with power, and the pervasive patriarchal character of many/most relationships – whether in state government, local government or the family – plays a crucial role in the way governance is constructed and experienced by individuals and groups. We thus need to understand the workings of power, and its intersection with gender, if we are to understand the way gender affects (and is affected by) governance structures and practices at all levels of society.

# GENDER AND EM(POWER)MENT

In order to think about power and em(power)ment in new ways, we need to explore its diverse and complex history. While Paulo Freire (1973) did not use the term, his emphasis on education as a means for conscientizing and inspiring individuals and groups to challenge social inequality inspired social activists concerned with empowering the poor and the marginalized. Intellectuals and activists in the South, and to a lesser extent in the North, drew on Freire and others to expand the concept of power and empowerment. Social activists focused on local, grass-roots activism as a means for empowering the poor so they could/would challenge the status quo. Others took a more reformist position, seeing empowerment as a way to improve productivity and effectiveness within established structures. Mainstream development agencies adopted this approach in the 1990s, when they too began to use the language of empowerment, participation and people's development (World Bank 1995).

How can we explain these different, even contradictory definitions? The explanation may lie in the fluidity of the term 'power'. To empower implies the ability to exert *power over*, to make things happen. It is an action verb, suggesting the ability to change the world. It has a transformatory sound, an implicit promise of change, often for the better. Consequently, empowerment has often been the watchword of crusaders trying to make the world a better, more equitable place – generally through revolution or, at least, fundamental social transformation (Wolf 1998: 4–8). Others adopt a more benign view of power, one that emphasizes the potential for rational discussion and evolutionary change within modern societies. Associated with liberal arguments about modernization and democracy, this approach assumes even marginalized people can bring about change by mobilizing to convince the powerful of the need for change. While apparently different, both perspectives are captured by the notion that power is largely the ability to exert *power over* institutions, resources and people (Held et al. 1999).

In order to understand the limitations of these approaches to empowerment and power, we need to explore various thoughts on the subject. In the 1970s, Steven Lukes rejected the notion that power is simply control over institutions and resources, and argued instead that power also involves controlling the agendas and thinking of others (1974: 23–4). Michel Foucault pushed the analysis further. Rejecting the notion that power is something held by individuals or groups (and not others), he argues that it permeates society. It is fluid, relational and exists only in the everyday relationships of people, both individually and in institutions. Such power can lead to repressive practices that are expressed in disciplined bodies, actions and thoughts/discourses. While much of Foucault's work has centred on the disciplinary, disempowering nature of modern power, he recognizes that relations of power inspire resistance as well (Foucault 1979, 1991; McNay 1992). In this regard, Akhil Gupta and James Ferguson's reading of Foucault is useful, particularly the argument that Foucault did not see resistance 'in a disembodied duel with power' (Gupta and Ferguson 1997: 19), but rather as a complex interaction. People are empowered and changed through resisting disciplinary power relations, but this very action/agency may also strengthen their incorporation into the status quo. While this analysis illuminates the workings of power (and empowerment) at the individual and institutional level, Foucault has less to say about the impact of larger political and economic structures. Moreover, his analysis is relentlessly European and male-focused. A more feminist and global analysis is required if we are to rethink women's empowerment in comparative perspective.

Since the 1980s, feminists have in fact contributed important insight to these debates. Most feminists have started from querying the concept of power as simply *power over* people and resources. Some have found Foucauldian theory useful to challenge the dominant assumption that power is a possession exercised over others within familiar boundaries of state, law or class. They have been attracted to his focus on bodies as sites of power and to his notion of power as fluid, relational and embedded in struggles over meanings/discourses (Hekman 1996). Others have used the expanded boundaries of power that Foucauldian thought opens up to query the concept of empowerment itself. Anna Yeatman, for example, worries that the term reproduces the hierarchy between the powerful protector (the state, the elite) and the powerless (i.e., women, children and the poor) who are seen as helpless, passive and needy. She would rather use the term 'empowering', which is interchangeable with 'capacitating' or 'enabling' (1999). Other feminists argue that Foucault's vision of power encourages a relativist position where all transformative politics become suspect (Fraser 1989; Hartsock 1990).

Black and Third World feminists approach empowerment somewhat differently. Most regard the issue of participation as central to empowerment. They argue that participation in challenges to hegemonic systems and discourses has often inspired both greater self-understanding and political action in women's private and public lives. Involvement in the politics of subversion is thus empowering in itself, even if it does not immediately transform dominant power relations. As Patricia Hill Collins points out, 'change can also occur in the private, personal space of an individual woman's consciousness. Equally fundamental, this type of change is also empowering' (1991: 111). At the same time, individual conscientization does not necessarily lead to progressive politics. The language of women's empowerment has been used by right-wing political groups and parties to inspire Hindu women to resist the 'pseudo-secularism' of the male, Westernized elites who have granted Muslims and other minorities 'concessions' not available to the Hindu majority (Butalia and Sarkar 1996). While this rhetoric has inspired Hindu women's agency in defense of the *dharma* (faith), such empowerment obviously poses important questions for other communities, as well as for Hindu women who do not subscribe to this interpretation.

These different approaches/arguments need to be brought together if we are to think about empowerment, power and gender in new ways. Foucault's exposition of power allows us to move away from more traditional notions of power as the ability to exert *power over* structures, people and resource. He reminds us that power is fluid, relational and connected to discourses/knowledge. This is an important insight for feminist analyses of power and empowerment. However, the relationship between structures, agency and discourse is crucial (Deveaux 1996: 230–7). We need to integrate concerns with the limitations (and possibilities) set in place by structures and discourses of power, with attention to individual consciousness/understanding (*power within*), and its role in collective action (*power with*). This broader understanding is necessary if women are going to successfully organize and exert *power to* challenge gender hierarchies, both in daily life and in state and local governance (Rowlands 1997: 13).

Efforts to improve governance in the South have become the business of development agencies as well as various world bodies such as the United Nations and other international institutions. These efforts are shot through with power and highly gendered. This chapter is particularly interested in the attempts by development agencies (both mainstream and alternative) to foster good governance and the possibility that gender could be brought more squarely into this process. This requires further examination of the intersection between em(power)ment, gender and development, both in theory and practice.

## EM(POWER)MENT, GENDER AND DEVELOPMENT

Initially development was a largely gender-blind endeavour, but by the 1970s some practitioners had recognized the need to help women, albeit rarely questioning existing relations between the sexes. The limitations of this approach inspired a shift to a gender and development (GAD) approach that highlighted the role of culture as well as political and economic factors in women's subordination (Young 1993; Sen and Grown 1988). Nevertheless, this approach remained largely captured by Western notions of development, with its focus on economic solutions to development problems (Hirshman 1995).

By the late 1980s, activists and theorists from the South, and to a lesser extent from the North, began to discuss the need for a new approach, one that emphasized the importance of empowerment as well as economic well-being. Gita Sen and Caren Grown used the term in their landmark book, *Development, Crises and Alternative Visions: Third World Women's Perspectives* (1988). They offered a vision of empowerment rooted in a commitment to collective action to challenge the specific problems and contexts facing women (and men) in the South – economic, political and cultural. While rather utopian in tone, the book calls for a collective vision that would inspire social transformation through 'political mobilization, legal changes, consciousness raising, and popular education' (p. 87).

Writings on empowerment and gender as an approach to development have become increasingly dominant in the alternative development literature, especially from the South. In 1994, for example, Srilatha Batliwala warned that 'empowerment', which had virtually replaced terms such as poverty alleviation, welfare and community participation, was in danger of losing its transformative edge. She called for a more precise understanding of both power and empowerment, one that sees power 'as

control over material assets, intellectual resources, and ideology'
(Batliwala 1994: 129). For Batliwala, empowerment is 'the process of
challenging existing power relations, and of gaining greater control over
the sources of power' (p. 130). It requires political action and collective
assault on cultural as well as national and community power structures
that oppress women and some men. Like Batliwala, Naila Kabeer (1994)
emphasizes collective, grass-roots participatory action – the *power to* work
*with* others 'to control resources, to determine agendas and to make
decisions' (Kabeer 1994: 229). More concerned with action than theory,
she continues to explore practical, measurable ways to empower women,
especially at the local level (Kabeer 1999).

Jo Rowlands (1997, 1998) brings a broader analytical perspective to the
discussion of gender, empowerment and development. Drawing on
Foucault and feminist thinking about power and gender, she argues that
'empowerment is more than participation in decision-making; it must also
include the processes that lead people to perceive themselves as able and
entitled to make decisions' (Rowlands 1997: 14). It is personal, relational
and collective. She recognizes that empowerment is not only a gender
issue, but also a development issue affecting women and men. While
acknowledging the complexity and difficulties of empowerment as a
concept and a practice, she remains convinced that the key to
empowerment lies in mobilizing marginalized people, especially women.
She cautions, however, that empowerment is a process rather than an end
product, neither easily defined nor measured. At the same time, she
believes 'there is a core to the empowerment process . . . which consists of
increases in self-confidence and self-esteem, a sense of agency and of
"self" in a wider context, and a sense of *dignidad* (being worthy of having a
right to respect from others)' (pp. 129–30).

These debates around gender, empowerment and development have
influenced both mainstream and alternative development practitioners
and scholars. The language of empowerment and participation was
particularly pronounced in what is often called alternative development
approaches (Pieterse 2001; Munck and O'Hearn 1999). Robert Chambers
(1997), for example, has crafted a participatory, people-first approach to
development known as participatory rural appraisal (PRA). This set of
methodological tools is both easily understood and user-friendly,
particularly in poor, grass-roots communities. While not deliberately
aimed at women, his approach targets the very poor, many of who are
women. Amartya Sen has contributed to these discussions as well. He sees
human capabilities/development as a process of developing individual
capacities through gaining education and skills which can empower
individuals and improve their quality of life (Sen 1990, 1995). Sen argues
that poverty reflects poor people's inability to meet their basic needs,
whether material or more intangible – what Sen calls 'agency
achievements' – of participation, empowerment and community life
(Dreze and Sen 1989). Sen criticizes development economics for
emphasizing quantity, such as longevity, rather than the quality of lives
led (Crocker 1995: 156). He points out that women in particular face social
as well as physical problems and that 'the remedies sought have to take

GENDER AND GLOBAL GOVERNANCE   213

note of the nature of the constraints involved and extent to which they can be removed' (Dreze and Sen 1989: 44). While one may quarrel with Sen's lack of attention to the political processes required for equitable resource distribution, he raises some important issues for the study of empowerment. However, both Chambers and Sen focus on the local, arguing that empowerment most often occurs at the point where most people live their lives.

Initially, mainstream development agencies ignored discussions of empowerment, but as top-down development failed to alleviate poverty in the 1990s, especially among women, empowerment began to enter the lexicon of mainstream women and development discourse. For example, the Beijing Platform of Action states emphatically women's empowerment is 'fundamental for the achievement of equality, development and peace' (UN 1996: para. 13). The Canadian International Development Agency's (CIDA) 'Policy on gender equality' includes women's empowerment as one of the eight guiding principles for its policy goals (CIDA 1999). Of course, mainstream development agencies generally interpret empowerment for women as a means for improving productivity within the status quo, rather than challenging and transforming established structures and practices (World Bank 1995). Nevertheless, mainstream development 'experts' increasingly use the language of empowerment when discussing women/gender and development, albeit largely within the rubric of small-scale, grass-roots community development (Friedmann 1992; Craig and Mayo 1995).

The link between empowerment and local communities has encouraged development practitioners and many scholars to ignore the crucial relationship between empowerment and national and global structures and discourses. Jane Parpart, Shirin Rai and Kathleen Staudt, in their recent collection, *Rethinking Empowerment* (2002), argue that empowerment is an empty term if it ignores these factors. Indeed, they claim that the tension between agency and structures, and their interrelationships, lies at the heart of the empowerment debate. While Caroline Moser's (1993) warning that challenges to structural power will alienate mainstream development agencies is well taken, one also needs to reflect upon how the agency and empowerment of women (and poor men) can be achieved without some transformation of existing power relations (both structural and discursive). Anne Phillips has addressed this question by pointing out that empowerment must include the ability to challenge the distribution of power and goods (Phillips 1999: 17). Negotiations with, and challenges to the state (and global forces) then become an important part of collective action leading to women's empowerment. As David Marquand points out, only an empowered and active citizenry can make progress towards social equality (Marquand 1997: 41). Thus, both agency and structures need to be held together, sometimes in tension, to understand the nature of change through the politics of collective (and individual) action at all levels of political institutions – local, national and global. This requires attention to the specific historical struggles (and capitulations) of women (and some men) determined to challenge the way particular structures and discourses of power operate to reinforce a gender-biased, unequal social and political system.

## EMPOWERMENT, GENDER AND GOVERNANCE

How do these debates relate to issues of gender and governance? Adopting the framework of Parpart, Rai and Staudt put forward in *Rethinking Empowerment* (2002), I believe governance and gender cannot be understood without addressing issues of gender and empowerment. However, much of the literature on empowerment ignores national and global forces. While recognizing that local political struggles are important for understanding larger questions of gender and governance, we need to attend to gendered struggles at the national and global levels as well. In our rapidly globalizing world, economic and political issues cannot be understood separately from the global. The growing power of global corporate and financial forces in an increasingly unequal world has been a double-edged experience for women. Free trade and global shifts in productivity have led to casualization and feminization of certain labour sectors, resulting in additional burdens on women and tensions within the family as gender relations get reconfigured. However, new opportunities for women are emerging as well, albeit often affected by race and class. Professional women inhabiting the world of international finance or involved in international bureaucratic machineries are positioned very differently to white Russian women looking to improve their life chances by consenting to become 'catalogue brides', and still more differently from Filipina domestic workers in Canada. Thus globalization is a two-edged sword for women – many are losing, but some have gained and are now in a position to negotiate better conditions – albeit more often as individuals than as a group (Marchand and Runyan 2000).

Consequently, some women should be in a better position to push for more gender-equitable governance practices, and many more may be able to exert pressure through collective action. Yet discussions about governance remain largely gender-neutral (Rai 2002). The current debates focus on whether governance in an increasingly global world is best achieved at the global or the national level. Some 'globalists' argue that the state's regulatory role is being taken over by multilateral organizations. They look to international organizations and legal instruments for solutions, pinning their hopes on the regulatory effect of the United Nations, the World Court and bodies such as the World Trade Organization (WTO), the World Bank and the International Monetary Fund (IMF). However, recent protests at the WTO meeting in Seattle and the World Bank/IMF meeting in Washington reveal a growing scepticism about this option. Although some authors argue that recent protests demonstrate the capacity of citizen activists to reign in global institutions (Liebowitz 2000: 41; Finnegan 2000; Naim 2000), others believe these global organizations are no longer accountable to citizens of nation-states, but more to global civil society. None of this discussion attends to the gendered implications of global governance.

Increasingly, scholars and activists are looking to the nation-state for solutions. Nation-states, of course, vary markedly in their ability and/or desire either to confront and/or negotiate with global forces, corporations and finance. And within states, considerable variation exists in the degree to which democratic accountability exists to all or most people, who are never monolithically equal in political and power terms. Class, geography and gender are notable factors determining access to and/or experience with state power. Nevertheless, national politics is increasingly seen as a key arena for struggles against poverty and marginalization. Not surprisingly, good governance and the empowerment of citizens and groups, so they can ensure responsible governance, is beginning to become a more central issue for some scholars and activists (Stiles 2000; Staudt 1998).

At the same time, it is important to remember that states have historically institutionalized male interests (see for example, Charlton et. al. 1989; Parpart and Staudt 1989; Rai and Lievesley 1996). This is reflected in the small numbers of women holding decision-making positions in state structures – a mere tenth or less of women legislators is the global norm (UNDP 1995; Staudt 1996). Such minority positioning often constrains women legislators from raising strategic issues for women. Challenges to this situation are being pursued at two levels. First, greater participation of women in national political bodies is argued for as part of the processes of democratization. Second, some call for mainstreaming gender in both national and global policy-making and institutional politics (see McBride-Stetson and Mazur 1995; Rai 2002). Empowerment in this context depends upon the space women are able to create within political structures, as well as the issues they are able to raise (or not) in their own strategic interests. We need much more careful, historically specific, analyses of women's attempts to develop political strategies and networks that challenge male power structures and improve state responsiveness to women's issues, both locally and nationally (Cockburn 1999).

## CONCLUSION

There is much to be done, and this chapter is more a call for action and reflection than a list of guidelines for engendering governance. However, certain issues are clear. Governance is highly gendered, and women's participation in positions of authority within governance structures at all levels is problematic. However, if we focus entirely on formal positions of authority, the chance for altering this imbalance is minimal. The literature on gender, power and empowerment suggests the need for a different approach, one that acknowledges the fluid, relational and pervasive character of power and the need to interrogate the workings of gender and power at all levels of society. Women who are held hostage in family structures are scarcely going to be able to come together to effect change. Cultural practices that inhibit conscientization about gender inequality often inhibit the chance that women and sympathetic men may understand and feel inspired to act for change (Afshar 1998). Without individual conscientization and commitment, the chances of transformation at the level of national and global governance are slim.

At the same time, we need to know more about the factors that enable women and men to press for change, to take the risks involved in fighting for a more gender-equitable community. The collective and individual actions at the community level, even in the poorest, most remote places, are key building blocks for engendering governance. A political culture that demands gender equity, and holds local actors accountable, is essential for improved gender relations at all levels. Similarly, the national level is a place where gender, power and governance intersect in many subtle ways. It is not enough to count the number of women working in bureaucracies. We must understand the many ways women have pressured bureaucracies and political parties for more gender-equitable practices – and the many ways they have not (or have tried and failed).

The lessons of history allow us to learn from the past and to construct a new future. Past experiences, the stories and strategies from struggles for gender equality at all levels, can inspire action as well as warning against easy promises and quick fixes. For example, gender mainstreaming is often presented as the panacea for more gender-equitable governance. Yet do we know enough about the way these policies have worked out on the ground? The lessons of the past call for critical assessment and in-depth analysis of the successes and limitations of this 'solution'. Moreover, a more fluid, relational notion of power also helps to move beyond simply counting numbers of women in institutions to a more creative and nuanced evaluation of policies such as gender mainstreaming (Gibb 2001). Often empowerment happens in unexpected and apparently trivial ways. Yet it can make a difference. For example, the women's budget campaign has not effected much legislative change, but it has highlighted the gendered nature of most government budgets and created a rallying point for women in a number of countries (Budlender 1996).

Finally, globalizing issues of governance, as well as networking globally to challenge hegemonic institutional politics within the local/national space are also critically important elements in the struggles for women's empowerment. Efforts to empower women that do not take into account the way women (and men) are situated in an increasingly global world economy are bound to fail (Rai 2002; Marchand and Runyon 2000).

However, none of these efforts can be understood alone. Gender struggles take place in the home, in the community, in NGOs, in institutions such as the media, schools and churches, in the workplace and in national and global structures. While the limits on personal and institutional energies often constrain action to particular arenas, it is essential that all efforts to challenge gender hierarchies understand the multi-level nature of the struggle. Only then will we begin to discover ways to bring about more gender-equitable, accountable governance structures and practices at all level of society. This is a challenge for all people who believe that good governance without gender equity is *not* an acceptable recipe for a fairer, more accountable world.

### References

Afshar, H. (ed.) 1998: *Women and Empowerment: Illustrations from the Third World.* New York: St Martin's Press.

Batliwala, S. 1994: The meaning of women's empowerment: new concepts from action. In G. Sen, A. Germain and L. C. Chen (eds), *Population Policies Reconsidered: Health, Empowerment and Rights,* Boston: Harvard University Press, 127–38.

Budlender, D. 1996: *The Women's Budget.* Cape Town, South Africa: Institute for Democracy in South Africa.

Butalia, U. and Sarkar, T. (eds) 1996: *Women and Right-Wing Movements: Indian Experiences.* London: Zed Books.

Canadian International Development Agency (CIDA) 1999: *Policy on Gender Equality.* Ottawa: CIDA.

Chambers, R. 1997: *Whose Reality Counts? Putting the First Last.* London: Intermediate Technology Publications.

Charlton, S. E., Everett, J. and Staudt, K. 1989: *Women, the State and Development.* Albany, N.Y.: SUNY/Albany Press.

Collins, P. H. 1991: *Black Feminist Thought: Knowledge, Consciousness, and the Politics of Empowerment.* New York: Routledge.

Cockburn, C. 1999: *The Space Between Us: Negotiating Gender and National Identities in Conflict.* London: Zed Press.

Craig, C. and Mayo, M. (eds) 1995: *Community Empowerment.* London: Zed Press.

Crocker, D. A. 1995: Functioning and capability: the foundations of Sen's and Nussbaum's development ethic. In J. Glover and M. Nussbaum (eds), *Women, Culture and Development: A Study of Human Capabilities.* Oxford: Clarendon Press.

Deveaux, M. 1996: Feminism and empowerment: a critical reading of Foucault. In S. Hekman (ed.), *Feminist Interpretations of Michel Foucault.* University Park, Pa.: Pennsylvania State University Press.

Dreze, J. and Sen, A. 1989: *Hunger and Public Action.* Oxford: Clarendon Press.

Enloe, C. 1990: *Bananas, Beaches and Bases: Making Feminist Sense of International Politics.* Los Angeles: University of California Press.

Enloe, C. 1993: *The Morning After: Sexual Politics at the End of the Cold War.* Los Angeles: University of California Press.

Finnegan, W. 2000: After Seattle: anarchists get organized. *The New Yorker* (17 April), 40–51.

Foucault, M. 1979: *Discipline and Punish: The Birth of the Prison.* Harmondsworth: Penguin.

Foucault, M. 1991: *The Foucault Reader: An Introduction to Foucault's Thought,* ed. P. Rabinow. Harmondsworth: Penguin.

Fraser, N. 1989: *Unruly Practices: Power, Discourse and Gender in Contemporary Social Theory.* Minneapolis, Minn.: University of Minnesota Press.

Freire, P. 1973: *Education for Critical Consciousness.* New York: Seabury Press.

Friedmann, J. 1992: *Empowerment: The Politics of Alternative Development.* London: Zed Press.

Gibb, H. 2001: *Gender Mainstreaming: Good Practices from the Asia Pacific Region.* Ottawa: North-South Institute.

Gupta, A. and Ferguson, J. (eds) 1997: *Culture, Power, Place: Explorations in Critical Anthropology*. Durham, N.C.: Duke University Press.

Hartsock, N. 1990: Foucault on power: a theory for women? In L. Nicholson (ed.), *Feminism/Postmodernism*, New York: Routledge.

Hekman, S. (ed.) 1996: *Feminist Interpretations of Michel Foucault*. University Park, Pa.: Pennsylvania State University Press.

Held, D., McGrew, A. M., Goldblatt, D. and Perraton, J. 1999: *Global Transformation: Politics, Economics, Culture*. Cambridge: Polity.

Hirshman, M. 1995: Women and development: a critique. In M. Marchand and J. Parpart (eds), *Feminism/Postmodernism/Development*, London: Routledge.

Kabeer, N. 1994: *Reversed Realities: Gender Hierarchies in Development Thought*. London: Verso.

Kabeer, N. 1999: Resources, agency, achievements: reflections on the measurement of women's empowerment. *Development and Change*, 30, 435–64.

Liebowitz, D. 2000: Explaining absences, analyzing change, looking toward the future: U.S. women's participation in transnational feminist organizing in North America. Presented at ISA, Los Angeles.

Lukes, S. 1974: *Power: A Radical View*. London: Macmillan.

Marchand, M. and Sisson Runyan, A. 2000: *Gender and Global Restructuring: Sightings, Sites and Resistances*. London: Routledge.

Marquand, D. 1997: *The New Reckoning: Capitalism, States and Citizens*. Cambridge: Cambridge University Press.

McBride-Stetson, D. and Mazur, A. (eds) 1995: *Comparative State Feminism*. London: Sage Press.

McNay, L. 1992: *Foucault and Feminism: Power, Gender and Self*. Cambridge: Cambridge University Press.

Moser, C. 1993: *Gender Planning and Development: Theory, Practice and Training*. London: Routledge.

Munck, R. and O'Hearn, D. (eds) 1999: *Critical Development Theory: Contributions to a New Paradigm*. London: Zed Books.

Naim, M. 2000: The FP interview: Lore's war. *Foreign Policy*, 118, 29–55.

Parpart, J., Rai, S. and Staudt, K. (eds) 2002: *Rethinking Empowerment: Gender and Development in a Global/Local World*. London: Routledge.

Parpart, J. and Staudt, K. (eds) 1989: *Women and the State in Africa*. Boulder, Colo.: Lynne Rienner Press.

Peterson, S. and Sisson Runyan, A. 1993: *Global Gender Issues*. Boulder, Colo.: Lynne Rienner.

Phillips, A. 1999: *Which Equalities Matter?* Cambridge: Polity.

Pieterse, J. 2001: *Development Theory: Deconstructions/Reconstructions*. London: Sage Publications.

Prakash, A. and Hart, J. A. 1999: *Globalization and Governance*. London: Routledge.

Rai, S. 2002: *Gender and International Political Economy: From Nationalism to Globalization*. Cambridge: Polity.

Rai, S. and Lievesley, G. 1996: *Women and the State: International Perspectives*. London: Taylor and Francis.

Rowlands, J. 1997: *Questioning Empowerment: Working with Women in Honduras.* Oxford: Oxfam Publications.

Rowlands, J. 1998: A word of the times, but what does it mean?: Empowerment in the discourse and practice of development. In H. Afshar (eds), *Women and Empowerment,* New York: St Martin's Press.

Sen, A. 1990: Gender and cooperative conflicts. In I. Tinker (ed.), *Persistent Inequalities,* New York: Oxford University Press.

Sen, A. 1995: Gender inequality and theories of justice. In J. Glover and M. Nussbaum (eds), *Women, Culture and Development,* Oxford: Oxford University Press.

Sen, G. and Grown, C. 1988: *Development, Crises and Alternative Visions: Third World Women's Perspectives.* New York: Monthly Review Press.

Staudt, K. 1996: Political representation: engendering politics. In *Background Papers: Human Development Report 1995.* New York: UNDP.

Staudt, K. 1998: *Policy, Politics and Gender: Women Gaining Ground.* Hartford, Conn.: Kumarian Press.

Stiglitz, J. 2002: *Globalization and its Discontents.* London: Norton.

Stiles, K. 2000: *Global Institutions and Local Empowerment: Competing Theoretical Perspectives.* London: Macmillan.

United Nations 1996: *Platform for Action and the Beijing Declaration.* Fourth World Conference on Women, Beijing, China, 4–15 September 1995.

United Nations Development Program 1995: *The Human Development Report 1995.* New York: UNDP.

Wolf, Eric. 1998: *Envisioning Power: Ideologies of Dominance and Crisis.* Berkeley: University of California Press.

World Bank 1995: *World Bank Participation Source Book.* Washington, D.C.: World Bank Environment Department Papers.

Yeatman, A. 1999: *Activism and the Policy Process.* London: Allen and Unwin.

Young, K. 1993: *Planning Development with Women: Making a World of Difference.* London: Macmillan.

# Index